Design and Analysis of Algorithms

Design and Analysis of Algorithms

Dr. Venugopal Temberveni
HOD & Associate Professor
Department of Computer Science and Engineering
JNTUH College of Engineering,
Sultanpur, Medak (Dist.), Telangana State, India.

and

Dr. Sammulal Porika
Assistant Professor
Department of Computer Science and Engineering
JNTUH College of Engineering,
Jagtial, Nachupally (Kondagattu), Karimnagar (Dist.),
Telangana State, India.

BSP **BS Publications**
A unit of **BSP Books Pvt. Ltd.**
4-4-309/316, Giriraj Lane, Sultan Bazar,
Hyderabad - 500 095
Phone : 040 - 23445605, 23445688

Design and Analysis of Algorithms *by Dr. Venugopal Temberveni & Dr. Sammulal Porika*

© 2016, *by Publisher*

Published by :

 **BS Publications**
A unit of **BSP Books Pvt. Ltd.**

4-4-309/316, Giriraj Lane, Sultan Bazar,
Hyderabad - 500 095
Phone : 040 - 23445605, 23445688
e-mail : info@bspbooks.net

ISBN : 978-93-5230-133-1 (HB)

Dedicated to,

Late T. Lakshmi Rajam & Smt. T. Vijaya Lakshmi (Parents)

Geeta (Wife)

Harshitha & Pranavi (Childrens)

- Dr. Venugopal Temberveni

Sri P. Manjee Nayak & Smt. *P. Rajamma* (Parents)

Kavitha (Wife)

Vishwa Teja & Nakshatra (Childrens)

- Dr. Sammulal Porika

Preface

Writing efficient algorithms is also a technology. Programming is seeing an exponential growth. The performance of a program basically depends upon the algorithm of a program. Therefore, designing of the algorithm must be correct for the better performance of a program. This book aims at bringing classical designing techniques of an algorithm. To write good algorithm knowledge of design is required.

The quality of an algorithm is determined by the analysis of an algorithm. It is an important aspect which controls the designing of an algorithm. This book deals with design and analysis of algorithms, and provides in-depth knowledge about developing efficient algorithms, but knowledge of data structure is desirable. In this book, the emphasis is on well-accepted, tested and proven algorithms. In short, this book is for anyone who needs to understand the design and analysis of algorithms.

This book is divided into eight chapters. Chapter 1 reviews the basic concepts of algorithms. It discusses how to calculate the time and space complexity of algorithm. A major emphasis is given on asymptotic notations. Chapter 2 explores various searching and traversal techniques. It also puts emphasis on graph, and covers the basic concept of graph and various algorithms related to the graph data structure. Chapter 3 covers divide and conquer technique in which quick sort and merge sort methods are discussed along with their best, average and worst case analysis. Chapter 4, 5, 6 and 7 of this book deal with the advanced design and analysis techniques which includes Greedy Algorithms, Dynamic Programming, Backtracking and the Branch and Bound algorithms. Chapter 8 is devoted to some advanced topics of algorithms such as P, NP and non-deterministic algorithms.

The objective of this book is to give the reader the basic concepts, theory of design and analysis of algorithms and its application in computer science. This text includes important features such as solved examples with problems for practice, old questions and multiple choice questions.

-Authors

Acknowledgements

We strongly believe that everything in the universe is planned and executed by the Almighty God. It is our duty to thank Him for selecting us for this project of writing this Textbook. We pray the Almighty God to bless all the readers of this book and lead them to a successful & prosperous career in their life.

We express deep sense of gratitude and thankfulness to Smt. Shailaja Ramaiyer, IAS, Vice Chancellor I/c, JNT University Hyderabad and Dr. N. Yadaiah, Registrar, JNT University Hyderabad for their encouragement in writing this book.

We are very much thankful to Dr. A. Govardhan, Principal, JNTUH CEH, Dr. S. Durga Bhavani, BOS, Professor & Director of SIT, Dr. A. Vinaya Babu, Professor of CSE, JNTUH CEH, Dr. V. Kamakshi Prasad, Professor & Head of CSE, JNTUH CEH and Dr. M. Sreenivasa Rao, Professor of Computer Science & Director, Academic Audit Cell, JNTUH, Dr. K.V. Raman Chairman BOS, Prqin CSE, JNTU K, Dr. Ch. Satyanarayana Prof. in CSE, JNTU K for their motivation and constant encouragement.

We thank Mr. Anil Shah, Director of BS Publications, Mr. Naresh Davergave, Production Manager and Mr. Vasudev Rao, Marketing Manager of BS Publications for their continuous support and cooperation in completing this book. We are ever grateful to the Team of BS Publications for giving us an opportunity to compile this book. They have provided the complete assistance in bringing out the book into the market.

We would like to express our sincere thanks to Dr. N. V. Ramana, Principal, JNTUH College of Engineering, Nachupally, and Dr. N.V.S Raju, Vice-Principal, JNTUH College of Engineering, Nachupally, Karimnagar, Telangana for their consistent and constant encouragement.

We would like to express our sincere thanks to Dr. M. Manzoor Hussain, Principal, JNTUH College of Engineering Sultanpur, and Dr. G. N. Sreenivas, Vice-Principal, JNTUH College of Engineering Sultanpur, Pulkal, Medak, Telangana for their consistent and constant encouragement.

We express our thanks to Sri M. Uday Kumar, HOD of CSE, Dr. Vishwanatha Raju, Dr. B. Vishnuvardhan, Dr. G. Narasimha, Dr. D. Ramesh, Mrs. P. Swetha, Sri P. Sreenivasa Rao, Sri Joshi Sripada, Dr. B. Kranthi Kiran, Sri. B.V. Ram Naresh Yadav, Sri. B. Sateesh Kumar, Dr. K. Shahu Chatrapati, Dr. M. Dhana Lakshmi, HOD of IT, Dr. S. Suresh

Kumar, Smt. Ch. Asha Jyothi for suggesting modifications and providing valuable suggestions for the improvement of the manuscript.

We also would like to thank all our friends and well-wishers who helped us directly or indirectly in completing this project.

We owe special thanks to our spouses for their support and encouragement during the preparation of the manuscript.

Last but not the least we thank all our family members for their endless support and cooperation during the course of completing this project.

-Authors

Contents

1

Introduction

2

Searching and Traversal Techniques

3

Divide and Conquer

4

The Greedy Method

5

Dynamic Programming

6

Backtracking

7

Branch and Bound

8

NP-Hard and NP-Complete Problems

1

INTRODUCTION

1.1 ALGORITHM

Algorithm originates from the name of Latin translation of a book written by al-khwarizmi a Persian mathematician. The book was entitled: "Algoritmi de numero Indorum". The term "Algoritmi" in the title of the book led to the term "Algorithm". In mathematics and computer science, an algorithm is a step-by-step procedure for calculations.

An algorithm is an effective method for finding out the solution for a given problem. It is a sequence of instructions that conveys the method to address a problem. Algorithm is the basis for any program in computer science. Algorithm helps in the organization of the program. Every program is structured and follows the specified guidelines and algorithm gives steps for the program. A problem can be solved by means of logical induction but in order to implement it in the form of a program, we require an appropriate algorithm.

Formal Definitions

Definition 1: Step by step procedure to solve a problem is called Algorithm.

Definition 2: A countable set of instructions followed to complete the required task is called an algorithm.

Definition 3: An algorithm is a finite set of instructions to do a particular task.

Various criteria are considered to evaluate an algorithm among which the essential ones are as follows:

1. **Input:** The algorithm should be given zero (or) more inputs explicitly. (≥ 0)

1

2. **Output:** One or more quantities are produced as an outcome. (> 0)

3. **Definiteness:** Every instruction must be free from ambiguity. (A = B + 3 or 5)

4. **Finiteness:** The algorithm must halt after finite number of steps for all the cases.

5. **Effectiveness:** Every step in the algorithm should be easy to understand and must be implementable through any of the programming languages.

Each step of algorithm must be subjected to one or more operations. For a computer to operate on the algorithm, certain constraints must be imposed on the operations performed on it. The time required to terminate an algorithm must be short sensibly. All the operations performed on an algorithm must be solvable manually within a limited amount of time. Computational procedures are those algorithms which are definite and effective. When an algorithm is implemented in a programming language, it gains this criterion.

1.2 LIFE CYCLE OF DESIGN AND ANALYSIS OF ALGORITHM

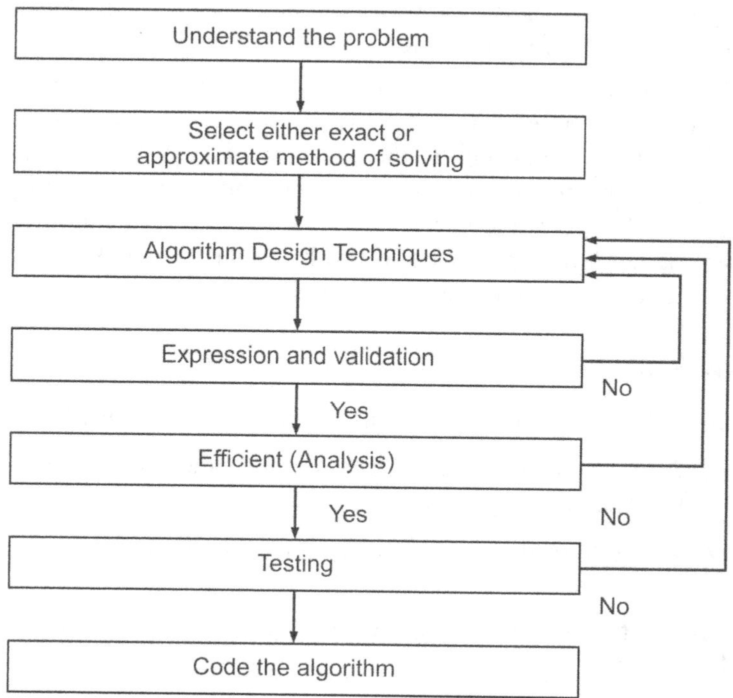

Understand the Problem: Before designing the algorithm, we need to understand the problem completely. This is a critical phase. If we do any mistake in this phase, the entire algorithm becomes wrong. So, we need to gather all the requirements from the user regarding problem. After that we have to find out the necessary inputs for solving that problem. The input to the algorithm is called "instance" of the problem.

Exact vs. Approximate Solving: Solve the problem exactly if possible, otherwise use approximation methods. Though some problems are solvable by exact method, they are solved faster using approximation method. So in such situations, we will use approximation method.

Algorithm Design Techniques: An important aspect of this book is to study different design techniques which yielded good algorithms. Designing new algorithms becomes easy once these design strategies are clearly understood. Designing an algorithm needs human intervention and cannot be done by a machine alone. Some of the techniques used in designing algorithms are:

1. Brute force
2. Divide and Conquer
3. Greedy Method
4. Dynamic Programming
5. Back Tracking
6. Branch and Bound

Depending on the nature of the problem suitable design technique is adopted.

Expressing an algorithm: The algorithms are written using structured programming principles. This includes writing comments where ever necessary, providing indentation, adhering to standards etc. Algorithms can be described in the following three ways.

1. Natural language like English: When this way is used, care should be taken and we should ensure that each and every statement is definite.
2. Graphic representation called flowchart: This method will work well when the algorithm is small and simple.
3. Pseudo-code Method: In this method, we should typically describe algorithms as program, which resembles language like Pascal and algol.

Algorithm validation: Checking whether the algorithm is producing appropriate outputs for all the valid inputs is called algorithm validation. The algorithm must be independent of limitations in a programming language in which it is implemented. It must not be effected by any programming language issues.

The solution can be expressed as a set of assertions about the input and output variables and also as expression in predicate calculus. If these two forms are proved to be equivalent, then it is a correct solution. Once the algorithm is built, next we have to prove its correctness. Usually validation is used for proving correctness of the algorithm i.e., it should be tested by proving all possible combinations of the inputs. Some of the techniques used for generating the inputs are:

1. ***Boundary Value Technique***: In Boundary Value Technique, if the correct value of a Variable is 10, it is tested by giving values in and around 10. (ex. 9,9.5, 10.5,11 etc.,)

2. ***Equivalence Partitioning***: In Equivalence Partitioning, the i/p is divided into different groups and tests the algorithm to work satisfactorily by giving values from these groups.

3. ***Random Generation***: Random Generation will test the algorithm by generating set of input values in random.

Analysis of an algorithm: Analyzing an algorithm involves study of data storage and processing of data which are performed by a computer. It measures the evaluation time of an algorithm and space required by it. Analysis is required to compare the performance of algorithms.

Algorithm analysis involves synthesizing a formula or guessing the fastness of algorithm depending upon the size of the problem it operates. Size of the problem can be

(a)   Number of inputs/outputs in an algorithm.

E.g., For a multiplication algorithm, the numbers to be multiplied are the inputs and the product of the numbers is the output.

(b)   Total number of operations involved in algorithm:

E.g., To find the minimum of all the elements in an array the number of comparisons made among the elements is the total number of operations.

Algorithm testing: Testing of an algorithm involves debugging and profiling. Debugging refers to finding out errors in the results and correcting the problem. Profiling refers to the measurement of performance of a correct program when executed on a data set. This includes calculation of time and space required for computation.

Coding an algorithm: After successful completion of all the phases, then an algorithm is converted into program by identifying a suitable computer language.

1.3 PSEUDO-CODE FOR EXPRESSING ALGORITHMS

1. Comments are denoted by '//'

2. Block of statements are enclosed within braces '{ }'.

3. No need of explicit declaration of a variables data type. Identifier starts with a character.

4. Records are used for the formation of complex data types. Here is an example,

```
Node = Record
{
   data type – 1   data – 1;
              .
              .
              .
   data type – n   data – n;
   node * link;
}
```

Here link is a pointer to the record type node. Individual data items of a record can be accessed with → and period operators.

5. Values can be assigned to variables as follows:

   <Variable>: = <expression>;

6. TRUE and FALSE are two Boolean values present.

   → Logical Operators   AND, OR, NOT

   → Relational Operators   <, <=, >, >=, =, !=

7. Loop control statements used are for, while and repeat-until.

   while Loop:

```
while < condition > do
{
        <statement-1>
             .
             .
             .
        <statement-n>
}
```

   for Loop:

```
for variable: = value-1 to value-2 step step do
{
<statement-1>
     .
     .
     .
<statement-n>
}
```

repeat-until:

```
        repeat
                <statement-1>
                        .
                        .
                        .
                <statement-n>
                until<condition>
```

8. A conditional statement has the following forms.

   If <condition> then <statement>
   If <condition> then <statement-1>
   Else <statement-2>

   Case statement:

```
   case
   {
   : <condition-1> : <statement-1>
                .
                .
                .
   : <condition-n> : <statement-n>
   : else : <statement-n+1>
   }
```

9. Input and output are done using the instructions read and write.

10. A single procedure exists which is of the form: Algorithm.

    the heading takes the form,

    Algorithm Name ___ of __ Algorithm (List of Parameter)

As an example, the following algorithm calculates first 'n' natural numbers and returns the result:

Algorithm

```
1: Algorithm Sum(n)   // n is number of natural numbers
2: {
3: NumSum:=0
4: for i:= 1 to n do
5: NumSum:= Numsum + i
6: return NumSum;
7: }
```

In the above example, Sum is the name of algorithm, 'n' is parameter. NumSum and 'i' are local variables.

Case study: Selection Sort

Here is an example that demonstrates the method of transforming a problem into an algorithm.

- Let us consider a problem of sorting 'n' arbitrary elements in non decreasing order for which algorithm must be devised.
- A Simple solution given by the following.
- Find the smallest among the unsorted elements and place it first in the sorted list.

Algorithm

```
1:   For i := 1 to n do
2:   {
3:   Examine  x[i]  to  x[n]  and  suppose  the  smallest
     element is x[min];
4:   swap x[i] and x[min];
5:   }
```

The above algorithm has two tasks:

(i) Finding the smallest element

(ii) Swap

The first task can be solved by assuming the minimum is x[i]; checking x[i] with x[I + 1], x[I + 2].......x[n], and whenever a smaller element is found, regarding it as the new minimum which is x[min]. x[n] is compared with the current minimum. The second task swap can be solved using the following code

```
temp:= x[i];
x[i]:=x[min];
x[min]:=temp;
```

Putting all these observations together, we get the algorithm Selection sort.

In the first step of this algorithm, the smallest element in the given list is identified. It is placed in the beginning of the list in the next step. A similar procedure is followed with the remaining elements where each time the least element among the elements is found and placed in appropriate position until the whole list is in sorted order.

Example: List L = 15, 25, 20, 5, 10

     5 is identified it is swapped with 15, → 5, 25, 20, 15, 10

     10 is identified it is swapped with 25, → 5, 10, 20, 15, 25

     15 is identified it is swapped with 20, → 5, 10, 15, 20, 25

     20 is identified it is swapped with 20, → 5, 10, 15, 20, 25

Algorithm

```
 1: Algorithm selection sort (x, n)
 2: // Sort  the  array  x[1:n]  into  non-decreasing
    //order.
 3: {
 4: for i:=1 to n do
 5: {
 6: min:=i;
 7: for k:=i+1 to n do
 8: if (x[k]<x[min]) then min:=k;
 9: temp:=x[i];
10: x[i]:=x[min];
11: x[min]:=temp;
12: }
13: }
```

1.4 RECURSIVE ALGORITHMS

Ability of a function to call itself is called recursion. Recursive algorithms are potential mechanisms and can express a convoluted code in a lucid manner. That is why, in certain cases, recursive algorithms are preferable. Recursion is of two types (i) Direct recursion (ii) Indirect recursion

A direct recursive algorithm straight away calls itself. If 'P' is an algorithm that calls an algorithm 'Q' in its body. If 'Q' in turn calls 'P', then it is said to be indirect recursive algorithm.

The following two examples show how to develop recursive algorithms.

In the first, we consider the Towers of Hanoi problem, and in the second, we generate all possible permutations of a list of characters.

1.4.1 Towers of Hanoi

Towers of Hanoi is a classical example of recursion problem. It is easier, efficient and do not make use of complex data structure. The task is to move all the three disks from source to destination without violating the following rules.

1. At a time, only one disk may be moved.
2. Larger disk should not be placed on top.
3. Each time a move is made, upper disk from one tower must be moved to another tower.
4. For the purpose of intermediate storage of disks, only one auxiliary tower should be used.

There is an interesting story behind the concept of Towers of Hanoi. It believed that when the world was brought into existence there was a tower accommodated with 64 golden disks. It is also called Tower of Brahma or Luca's Tower. The disks were of different sizes arranged in a stack in ascending order. There were two more empty towers beside the actual tower. Let them be auxiliary, destination and actual tower be source. The disks must be transferred from source to destination using the middle tower auxiliary.

It is said that Brahmin presents have been moving these disks, according to the unchangeable rules of the Brahma, since that time and when once this puzzle is completed, the world would come to an end.

Note: If there are 'n' disks then the minimum number of moves to solve the Towers of Hanoi problem is $2^n - 1$

Algorithm for Towers of Hanoi problem: Name of the algorithm is TOH and n disks are to be moved from source s to destination d using auxiliary tower a.

Algorithm

```
1:   Algorithm TOH(n, s, d, a)
2:   {
3:   If (n>=1) then
4:   {
5:   TOH(n-1,s,a,d);
6:   Write("move top disk from tower", s, "to top of
     tower", d);
7:   TOH(n-1,a,d,s);
8:   }
9:   }
```

1.4.1.1 Solution to Towers of Hanoi for Three Disks

In this problem, there are three towers named source, auxiliary and destination. The source tower consists of three disks of different sizes, where each disk resting on the one just larger than it.

Start: The source tower consisting of 3 disks.

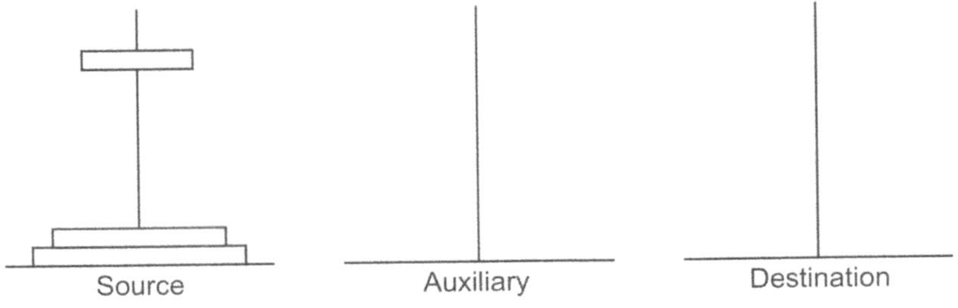

Step 1: Move disk 1 from source to destination.

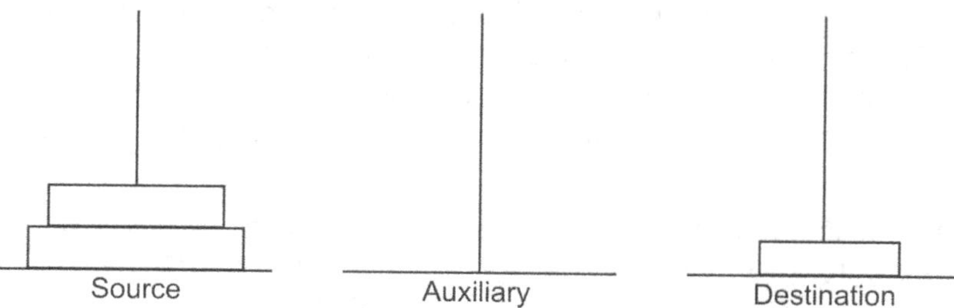

Step 2: Move disk 2 from source to auxiliary.

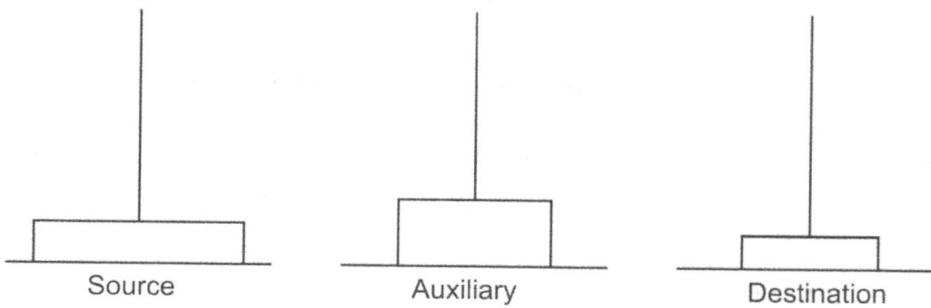

Step 3: Move disk 1 from destination to auxiliary.

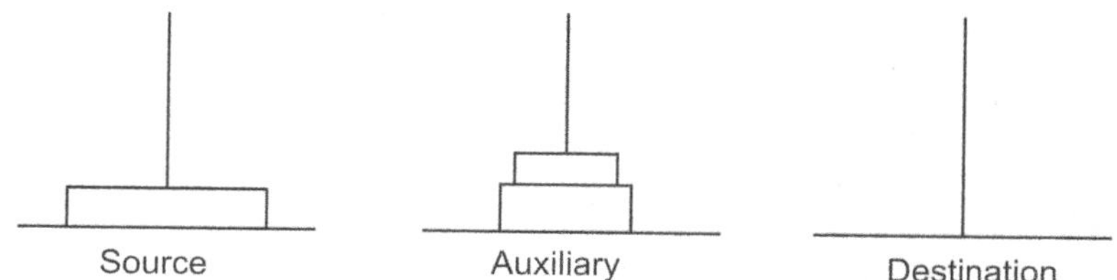

Step 4: Move disk 3 from source to destination.

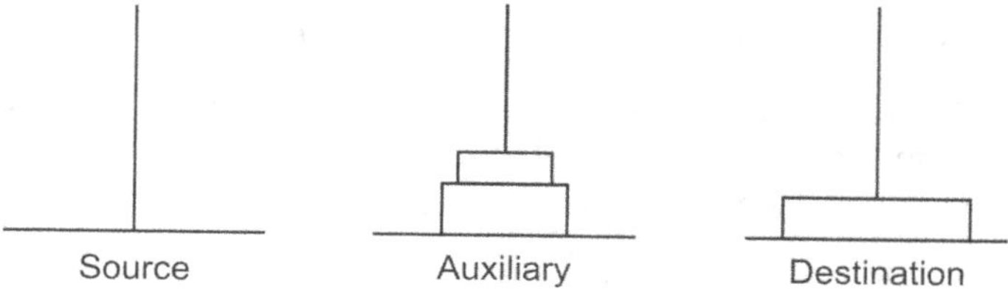

Step 5: Move disk 1 from auxiliary to source.

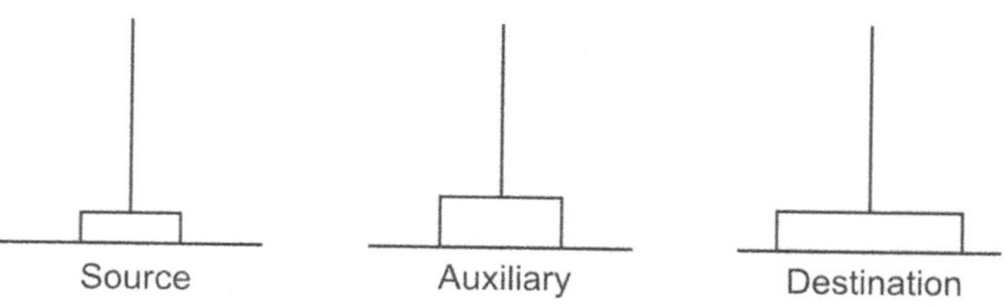

Step 6: Move disk 2 from auxiliary to destination.

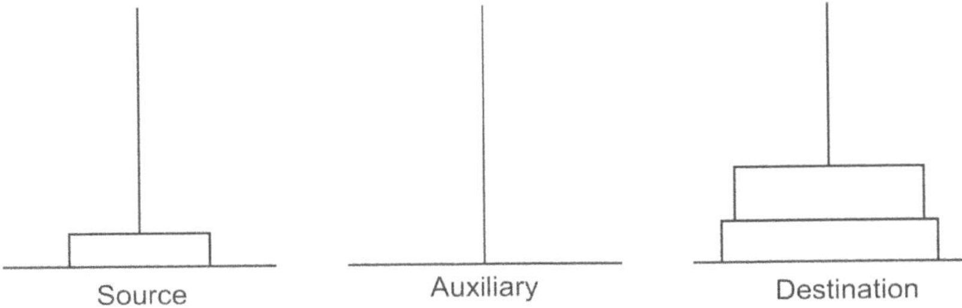

Step 7: Move disk 1 from source to destination.

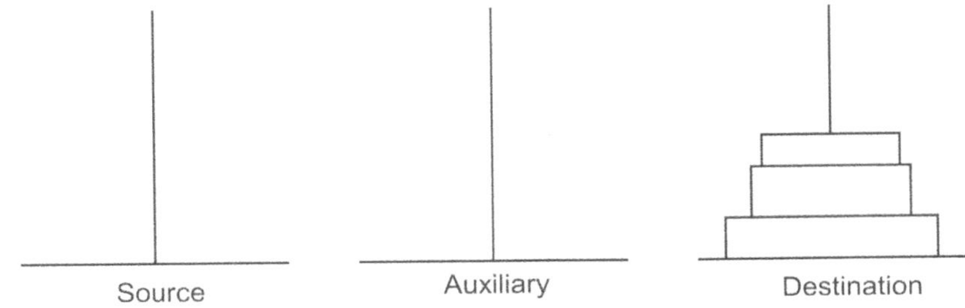

Thus, the destination consists of three disks satisfying the above rule.

Analysis:

Number of disks = 3

Number of times disk 1 moved = $2^2 = 4$

Number of times disk 2 moved = $2^1 = 2$

Number of times disk 3 moved = $2^0 = 1$

Total number of moves = $2^3 - 1 = 7$

Note: Number of movements of each disk is in power of 2

1.4.1.2 Solution to Towers of Hanoi for Four disks

Step 1: Move disk 1 from Source to Auxiliary.

Step 2: Move disk 2 from Source to Destination

Step 3: Move disk 1 from Auxiliary to Destination.

Step 4: Move disk 3 from Source to Auxiliary.

Step 5: Move disk 1 from Destination to Source

Step 6: Move disk 2 from Destination to Auxiliary

Step 7: Move disk 1 from Source to Auxiliary

***Step* 8:**   Move disk 4 from Source to Destination

***Step* 9:**   Move disk 1 from Auxiliary to Destination

***Step* 10:** Move disk 2 from Auxiliary to Source

***Step* 11:** Move disk 1 from Destination to Source

***Step* 12:** Move disk 3 from Auxiliary to Destination

***Step* 13:** Move disk 1 from Source to Auxiliary

***Step* 14:** Move disk 2 from Source to Destination

***Step* 15:** Move disk 1 from Auxiliary to Destination

Analysis:

Number of disks = 4

Number of times disk 1 moved = $2^3 = 8$

Number of times disk 2 moved = $2^2 = 4$

Number of times disk 3 moved = $2^1 = 2$

Number of times disk 4 moved = $2^0 = 1$

Total number of moves = $2^4 - 1 = 15$

NOTE: Number of movements of each disk is in power of 2

1.4.1.3 C Program to Solve Towers of Hanoi Problem

```c
#include<stdio.h>
#include<conio.h>
#include<math.h>
void Towers(int n, char from, char to, char aux)
{
   if(a>=1)
   {
     Towers(n-1,from,aux,to);
     printf("Move disk %d from %c to %c \n",n, from,to);
     Towers(n-1,aux,to,from);
   }
return;
}
void main()
{
   int disk, moves;
   clrscr();
   printf("Enter number of disks  : ");
scanf("%d",&disk);
```

```
moves=(pow(2,disk)-1);
printf("Number of moves needed are  :  %d\n",moves);
Towers(disk,'s','d','a'); getch();
  }
```

1.4.1.4 Permutation Generator

The problem is to print all possible permutations of a set containing 'k' elements (k>=1).

For example, if the set is {x, y, z}, then the set of permutation is,

{ (x, y, z),(y, z, x),(z, x, y),(x, z, y),(y, x, z),(z, y, x)}

- Hence for 'k' elements there are k! permutations
- A simple algorithm can be obtained by looking at the case of 4 statement(x, y, z, w)
- The Answer can be constructed by writing
1. x followed by all the permutations of (y, z, w)
2. y followed by all the permutations of (x, z, w)
3. z followed by all the permutations of (x, y, w)
4. w followed by all the permutations of (x, y, z)

Algorithm

```
 1:  Algorithm perm(a,k,n)
 2:  {
 3:  if(k=n) then write (a[1:n]); // output permutation
 4:  else   //a[k:n] ahs more than one permutation
 5:  // Generate this recursively.
 6:  for i:=k to n do
 7:  {
 8:  t:=a[k];
 9:  a[k]:=a[i];
10:  a[i]:=t;
11:  perm(a,k+1,n);
12:  //all permutation of a[k+1:n]
13:  t:=a[k];
14:  a[k]:=a[i];
15:  a[i]:=t;
16:  }
17:  }
```

1.5 PERFORMANCE ANALYSIS OF ALGORITHM

Study of algorithms is required for the following reasons:

- To estimate the computational time and space required while operating a problem.

- To prove that your method for obtaining solution ends after finite steps yielding a correct solution.

- To pick-up an efficient algorithm to solve a problem among the available algorithms.

1.5.1 Efficiency

Efficiency of an algorithm depends upon the amount of resources utilized by the algorithm. A maximum efficient algorithm will exhibit the property of minimal resource utilization and vice versa. Though two algorithms are designed to solve same problem, they may have different efficiencies.

For example, consider a problem of sorting 'n' elements. If an Insertion sort technique is adopted to solve this problem, it takes an approximate time equal to $C_1 n^2$ (C_1 is constant). If the same problem is solved using Merge sort technique, it takes $C_2\, n \log_2 n$ units of time (C_2 is constant). For small inputs Insertion sort is better than merge sort. But for larger inputs Merge sort is better than Insertion sort because its running time grows more slowly with increase in input size compared to that of Insertion sort (i.e., $n \log n$ grows more slowly than n^2)

Analysis of algorithm is the study of algorithm i.e., calculating the time and space complexity. Analysis of algorithms is of two types Priori analysis and posteriori analysis.

1.5.2 Priori Analysis

It is also known as performance analysis. Analysis of algorithm is done before running the algorithm on any computer machine i.e., before executing algorithm, we will study the behavior of the algorithm. It gives an estimate about the running time of the algorithm.

We find the order of magnitude of an algorithm before a program is written and executed. This analysis is machine and platform independent. The first objective of priori analysis is to associate a mathematical function in terms of input size 'n' representing the rate of growth of the time of algorithm as a function of input size. Some algorithm may follow a constant growth that is irrespective of the input size, it takes constant growth. While other algorithm may have logarithmic growth like $O(\log n)$ and some may have polynomial growth like n, n^2 while some may have exponential growth like 2n, 3n. It is desirable to have algorithm for problems that take polynomial growth as they take less time than in comparison to exponential time algorithm. It is less accurate when compared to posteriori analysis, but cost of analysis is low.

Advantage of priori analysis:
1. Analysis is done before implementing or running the algorithm on machine.
2. Simple and uniform. Hence easier for making performance.

Drawback: We get only estimated value i.e., not real values.

1.5.3 Posteriori Analysis

It is also called performance measurement. During the stage of analysis, the target must be identified. Algorithm is converted to a program and run on a machine. While algorithm is executed, then the information collected regarding execution time and primary memory requirements is called as posteriori analysis. It gives accurate values and is very costly.

Note: Priori algorithm is always better than posteriori analysis.

Advantage of posteriori: Values we get are real or exact in actual units of time.

Drawback
1. Difficulty in conducting experiments.
2. Difficulty in making performance comparison, because of non-uniform values of a single algorithm.

Analysis of algorithm means developing a formula or prediction of how fast the algorithm works on the problem size.

Problem size of an algorithm: Size of the problem is based on kind of the problem dealt with.

Example 1: If an element is to be searched a p-element array, size of problem = Size of array = p.

Example 2: If the elements of two arrays of sizes 'p' and 'q' are to be merged then size of problem = p + q.

Example 3: If factorial of a number 'p' is to be computed, then size of the problem = 'p'.

1.5.4 Complexity

Complexity is the time taken and the space required for an algorithm for its completion. It is a measurement through which one can judge the quality of an algorithm and can be used for finding and sorting out better algorithms. Complexity can be classified into two types. Normally:

1. Space complexity   2. Time complexity

1.5.4.1 Space Complexity

The complexity can be defined as the amount of space an algorithm requires.

The space needed by each of the algorithm is the sum of the following components.

1. A fixed part
2. A variable part

1. **Fixed part:** It depends on the characteristics of input and output. That consists of space needed by component variable whose size is dependent on the particular problem instance being solved.

2. **Variable part:** The space requirement denoted by S(p) of any algorithm 'p' can be given as $S(p) = C + S_p$ (Instance characteristics) where, C is constant.

1.5.4.2 Time Complexity

Time Complexity of a program 'p' can be defined as the sum of compile time and execution time (runtime). Let us suppose that we compile a program for once and we run it several times. Then runtime of program will be considered.

Time complexity is the amount of time required by the algorithm for the completion of the problem. In this we have three cases (i) best case (ii) worst case (iii) Average case.

1. **Best case:** If an algorithm takes minimum amount of time to run to completion for a specific set of input, then it is called best case time complexity.

   E.g., While searching a particular element by using sequential search we get the desired element at first place itself then it is called best case time complexity.

2. **Worst case:** If an algorithm takes maximum amount of time to run to completion for a specific set of input, then it is called worst case time complexity. Defining the other way, it is maximum amount of time taken by an algorithm to give an output is called as worst case.

   E.g., While searching an element by using linear searching method if desired element is placed at the end of the list then we get worst case time complexity.

3. **Average case:** The average time taken by an algorithm to run to completion is called average case.

This classification gives the complexity information about the behavior of the algorithm at a particular instance and of an algorithm on specific in random algorithm.

Case Study – Linear Search:

1	2	3	4	5	6	7	8	9
10	20	15	08	20	30	50	40	25

Output in this problem is of two types: 1. Successful Search 2. Unsuccessful Search

1. **Successful Search:** Element to be searched is present in the array. Minimum numbers of comparisons are required when we are searching for 1st element i.e., 10 in this problem and number of comparisons are 1, if numbers of elements are increased from 9 to 100 numbers of comparisons are not changed. This is best case for linear search.

   Here algorithm is same only we are changing the input, we get the output in least amount of time and it is $O(1)$ or $O(c)$ or $O(k)$ where c & k are constants, $O(1)$ does not mean 1 comparison, it means algorithm takes constant time independent of number of inputs.

   Maximum number of comparisons are required if we search for last element i.e., 25 in this problem, number of comparison equal to number of elements i.e., 9 in this problem. As number of elements is increasing, number of comparisons also increases. So time taken is dependent on number of elements and it is linear. This case falls under Worst case.

   Worst case for Linear Search $= O(n)$.

2. **Unsuccessful Search:** If the element to be searched is not present in the array, then search is unsuccessful. Number of comparison required is 'n'. So in this case Best case, Worst case and Average case, all are same and it is equal to $O(n)$.

   Best case = Worst case = Average case = $O(n)$

   Time complexity of an algorithm can be found in three ways:

   (i) Brute force method (ii) Step count method (iii) Asymptotic Notation

1.5.4.2.1 Brute Force Method

Time Complexity of a program 'p' can be defined as the sum of compile time and execution time (runtime). Let us suppose that we compile a program for once and we run it several times. Then runtime of program will be considered. Let the runtime be t_p.

t_p = time taken to perform all the operations present in the program(addition, subtraction, comparison etc).

As t_p is influenced by many other factors and these factors are unknown at the time of conceiving of the program, only estimation of t_p is possible.

Let us assume that we know the characteristics of the compiler to be used. Let us determine the number of additions, subtractions, multiplications, divisions, comparisons, loads, and stores etc., that are performed by code for p.

Hence, an expression for t_p is as follows:

$$t_p(k) = C_a\,ADD(k) + C_s\,SUB(k) + C_m\,MUL(k) + C_d\,DIV(k) + \ldots\ldots$$

'k' denotes instance characteristics and C_a, C_s, C_m, C_d etc., represent the time required for additions, subtractions, multiplications, divisions respectively. ADD, SUB, MUL, DIV are the functions that represent the number of additions, subtractions, multiplications, divisions etc that are performed when the code for 'p' is used on an instance with characteristic 'k'.

But it is difficult to obtain such an exact formula because the time of execution depends upon the numbers being operated upon. Also in the case of a multi-user system the execution time depends upon numerous factors such as system load, number of other programs being run on the computer at that particular instance.

1.5.4.2.2 Step Count Method

A program step is defined as a meaningful statement of a program that has an execution time that is independent of the instance characteristics. It is assumed that all statements have same cost (i.e., execution time). We can determine the total number of steps needed by the program by counting the total number of steps.

Order of Magnitude of an algorithm: Each algorithm contains a finite number of statements. Each statement occurs one or more times. The sum of number of occurrences of all the statements contained in an algorithm is called order of magnitude of an algorithm.

Example:

```
For (i = 0; i < n; i++)
    {
---------
---------        }  'k' statements
---------
    }
```

Let us assume in above program, there are 'k' statements enclosed in the for loop and statement taken one unit of time for execution. Hence the execution of 'k' statements requires 'k' units of time. If these 'k' statements are executed 'n' times, then execution time is n*k units.

Hence order of magnitude of above algorithm = n*k units.

1. Few examples for finding out number of steps using step count method:

Example:

```
Algorithm Sum()
{
read (a,b,c,d);        ← 1 unit
x=a+b+c+d;             ← 1 unit
write(c)               ← 1 unit
}                      -------------
                          3 units
                       -------------
```

The above algorithm has Four inputs, output and number of steps are three.

Step count =3;

2. Finding the sum of n numbers stored in the array a "n" is known as instance characteristics (input size):

```
Algorithm Sum(a,n)
{
    sum:=0.0;              ← 1 unit
    for i:=1 to n do       ← n+1 unit
    sum:=sum + a[i];       ← n unit
    write(sum);            ← 1 unit
}                          -------------
                            2n+3 units
                           -------------
```

Step count = 2n + 3

3. Read n values from keyboard find their sum and average:

```
Algorithm Avg( )
{
sum:=0.0;              ← 1 unit
Read n;                ← 1 unit
for i:=1 to n do       ← n+1 unit
  {
    Read num;          ← n unit
    Sum=sum + num;     ← n unit
  }
  Avg=sum/n            ← 1 unit
  Write(sum, avg);     ← 1 unit
  }
                       -------------
                         3n+5 units
                       -------------
```

Step count = 3n + 5

4. Addition of matrix A and matrix B of dimension m × n storing result in matrix C:

```
Algorithm matadd(a,b,c,m,n)
{
   for i:=1 to m do            ← m+1 unit
    for j:=1 to n do           ← m(n+1) unit
    c[i,j]=a[i,j]+b[i,j];      ← mn unit
}                              --------------
                              2mn+2m+1 units
                              --------------
```

Step count = 2mn + 2m + 1

5. Finding nth fibonacci number:

```
Algorithm Fibonacci(n)
{
   if (n<=1) then              ← 1 unit
        write(n);
   else
{
    fib1 := 0;                 ← 1 unit
    fib2 := 1;                 ← 1 unit
    for i := 2 to n do         ← n+1 units
    {
      fib := fib1 + fib2;      ← n units
      fib1 := fib2;            ← n units
      fib2 := fib;             ← n units
    }
      Write (fn);              ← 1 unit
   }
}                              --------------
                               4n+5 units
                              --------------
```

Step count = 4n + 5

6. Finding the sum of n numbers stored in the array a using recursion:

```
Algorithm RecSum(a,n)              ← T(n) unit
{
  if(n<=0) then                    ← 1 unit
  {
     Return 0;
}
else
{
return RecSum(a, n-1) + a[n]; ← T(n-1) + b units
}
}
```

Solution: $T(n) = 1 \quad n = 0$

$$T(n) = T(n-1) + b \quad n > 0$$

Step count method for C programs:

```
1. main ( )
   {
   int a,b,c;
   scanf("%d%d",&a,&b);          ← 1 unit
   c=a+b;                        ← 1 unit
   printf("%d",c)                ← 1 unit
   }                             ------------
                                     3 units
                                 ------------
```

Step count = 3;

```
2. main ( )
   {
   int n;
   printf("enter a number");    ← 1 unit
   scanf("%d", &n);             ← 1 unit
   for(int i=0;i≤n;i++)         ← 2n+2 unit
   printf("shyam");            ← n unit
   }                            -------------
                                   3n+4 units
                                -------------
```

Step count = 3n + 4;

1.5.5 Asymptoic Notation: [Formal Definitions]

We use same simple abstractions to simplify algorithm analysis. First we ignored the actual cost of each statement, assumed that all statements have same cost (i.e., execution time). Then we observed that handling these constants are also complex, the running time of any sorting algorithm is $an^2 + bn + c$ for some +ve constants a, b & c that depend on the statement cost.

As the Size of 'n' is very large we are interested only in growth function of the running time of the algorithm. We are interested in finding out as 'n' is increased running time is also increased or not. If running time is not increased as 'n' is increased then the running time is independent of 'n' and time complexity is O(1).

If the running time is increased as 'n' is increased, then running time is dependent on 'n'. If the running time of an algorithm is $an^2 + bn + c$. We consider only the leading term of the formula (eg. an^2) since the lower order terms are relatively insignificant for large n.

We also ignore the coefficient of the leading term, Since they are less significant then the rate of growth.

This study of growth functions are called Asymptotic analysis of algorithm, and they are denoted by Asymptotic notations.

This asymptotic notation contains five types they are as follows.
1. Big-Oh Notation(O-Notation)
2. Omega Notation(Ω-Notation)
3. Theta Notation (Θ Notation)
4. Little –oh Notation(o-Notation)
5. Little omega Notation (ω-Notation)

1.5.5.1 Big-Oh Notation (O- Notation)

Big –Oh notation denoted by 'O' is a method of representing the upper bound or worst case of algorithm's run time. Using big-oh notation, we can give longest amount of time taken by the algorithm to complete.

Definition: Let f(n) and g(n) are two non-negative functions. The function **f(n) = O(g(n))** if   there exist positive constants n_0 and c such that **f(n) $\leq$ c*g(n)** for all n, n>n_0.

$\rightarrow$ Means order at most

$\rightarrow$ Used to measure the worst case time complexity.

Find Big oh for the following functions:

```
1.  f(n)=2n² + 3n + 1
    f(n)  = O(g(n))
    f(n)  <= cg(n)                   n>=n₀
    2n² + 3n + 1 <= 1               false
    2n² + 3n + 1 <= 3n              false
    2n² + 3n + 1 <= n²             false
    2n² + 3n + 1 <= 2n²            false
    2n² + 3n + 1 <= 3n²            true for n > = 4
    f(n)<=3n²
    f(n) = O(n²) where c = 3 and n₀= 4
2.  f(n)  = 5n + 4                   n > = n₀
          5n + 4 < =4               false
          5n + 4 < = 5n             false
          5n + 4 < = 6n             true for n > = 4
    f(n)= O(n) where c = 6 and n₀ = 4
```

3. $f(n) = 10n^3 + 6n^2 + 6n + 2$
$$10n^3 + 6n^2 + 6n + 2 <= 11n^3 \quad n >= 7$$
$f(n) = O(n^3)$ where $c = 11$ $n_0 = 7$

Consider the function $f(n) = 2n + 2$ and $g(n) = n^2$ we have to find constant c so that $f(n) \leq g(n)$, in other words $2n + 2 \leq n^2$ then we find that for n = 1 or 2, f(n) is greater than g(n) that means for c = 1 when n = 1, f(n) = 4 and g(n) = 1, for n = 2, f(n) = 6 and g(n) = 4. When $n \geq 3$ we obtain $f(n) \leq g(n)$.

Hence $f(n) = O(g(n))$

$5n + 2 = O(n)$ as $5n + 2 <= 6n$ for all $n >= 2$.

$109n + 6 = O(n)$ as $109n + 6 <= 110n$ for all $n >= 6$.

$13n^2 + 6n + 2 = O(n^2)$ as $10n^2 + 4n + 2 <= 14n^2$ for all $n >= 6$.

$4*2^n + n^2 = O(2^n)$ as $4*2^n + n^2 <= 5*2^n$ for $n >= 4$.

Various meanings associated with Big-Oh are

$O(1)$ - Constant computing time

$O(n)$ – Linear

$O(n^2)$ – Quadratic

$O(n^3)$ – Cubic

$O(2^n)$ – Exponential

$O(\log n)$ – Logarithmic

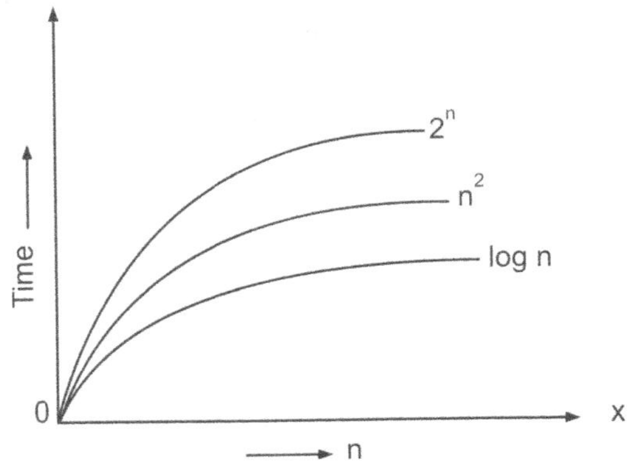

The relationship among those computing time is $0(1) < 0(\log n) < 0(n) < 0(n^2) < 0(2^n)$

$O(2^n)$ – rate of growth is very high (algorithm takes slower)

$O(\log n)$ – rate of growth is very less (algorithm takes faster)

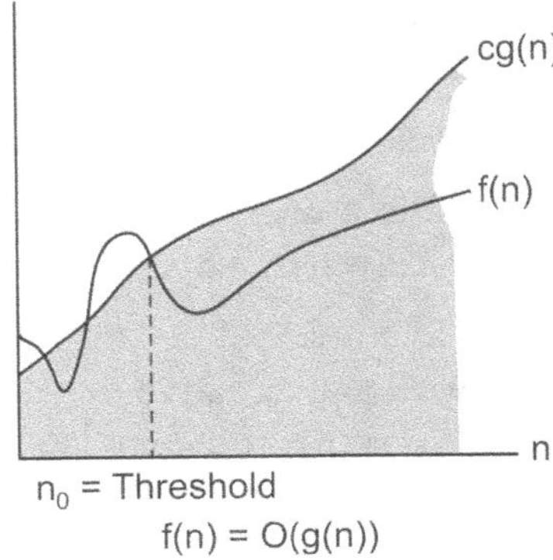

g(n) is an asymptotic upper bound for f(n).

1.5.5.2 Omega Notation (Ω-Notation)

Omega notation denoted as 'Ω' is a method of representing the bound of algorithm running time using omega notation we can denote shortest amount of time taken by algorithm to complete.

Definition: Let $f(n)$ and $g(n)$ are two non-negative functions. The function $f(n) = \Omega(g(n))$ if there exist positive constants C and n_0 such that $f(n) > c*g(n)$ for all n, $n \geq n_0$.

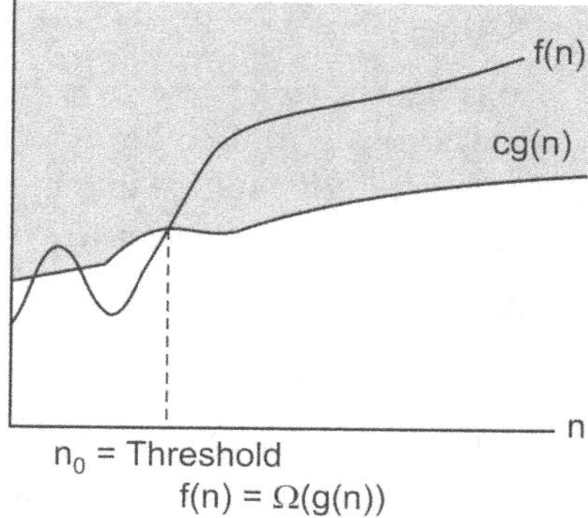

→ Means order at least.

→ Used to measure best case time complexity.

$g(n)$ is an asymptotic lower bound for $f(n)$.

Example: Consider $f(n) = 2n + 5$ and $g(n) = 2n$ then $2n + 5 \geq 2n$. for $n > 1$ hence $2n + 5 = \Omega(n)$ $5n + 2 = \Omega(n)$ as $5n + 2 >= 5n$ for $n >= 1$. (the inequality holds for $n >= 0$, but the definition of Ω requires an $n_0 > 0$).

$109n + 6 = \Omega(n)$ as $109n + 6 >= 109n$ for all $n >= 1$.

$13n^2 + 6n + 2 = \Omega(n^2)$ as $13n^2 + 4n + 2 >= 13n^2$ for all $n >= 1$.

$4*2^n + n^2 = \Omega(2^n)$ as $4*2^n + n^2 >= 4*2^n$ for $n >= 1$.

Observe also that

$5n + 2 = \Omega(1)$.

$13n^2 + 6n + 2 = \Omega(n)$.

$13n^2 + 6n + 2 = \Omega(1)$.

$4*2^n + n^2 = \Omega(n^2)$.

$4*2^n + n^2 = \Omega(n)$.

$4*2^n + n^2 = \Omega(1)$.

1.5.5.3 Theta Notation (Θ-Notation)

Theta notation denoted as 'Θ' is a method of representing running time between upper bound and lower bound.

Let $f(n)$ and $g(n)$ be two non negative functions. The function $f(n) = \sim (g(n))$ if there exist positive constants C_1, C_2 and n_0 such that $C_1 g(n) \leq f(n) \leq C_2 g(n)$ for all n, $n \geq n_0$.

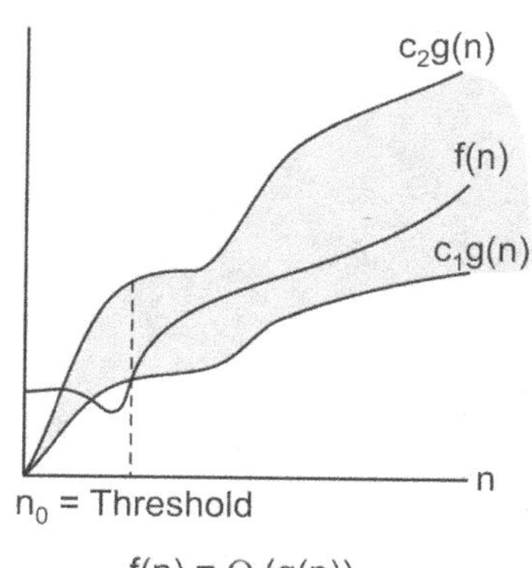

$\rightarrow$ Means order exactly.

$\rightarrow$ Used to find average case time complexity

g(n) is an asymptotically tight bound for f(n).

E.g., if f(n) = 2n + 8 > 5n where n $\geq$ 2; 2n + 8 $\geq$ 6n where n $\geq$ 2 and 2n + 8 < 7n when n $\geq$ 2. Hence 2n + 8 = Θ(n) such that constants C_1 = 5, C_2 = 7 and n_0 = 2.

The theta notation is more precise than both big-oh and omega notation.

1.5.5.4 Little "oh" Notation (o-Notation)

Little oh notation is denoted as o. It is used to denote proper upper bound that is not asymptotically tight.

Let f(n) and g(n) are two non-negative functions. The function f(n) = o(g(n)) if there exist positive constants n_0 and c such that f(n) < c*g(n) for all n, n > n_o .

$$\lim_{n \to \alpha} \frac{f(n)}{g(n)} = 0$$

E.g., The function 3n + 2 = o(n^2) since $\lim_{n \to \alpha} \dfrac{3n + 2}{n^2} = 0$

$$f(n) = 3n + 2$$

$$f(n) < c \, g(n)$$

$$3n + 2 < n^2 \qquad n >= 4$$

$$\lim_{n \to \alpha} \frac{3n + 2}{n^2} = 0$$

$$3n + 2 = o(n^2)$$

1.5.5.5 Little Omega Notation (ω-Notation)

Little omega notation is used to denote proper lower bound that is not asymptotically tight.

Let f(n) and g(n) are two non-negative functions. The function **f(n) = w(g(n))** if there exist positive constants n_0 and c such that **f(n) > c*g(n)** for all n, n > n_0 .

$$\lim_{n \to \alpha} \frac{g(n)}{f(n)} = 0$$

Ex: The function n^2 + 6 since $\lim_{n \to \alpha} \dfrac{n}{n^2 + 6} = 0$

$$f(n) = n^2 + 6$$

$$f(n) > cg(n)$$

$$n^2 + 6 > n \quad n >= 1$$

$$\lim_{n \to \alpha} \frac{n}{n^2 + 6} = 0$$

$$n^2 + 6 > \omega(n)$$

1.5.6 Properties of Asymptotic Notations

Many of the relational properties of real numbers apply to asymptotic comparisons as well. For the following, assume that f(n) and g(n) are asymptotically positive.

Transitivity

$f(n) = \Theta(g(n))$ and $g(n) = \Theta(h(n))$ imply $f(n) = \Theta(h(n))$,

$f(n) = O(g(n))$ and $g(n) = O(h(n))$ imply $f(n) = O(h(n))$,

$f(n) = \Omega(g(n))$ and $g(n) = \Omega(h(n))$ imply $f(n) = \Omega(h(n))$,

$f(n) = o(g(n))$ and $g(n) = o(h(n))$ imply $f(n) = o(h(n))$,

$f(n) = \omega(g(n))$ and $g(n) = \omega(h(n))$ imply $f(n) = \omega(h(n))$.

Reflexivity

$f(n) = \Theta(f(n))$,

$f(n) = O(f(n))$,

$f(n) = \Omega(f(n))$.

Symmetry

$f(n) = \Theta(g(n))$ if and only if $g(n) = \Theta(f(n))$.

Transpose symmetry

$f(n) = O(g(n))$ if and only if $g(n) = \Omega(f(n))$,

$f(n) = o(g(n))$ if and only if $g(n) = \omega(f(n))$.

Comparison of Asymptotic notations with real numbers: Let f(n) and g(n) be two non negative functions and a and b be two real numbers.

$f(n) = O(g(n)) \approx a \leq b,$

$f(n) = \Omega(g(n)) \approx a \geq b,$

$f(n) = \Theta(g(n)) \approx a = b,$

$f(n) = o(g(n)) \approx a < b,$

$f(n) = \omega(g(n)) \approx a > b.$

We say that f(n) is asymptotically smaller than g(n) if f(n) = o(g(n)), and f(n) is asymptotically larger than g(n) if f(n) = ω(g(n)).

One property of real numbers, however, does not carry over to asymptotic notation:

Trichotomy: For any two real numbers a and b, exactly one of the following must hold: a < b, a = b, or a > b, but all functions cannot be asymptotically comparable.

Any two real numbers can be compared, but not all functions are asymptotically comparable. Let f(n) and g(n) are two non-negative functions, a special case may exist for which neither f(n) = O(g(n)) nor f(n) = Ω(g(n)) are satisfied. For example, the functions n and $n^{1+\cos n}$ cannot be compared using asymptotic notation, since the value of 1 + cos (n) rotates between 0 and 2, taking on all values in between.

if f(n) = O(g(n)) and h(n) = O(g(n)) then f(n) + h(n) = O(max(g(n), d(n)))

if f(n) = O(g(n)) and h(n) = O(g(n)) then f(n) * h(n) = O(g(n) * d(n))

if f(n) = O(g(n)) Then a*f(n) = O(g(n)) where 'a' is constant.

1.5.6.1 Time Complexity of Program Segments with Loops

```
1. for i :=1 to n
   s;
   complexity: O(n)
2. for i:=1 to n
   for j:=1 to n
   s;
   complexity: O(n²)
3. i=1, k=1;
   While(k<=n)
   {
   i++;
   k=k+i;
   }
   complexity: O(√2)
4. for (i=1; i*i <=n;++i)
   S;
   complexity: O(√2)
5. j=1;
   while(j<=n)
   {
   j=j*2;
   }
   complexity: O(log n)
```

```
6. for i:=1 to n/2
   for j:=1 to n/3
   for k:=1 to n/4
   s;
```
complexity: $O(n^3)$

```
7. for i:=1 to n
   for(j=1; j<=n; j=j*2)
   s;
```
complexity: $O(n \log n)$

```
8. for i:=1 to n
   for j:=1 to n
   for k:=1 to n
   { s;
   break;
   }
```
complexity: $O(n^2)$

1.6 RECURRENCE RELATIONS

Definition 1: A recurrence relation is an equation or inequality that illustrates a function in terms of its value on smaller inputs. Special techniques are required to analyze the space and time required.

Definition 2: Recurrence relation is an equation that recursively defines a sequence, once one or more initial terms are given.

Each further term of the sequence is defined as a function of the preceeding terms.

A recurrence relation is the arrangement of a series of values in terms of previous values in the sequence and base values.

Solving Recurrence Relations: Solution to recurrence relation can be obtained using two methods: 1. substitution method 2. Masters method.

1.6.1 Substitution Method

In this method we consistently guess an asymptotic bound (upper or lower) on the solution, and trying to prove it by induction.

Example Problems:

1. $T(n) = T(n-1) + n$ 　　　$n > 1$

   $T(n) = 1$ 　　　　　　　$n = 1$

Solution:

$T(n) = T(n-1) + n$ 　　　　　　　　　　　.....(1)

$$T(n-1) = T(n-2) + n - 1 \quad\quad\quad\quad\quad .....(2)$$

Substituting (2) in (1)

$$T(n) = T(n-2) + n - 1 + n \quad\quad\quad\quad\quad .....(3)$$

$$T(n-2) = T(n-3) + n - 2 \quad\quad\quad\quad\quad .....(4)$$

Substituting (4) in (3)

$$T(n) = T(n-3) + n - 2 + n - 1 + n \quad\quad\quad\quad\quad .....(5)$$

General equation

$$T(n) = T(n-k) + (n - (k-1)) + n - (k-2) + n - (k-3) + n - 1 + n$$

$$.....(6)$$

$$T(1) = 1$$

$$n - k = 1$$

$$k = n - 1 \quad\quad\quad\quad\quad .....(7)$$

Substituting (7) in (6)

$$T(n) = T(1) + 2 + 3 + ... n - 1 + n$$

$$= 1 + 2 + 3 + ... + n$$

$$= n(n+1)/2$$

$$T(n) = O(n^2)$$

2. $T(n) = T(n-1) + b \quad\quad n > 1$

$T(n) = 1 \quad\quad\quad\quad\quad\quad n = 1$

***Solution*:**

$$T(n) = T(n-1) + b \quad\quad\quad\quad\quad .....(1)$$

$$T(n-1) = T(n-2) + b \quad\quad\quad\quad\quad .....(2)$$

Substituting (2) in (1)

$$T(n) = T(n-2) + b + b$$

$$T(n) = T(n-2) + 2b \quad\quad\quad\quad\quad .....(3)$$

$$T(n-2) = T(n-3) + b \quad\quad\quad\quad\quad .....(4)$$

Substituting (4) in (3)

$$T(n) = T(n-3) + 3b$$

General equation

$$T(n) = T(n-k) + k.b$$

$$T(1) = 1$$

$$n - k = 1$$

$$k = n - 1$$

$$T(n) = T(1) + (n-1)b$$

$$= 1 + bn - b$$

$$T(n) = O(n)$$

3. $T(n) = 2\,T(n-1) + b \qquad n > 1$

   $T(n) = 1 \qquad\qquad\qquad n = 1$

***Solution*:**

$$T(1) = 1$$

$$T(2) = 2.T(1) + b$$
$$= 2 + b$$
$$= 2^1 + b$$

$$T(3) = 2T(2) + b$$
$$= 2(2 + b) + b$$
$$= 4 + 2b + b$$
$$= 4 + 3b$$
$$= 2^2 + (2^2 - 1)b$$

$$T(4) = 2.T(3) + b$$
$$= 2(4 + 3b) + b$$
$$= 8 + 7b$$
$$= 2^3 + (2^3 - 1)b$$

General equation

$$T(k) = 2^{k-1} + (2^{k-1} - 1)b$$

$$\vdots$$

$$T(n) = 2^{n-1} + (2^{n-1} - 1)b$$
$$T(n) = 2^{n-1}(b + 1) - b$$
$$= 2^n(b + 1)/2 - b$$

Let $c = (b + 1)/2$

$$T(n) = c\,2^n - b$$
$$= O(2^n)$$

4. $T(n) = T(n/2) + b \qquad n > 1$

   $T(1) = 1 \qquad\qquad\quad n = 1$

***Solution*:**

$$T(n) = T(n/2) + b \qquad\qquad\qquad\qquad\qquad \text{.....(1)}$$
$$T(n/2) = T(n/4) + b \qquad\qquad\qquad\qquad\quad \text{.....(2)}$$

Substituting (2) in (1)

$$T(n) = T(n/4) + b + b$$
$$= T(n/4) + 2b \qquad\qquad\qquad\qquad\qquad \text{.....(3)}$$
$$T(n/4) = T(n/8) + b \qquad\qquad\qquad\qquad\quad \text{.....(4)}$$

Substituting (4) in (3)

$T(n) = T(n/8) + 3b$

$\quad = T(n/2^3) + 3b$

General equation

$T(n) = T(n/2^k) + kb$ $\qquad\qquad\qquad\qquad$ .....(5)

$T(1) = 1$

$n/2^k = 1$

$2^k = n$

$K = \log n$ $\qquad\qquad\qquad\qquad\qquad\qquad\qquad$ .....(6)

Substituting (6) in (5)

$T(n) = T(1) + b.\log n$

$\quad = 1 + b \log n$

$T(n) = O(\log n)$

1.6.2 The Master Method

This is a cookbook method for determining asymptotic solutions to recurrences of a specific form. Master method provides solution to recurrence relation of the function.

$$T(n) = aT(n/b) + f(n) \qquad n > d$$

$$\quad\quad\;\; = c \qquad\qquad\qquad\quad n = d$$

Where a, b, c and d are positive constants.

$\quad a >= 1, b > 1, c >= 1, d >= 1.$

$\quad T(n) = a\ T(n/b) + f(n),$

Where we interpret n/b to mean either $\lceil n/b \rceil \lfloor n/b \rfloor$. Then T(n) can be bounded asymptotically as follows:

Case 1: If $f(n) = O((n^{\log_b a - \epsilon})$ for some constant $\epsilon > 0$, then $T(n) = \theta(n^{\log_b a})$.

Case 2: If $f(n) = \theta(n^{\log_b a} \log^k n)$, then $T(n) = \theta (n^{\log_b a} \log^{k+1} n)$.

Case 3: $f(n) = \Omega(n^{\log_b a + \epsilon})$ for some constant $\epsilon > 0$, and if $af(n/b) <= cf(n)$ for some constant $c < 1$ and all sufficiently large n, then $T(n) = \theta(f(n))$.

Use the master method to give tight asymptotic bounds for the following recurrences:

1. $T(n) = 4T(n/2) + n \qquad\qquad n > 1$

$\quad T(n) = 1 \qquad\qquad\qquad\qquad n = 1$

From the above recurrence relation we obtain

$a = 4, b = 2, c = 1, d = 1, f(n) = n$

$\log_b a = \log_2 4 = \log_2 2^2 = 2 \log_2 2 = 2$

$n^{\log_b a} = n^2$

$$f(n) = O(n^2)$$
$$n = O(n^2) \quad \text{It will fall in Case 1. So that}$$
$$T(n) = \theta(n^2)$$

2. $T(n) = 4T(n/2) + n^2 \qquad\qquad n > 1$

   $T(n) = 1 \qquad\qquad n = 1$

   From the above recurrence relation we obtain

   $a = 4, b = 2, c = 1, d = 1, f(n) = n^2$

   $n^{\log_b a} = n^2$

   $f(n) = \theta(n^2)$

   $n^2 = \theta(n^2)$

   It will fall in case 2.

   $T(n) = \theta(n^2 \log n)$

3. $T(n) = 4T(n/2) + n^3 \qquad\qquad n > 1$

   $T(n) = 1 \qquad\qquad n = 1$

   From the above recurrence relation we obtain

   $a = 4, b = 2, c = 1, d = 1, f(n) = n^3$

   $n^{\log_b a} = n^3$

   $f(n) = \Omega(n^{\log_b a + \epsilon})$

   $\qquad = \Omega(n^{2 + \epsilon})$

   $n^3 = \Omega(n^{2 + \epsilon})$

   This will fall in case 3.

   $T(n) = \theta(n^3)$

4. $T(n) = 2T(n/2) + n \qquad\qquad n > 1$

   $T(n) = 1 \qquad\qquad n = 1$

   From the above recurrence relation we obtain

   $a = 2, b = 2, c = 1, d = 1, f(n) = n$

   $n^{\log_b a} = n^{\log_2 2} = n$

   $f(n) = \theta \, n^{\log_b a})$

   $\qquad = \theta(n)$

   It will fall in case 2.

   $T(n) = \theta(n \log n)$

1.7 PROBABILISTIC ANALYSIS

To analyze the running time of an algorithm we use theory of probability. Probabilistic analysis is used to find out average running over all possible inputs. It is required to know about the distribution of the inputs to perform probabilistic analysis to compute an expected running time.

In some problems, the set of all possible inputs can be assumed, for other problems set of all possible inputs cannot be determined. Probabilistic analysis can be used to all problems where the set of all possible inputs can be assumed for other problems we cannot apply probabilistic analysis.

Input distribution should be known to apply probabilistic analysis. Some part of the algorithm behavior is randomized, for analysis and design of algorithms probability and randomness is used very frequently and these algorithms are called probabilistic or randomized algorithms.

In these algorithms a random bits generated through pseudo random generator are used as an auxiliary input to get the good 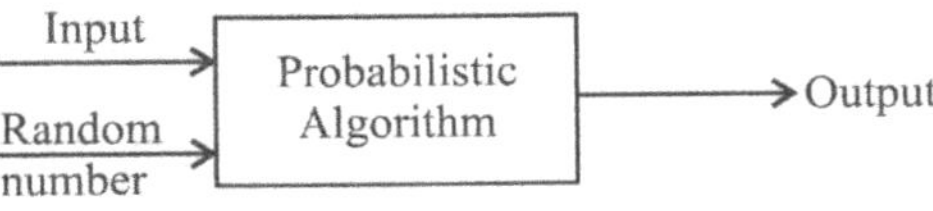

performance in the average case. The performance of the algorithm will be determined by the random input and it is called the expected run time. The worst case is ignored as the probability of its occurrence is very less.

Example: An array of n elements having n/2 '1's and n/2 '0's, the problem is to search a '1' in this array. If we use any deterministic algorithm it will take n/2 comparisons, which is very long, and it is not guaranteed for all possible inputs that the algorithm will complete quickly.

With high probability we can search quickly '1' if we check elements at random for all possible inputs.

Randomized Algorithm is used in Quick sort where the complexity of the problem is reduced from $O(n^2)$ to $O(n \log n)$ for some set of input such as when the elements are already in sorted order.

1.8 AMORTIZED ANALYSIS

An important analysis tool useful for understanding the run times of algorithms that have steps with widely varying performance is "amortization". The term "amortization" itself comes from the field of accounting, which provides an instance monetary metaphor for algorithm analysis.

Example: The above example provides a motivation for the amortization technique, which gives us a worst case way of performing an average case analysis. Formally, we define the amortized running time of an operation within a series of operations as the worst case running time of the series of operations divided by number of operations. When the series of operations is not specified, it is usually assumed to be a series of operations from the repertoire of a certain data structure starting from an empty structure. Thus amortized running time of each operation in the clearable table ADT is

'O(n)'. When we implement that clearable table with an array. Note that the actual running time of operation may be much higher than the amortized running time.

For example, a particular clear operation may take 'O(n)' time.

The advantage of using amortization is that it gives us a way to a robust average case analysis without using any probability.

Amortized complexity: In amortized complexity we change sum of the actual cost of an operation to other operation. The amortized cost of each insertion is no more than 2 and that of each deletion is no more than 6.

The actual cost of any insertion or deletion is no more than   '2 * I + 6 * D'.

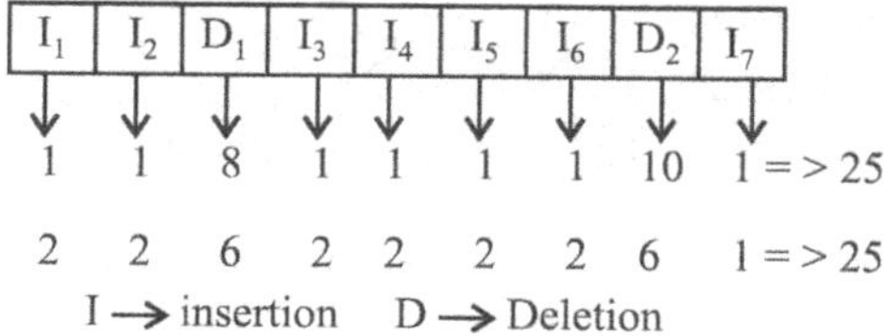

Amortized means finalizing the average run time per operation over a worst case sequence of operations.

Note: The only requirement is that the sum of the amortized complexity of all operations in any sequence of operations be greater than or equal to their sum of actual complexity.

$$\sum_{1<=i<=n} \text{amortized}(i) \geq \sum_{1<=i<=n} \text{actual}(i)$$

Case Study 1: Linear Search

1	2	3	4	5	6	7	8	9
10	20	15	08	20	30	50	40	25

Number of comparisons required to search: 10   → 1 comparison
Number of comparisons required to search: 20   → 2 comparisons
Number of comparisons required to search: 15   → 3 comparisons
Number of comparisons required to search: 08   → 4 comparisons
Number of comparisons required to search: 20   → 5 comparisons
Number of comparisons required to search: 30   → 6 comparisons
Number of comparisons required to search: 50   → 7 comparisons
Number of comparisons required to search: 40   → 8 comparisons
Number of comparisons required to search: 25   → 9 comparisons

Total number of comparisons required to search all the elements in the array are 45.

Then amortized cost = total number of comparison/ total number of elements

$$= 45/9 = 5$$

Case Study 2: Binary Search

1	2	3	4	5	6	7
10	15	20	21	40	45	70

Number of comparisons required to search: 10 $\rightarrow$ 3 comparisons

Number of comparisons required to search: 15 $\rightarrow$ 2 comparisons

Number of comparisons required to search: 20 $\rightarrow$ 3 comparisons

Number of comparisons required to search: 21 $\rightarrow$ 1 comparison

Number of comparisons required to search: 40 $\rightarrow$ 3 comparisons

Number of comparisons required to search: 45 $\rightarrow$ 2 comparisons

Number of comparisons required to search: 70 $\rightarrow$ 3 comparisons

Total number of comparisons required to search all the elements in the array are 17.

Then amortized cost = total number of comparison/ total number of elements

$$= 17/7 = 2.43$$

1. low = 1, high = 7, mid = (1+7)/2 = 4 $\rightarrow$ 1 comparison
2. low = mid +1 = 5, high = 7, mid = (5 + 7)/2 = 6 $\rightarrow$ 2 comparisons
3. low = 1, high = mid − 1 = 3, mid = (1 + 3)/2 = 2 $\rightarrow$ 2 comparisons
4. low = mid +1 = 7, high = 7, mid = (7 + 7)/2 = 7 $\rightarrow$ 3 comparisons
5. low = 5, high = mid − 1 = 5, mid = (5 + 5)/2 = 5 $\rightarrow$ 3 comparisons
6. low = mid +1 =3, high = 3, mid = (3 + 3)/2 = 3 $\rightarrow$ 3 comparisons
7. low = 1, high = mid − 1 = 1, mid = (1 + 1)/2 =2 $\rightarrow$ 3 comparisons

Previous Gate Questions and Solutions

1. Consider the following three claims
    1. $(n + k)^m = \Theta(n^m)$, where k and m are constants
    2. $2^{n+1} = O(2^n)$
    3. $2^{2n+1} = O(2^n)$

Which of these claims are correct?

(a) 1 and 2   (b) 1 and 3

(c) 2 and 3   (d) 1, 2 and 3

Answer: (a)

Solution:

Consider each statement separately

I. $f(n) = (n + k)^m$

So, $f(n) = (1 + n)^m$

Assume $k = 1$ constant

$f(n) = 1 + {}^mC_{1n} + {}^mC_{2n} + \text{---------} {}^mC_m \, n^m$

$f(n) = O(n^m)$ which is correct

II. $f(n) = 2^{n+1}$

$f(n) = 2^n \cdot 2^1$

$f(n) = 2.2^n$

$f(n) = O(2^n)$ which is correct

III. $f(n) = 2^{n+1}$

$f(n) = 2^{2n} . 2^1$

$f(n) = 2.2^{2n}$

$f(n) = O(2^{2n})$ which is false

Then I and II are correct.

2. Let A $[1,...., n]$ be an array storing a bit(1 or 0) at each location, and $f(m)$ is a function whose time complexity is $\theta(m)$. Consider the following program fragment written in a C like language:

```
Counter = 0;
for(i=0;i<n;i++)
{if (A[i]==1)counter++;
else {f(counter);counter=0;
}}
```

The Complexity of the program fragment is:

(a) $\Omega(n^2)$ (b) $\Omega(n \log n)$ and $O(n^2)$

(c) $\theta(n)$ (d) $o(n)$

Answer: (c)

Solution:

The given code is:

```
1.  Counter = 0;
```

```
2.  for(i=0;i<n;i++)
3.  {if (A[i]==1)counter++;
4.  else {f(counter);counter=0};
5.  }
```

The time complexity of the program fragment depends on the frequency (Number of steps) of line 3 and 4. In line 4 the frequency depends on the variable counter and there is no increment in the counter variable which is initialize to 0, so f(0) then counter = 0 means there is no cell in an array which having a bit 0, so all cells in the array contain 1. Consider the line 3 if (A[i] = 1)counter++; the value of i will be increases up to n so the value of counter will be n. Since n is the frequency of the line 3 and the frequency of the line 4 is 0. So the time complexity of the line 3 is O(n) on average n and f(0) = O(1) is the time complexity of line 4. So the time complexity of the program fragment is maximum of line 3 and 4 which is O(n) on average.

3. The time complexity of the following C function is (assume n>0)
```
int recursive(int n) {
if(n==1)
return(1);
else
return(recursive(n-1) + recursive(n-1));
}
```

(a) O(n)   (b) O(n log n)   (c) $O(n^2)$ (d) $O(2^n)$

Answer: (d)

Solution:

The given C function is recursive. The best way to find the time complexity of recursive function is that convert the code (algorithm) into recursion equation and solution of the recursion equation is time complexity of the given algorithm.

```
1. int recursive(int n) {
2. if(n==1) return(1);
3. else
4. return(recursive(n - 1) + recursive(n - 1));
5. }
```

The name of the function is recursive

Let recursive(n) = T(n)

According to line 2 if(n = 1) return(1)

Then the recursion equation is

$T(n) = 1 \quad n = 1$

According to line 4 recursion equation is

$T(n) = T(n-1) + T(n-1) \; n > 1$

Or $\quad T(n) = 2T(n-1) \; n > 1$

So the complete recursion equation is

$T(n) = 1 \; n = 1$

$T(n) = T(n-1) + T(n-1) \; n > 1$

Or $T(n) = 2T(n-1) \; n > 1$

$T(1) = 1 = 2^0$

$T(2) = 2T(1) = 2.1 = 2^1$

$T(3) = 2T(2) = 2.2 = 2^2$

$T(4) = 2T(3) = 2.3 = 2^3$

$$\cdot \quad \cdot \; \cdot \qquad \cdot$$

$$\cdot \quad \cdot \; \cdot \qquad \cdot$$

$$\cdot \quad \cdot \; \cdot \qquad \cdot$$

$T(n) = 2^{n-1}$

Or $T(n) = 2^n . 1/2$

So $T(n) = O(2^n)$

4. Suppose $T(n) = 2T(n/2) + n$, $T(0) = T(1) = 1$ Which one of the following is FALSE?

   (a) $T(n) = O(n^2)$ (b) $T(n) = \theta(n \log n)$

   (c) $T(n) = \Omega(n^2)$ (d) $T(n) = O(n \log n)$

Answer: (a)

Solution:

$T(0) = T(1) = 1$

$T(n) = 2T(n/2) + n$

$T(n) = 2T(n/2) + n \qquad\qquad n > 1$

$T(n) = 1 \qquad\qquad n = 1$

From the above recurrence relation we obtain

$a = 2, \quad b = 2, c = 1, \quad d = 1, f(n) = n$

$n \log_b a = n\log_2 2 = n$

$f(n) = \theta(n \log_b a)$

$\qquad = \theta(n)$

It will fall in case 2.

$T(n) = \theta\ (n \log n)$

Implies $T(n) = O(n \log n)$

Implies $T(n) = \Omega(n \log n) \Rightarrow \Omega\ (n^2)$

$T(n)$ is not $O(n^2)$.

5. Consider the following is true?

$T(n) = 2T([\sqrt{2}\ ]) + 1,\ T(1)=1$

Which one of the following is true?

   (a) $T(n) = \theta(\log \log n)$ (b) $T(n) = \theta(\log n)$

   (c) $T(n) = \theta(\sqrt{2}\ )$ (d) $T(n) = \theta(n)$

Answer: (a)

Solution:

$T(1) = 1$

$T(n) = 2T([\sqrt{2}\ ]) + 1$

We know that $\log^2_2 = 1$

So, all the level sums are equal to $\log^2_2$

The problem size at level k of the recursion tree is n^{2-k} and we stop recursing this value is a constant. Setting $n^{2-k} = 2$ and solving for k gives us $2^{-k} \log_2 n = 1 \Rightarrow 2^k = \log_2 n \Rightarrow k = \log\log_2 n)$

So $T(n) = \theta(\log \log n)$

6. Consider the following functions:

$f(n) = 2^n$

$g(n) = n!$

$h(n) = n \log n$

Which of the following statements about the asymptotic behavior of f(n), g(n) and h(n) is true ?

   (a) $f(n) = O(g(n));\ g(n) = O(h(n))$

   (b) $f(n) = \Omega\ (g(n));\ g(n) = O(h(n))$

   (c) $g(n) = O(f(n));\ h(n\ ) = O(f(n))$

   (d) $h(n) = O(f(n));\ g(n) = \Omega\ (f(n))$

Answer: (d)

Solution:

$$f(n) = 2^n$$

$$\Rightarrow f(n) = O(2^n)$$

$$g(n) = n!$$

$$\Rightarrow g(n) = O(n!)$$

$$h(n) = n^{\log n}$$

$$\Rightarrow h(n) = O(n^{\log n})$$

The Asymptotic order of the function is as follows $1 < \log \log n < \log n < n^{\epsilon} < n^c < n^{\log n} < c^n < n^n < c^{cn} < n!$

Where $0 < \epsilon < 1 < c$ [$n < n^2$ means n grows more slowly than n^2]

So $n^{\log n} < c^n < n!$

$$n^{\log n} < 2^n < n!$$

Assume $C = 2$

$$h(n) < f(n) < g(n)$$

From the above relation we can arrive at $h(n) \in O(f(n))$ and $g(n) = O(f(n))$

7. Consider the Quick sort algorithm. Suppose there is a procedure for finding a pivot element which splits the list into sub-lists each of which contains at least one-fifth of the elements. Let $T(n)$ be the number of comparisons required to sort n elements. Then

   (a) $T(n) \leq 2T(n/5) + n$ (b) $T(n) \leq T(n/5) + T(4n/5) + n$

   (c) $T(n) \leq 2T(4n/5) + n$ (d) $T(n) \leq 2T(n/2) + n$

Answer: (b)

Solution:

If we want to sort n elements with the help of quick sort algorithm. If pivot elements which split the lists into two sub lists each in which one list contains one-fifth element or n/5 and other list contains 4n/5 and balancing takes n so

$$T(n) \leq T(n/5) \leq T(4n/5) + n$$

[**Note:** $n - n/5 = 5n - n/5 = 4n/5$]

8. The running time of an algorithm is represented by the following recurrence relation

$$T(n) = \begin{cases} n & n \geq 3 \\ T\left(\dfrac{n}{3}\right) + cn & \text{otherwise} \end{cases}$$

Which one of the following represents the time complexity of the algorithm?

(a) $\theta(n)$

(b) $\theta(n \log n)$

(c) $\theta(n^2)$

(d) $\theta(n^2 \log n)$

Answer: (a)

Solution:

Complexity is decided for large values of n only,

So, $T(n) = T(n/3) + cn$ for $n > 3$

Using masters theorem

Here $a = 1, b = 3, \log_b a = \log_3 1 = 0$

$f(n) = cn = \theta(n^1)$

Since $n^{\log a} = n^0$ is below $f(n) = \theta(n^1)$

This belongs to case III of masters theorem,

Where the solution is

$T(n) = \theta(f(n)) = \theta(n)$

9. Two alternative packages A and B are available for processing a database having 10^k records. Package A requires $0.0001\ n^2$ time units and Package B requires $10n\log_{10}n$ time units to process n records. What is the smallest value of k for which package B will be preferred over A ?

(a) 12

(b) 10

(c) 6

(d) 5

Answer: (c)

Solution:

A requires $0.0001\ n^2$ time units. A and B require $10\ n\log_{10}n$ time unit to process n records for package B will be preferred over A

So $0.0001\ n^2 < 10\ n\log_{10}n$

$n^2/10^5 < 10\ n\log_{10}n$

$n^2 = 10^6\ n\log_{10}n$

compare this constant with 10^K

So minimum value of $K = 6$ for which package B will be preferred over A.

10. Procedure A(n)

```
{
if (n<=2) return(1)
else
    return(A √2 ))
}
```

Solution:

$$T(n) = c, n < = 2$$

$$T(n) = T(\sqrt{2}) + 6, n > 2$$

$$T(n) = T(\sqrt{2}) + 6$$

$$T(n) = T(n^{1/2}) + b \Rightarrow T(n^{1/2}) = T(n^{1/4}) + b$$

$$T(n) = T(n^{1/4}) + 2b$$

$$T(n) = T(n^{1/8}) + 3b$$

$$T(n) = T(n^{1/2^k}) + kb \Rightarrow T(n) = T(2^{1/2^k}) + kb$$

$$T(n) = T(2) + b \log_2^1 \Rightarrow T(n) = c + b \log_2^1 \Rightarrow T(n) = c + b \log \log_2 x \Rightarrow$$

$$O(\log \log n)$$

Objective Question Bank

1. The step-by-step instructions that solve a problem are called _______ .

    [   ]

    A. An algorithm   B. A plan
    C. A sequential structure   D. None of the above

2. The primary tool used in structured design is a: [   ]

    A. Structure chart   B. Data-flow diagram
    C. Program flowchart   D. None of the above

3. System Study involves   [   ]

    A. Study of an existing system

    B. Documenting the existing system.

    C. Identifying current deficiencies and establishing new goals

    D. All of the above

4. A problem's _____ will answer the question, "What information will the computer need to know in order to either print or display the output times?"   [   ]

    A. Input   B. Output
    C. Purpose   D. None of the above

5. Documentation is prepared   [   ]

    A. At every stage   B. At system design
    C. At system analysis   D. At system development

6. Problem analysis is done during   [   ]

    A. System design phase   B. Systems analysis phase
    C. Before system test   D. All of the above

7. Two main measures for the efficiency of an algorithm are   [   ]

    A.   Processor and memory   B.   Complexity and capacity

    C.   Time and space   D.   Data and space

8. The time factor when determining the efficiency of algorithm is measured by   [   ]

    A.   Counting microseconds

    B.   Counting the number of key operations

    C.   Counting the number of statements

    D.   Counting the kilobytes of algorithm

9. The space factor when determining the efficiency of algorithm is measured by   [   ]

    A.   Counting the maximum memory needed by the algorithm

    B.   Counting the minimum memory needed by the algorithm

    C.   Counting the average memory needed by the algorithm

    D.   Counting the maximum disk space needed by the algorithm

10. Which of the following case does not exist in complexity theory?

                                                      [   ]

    A.   Best case   B.   Worst case

    C.   Average case   D.   Null case

11. Which of the following data structure store the homogeneous data elements?   [   ]

    A.   Arrays   B.   Records

    C.   Pointers   D.   None

12. An algorithm that calls itself directly or indirectly is known as   [   ]

    A.   Sub algorithm   B.   Recursion

    C.   Polish notation   D.   Traversal algorithm

13. _________ is a method of expressing algorithms by a collection of geometric shapes with imbedded descriptions of algorithmic steps [   ]

    A.   Flow chart   B.   Chart

    C.   Numerical method   D.   Differential method

14. _________ is the maximum no. of steps that can be executed for a given parameter   [   ]

    A.   Best case   B.   Worst case

    C.   Average case   D.   None

15. The number of times a statement is executed is usually referred as

    [   ]

    A. Complexity   B. Frequency count
    C. Both A & B   D. None

16. Theta notation expresses   [   ]
    A. Tight bounds   B. Upper bounds
    C. Lower bounds   D. Worst cases

17. Function g is an upper bound on function f if for all x,   [   ]
    A. $g(x) \le f(x)$ B. $g(x) \ge f(x)$
    C. $g(x) = f(x)$ D. $f(x) < g(x)$

18. An Algorithm must be always   [   ]
    A. Terminate   B. Executable
    C. Well-ordered   D. All

19. Which of the following needed to Design an Algorithm   [   ]
    A. Pseudo code   B. Methodology
    C. Both A&B   D. None

20. Transferring the values from the user to a variable, or vice-versa is

    [   ]

    A. Function   B. Algorithm
    C. Expression   D. All

21. Which one of the following search is not very efficient for large lists

    [   ]

    A. Binary   B. Sequential
    C. Both A&B   D. None

22. What are the major phases of performance evaluation   [   ]
    A. A prior estimates   B. A posterior testing
    C. Both A&B   D. None

23. Theta notation expresses   [   ]
    A. Tight bounds   B. Upper bounds
    C. Lower bounds   D. Worst cases

24. Consider the following functions:

    $f(n) = 2n$

    $g(n) = n!$

    $h(n) = n \log n$

Which of the following statements about the asymptotic behavior of f(n), g(n) and h(n) is true?   [   ]

A. $f(n) = O(g(n)); g(n) = O(h(n))$

B. $f(n) = \Omega(g(n)); g(n) = O(h(n))$

C. $g(n) = O(f(n)); h(n) = O(f(n))$

D. $h(n) = O(f(n)); g(n) = \Omega(f(n))$

Fill in the Blanks

1. _________________ is composed of a finite set of steps, each of which may require 1 or more operations.

2. A _________________ is the expression of an algorithm in a programming language.

3. Algorithms that are definite and effective are also called _________________

4. Program proving is also called _________________

5. _________________ refers to the task of determining how much computing time and storage an algorithm requires.

6. _________________ is the process of executing programs on sample data sets to determine whether faulty results occur and, if so, to correct them.

7. Compound data types can be formed with _________________

8. Input and Output instructions are done using the instructions _________________ and _________________

9. The _________________ of an algorithm is the amount of memory it needs to run to completion.

10. The _________________ of an algorithm is the amount of time it needs to run to completion.

11. The time T(P) taken by a program P is the sum of the _________________ and _________________

12. The function _________________ if there exist positive constants c and n_0 such that $f(n) \leq c*g(n)$ for all n, $n \geq n_0$.

13. The function _________________ if there exist positive constants c and n_0 such that $f(n) \geq c*g(n)$ for all n, $n \geq n_0$.

14. _________________ notation provides an asymptotic lower bound on a function.

15. We use _________________ to denote an upper bound that is NOT asymptotically tight.

16. Big oh provides an _______________ upper bound on a function.

17. $\sum(1 \leq k \leq n)[O(n)]$ where $O(n)$ stands for order n is: __________

Review Questions

1. (a) Compare Big-oh notation and Little-oh notation. Illustrate with an example.

   (b) Find Big-oh notation and Little-oh notation for $f(n) = 7n^3 + 50n^2 + 200$.

      R09 April-May 2012

2. Solve the following recurrence relations and give a bound for each of them.

   (a) $T(n) = 2\ T(n/3) + 1$ (b) $T(n) = 5\ T(n/4) + n$

   (c) $T(n) = 9\ T(n/3) + n2$ (d) $T(n) = 49\ T(n/25) + n^{3/2} \log n$

   (e) $T(n) = T(n-1) + nc$, where $c >= 1$, a constant.

      R09 set no 4 December-January, 2011-2012

3. (a) Explain the asymptotic notations used in algorithm analysis.

   (b) What is big "oh" notation? Show that if $f(n) = a_m n^m + .. + a_1 n + a_0$ then $f(n) = O(n^m)$.

      R09 June-2014

4. Solve the following recurrence relations and give a Ω bound for each of them:

   (a) $T(n) = 7\ T(n/7) + n$

   (b) $T(n) = 8\ T(n/2) + n3$

   (c) $T(n) = 8\ T(n-1) + 2$

   (d) $T(n) = T(n-1) + cn$, where $c > 1$, a constant.

      R09 set no 1 December-January, 2011-2012

5. (a) Write a recursive algorithm that converts a string of numerals to an integer, for example "34567" to 34567.

   (b) Write a recursive algorithm that calculates and returns the length of a list.

      R09 set no 3 December-January, 2011-2012

6. Define time complexity, Describe different asymptotic notations used to represent the time complexities with suitable examples.

      R09 May 2013

7. (a) Write an algorithm to find the largest Element in an array of n elements. Find its time complexity.

   (b) Explain about amortized analysis and probabilistic analysis.

      R09 November-December 2012

8. The Fibonacci numbers are defined as $f_0 = 0$ and $f_1 = 1$ and $f_i = f_i - 1 + f_i - 2$ for i >1. Write both recursive and iterative algorithm to compute f_i. Also find their time complexities using step count method?

R09 December 2011

9. (a) Present an algorithm that searches for the element x in unsorted array a[1:n]. If x occurs, then return a position in the array; else return zero. Evaluate its time complexity.

    (b) Obtain a non-deterministic algorithm of complexity O(n) to determine whether there is a subset of n numbers a_i, $1 \le i \le n$, that sums to n.

R09 December 2011

10. Define Time complexity. Explain the following Asymptotic notations:

    (a) Big Oh notation   (b)   Theta notation
    (c) Little oh notation   (d)   Amortized analysis.

R09 November/December-2013

11. (a) Define the terms Time and Space complexities. Explain about space analysis of an algorithm with example.

    (b) Explain various approaches to time complexity.

12. (a) Define the terms "Time complexity" and "Space complexity" of algorithms. Give a notation for expressing such a complexity and explain the features of such a notation.

    (b) Explain in detail about Little oh notation.

13. (a) Define Omega notation. Explain the terms involved in it. Give an example.

    (b) Explain in detail about Amortized analysis.

14. (a) For the Travelling sales person algorithm show that the time complexity is $0(n^2 2^n)$ and space complexity is $O(n2^n)$.

    (b) Write an algorithm of matrix chain multiplication.

SEARCHING AND TRAVERSAL TECHNIQUES

2.1 BINARY TREE TRAVERSAL TECHNIQUES

Visiting each node once in a called binary tree is called binary tree traversal. There are three types of binary tree traversal algorithms:

1. In-order traversal
2. Pre-order traversal
3. Post-order traversal

2.1.1 Recursive Binary Tree Traversal Algorithms

1. In-order Traversal (LNR)
   (a) Traverse the left sub tree in inorder
   (b) Process the Node
   (c) Traverse the right sub tree in inorder
2. Pre-order Traversal (NLR)
   (a) Process the Node
   (b) Traverse the left sub tree in preorder
   (c) Traverse the right sub tree in preorder
3. Post-order (LRN)
   (a) Traverse the left sub tree in postorder
   (b) Traverse the right sub tree in postorder
   (c) Process the Node

2.1.2 Non-recursive Binary Tree Traversal Algorithms

1. **In-order Traversal of a Binary Tree**
   (a) Set the node pointer to root node of the given binary tree.
   (b) The following sets of operations are performed until the stack becomes empty.

(i) Starting from the node, we keep moving left as much as possible. By this, we reach a node which does not contain a left child. Let us denote this node by P.

(ii) During the process of moving down the tree to the left, we push each node pointer on the path onto the stack.

(iii) Now P contains NULL

(iv) A node pointer is popped from the stack and stored in P

(v) Display value of node P

(vi) Now P points to right child of P.

Algorithm

```
 1:  void inorder(BTNODE *root)
 2:  {
 3:  stack st;                    // step 1
 4:  BTNODE *p = root ;
 5:  while (!st.empty( ) || p)
 6:  {
 7:  if(!p)                       // step 2(iii)
 8:  {
 9:  p = st.pop( );// step 2(iv) get the left most node
10:  display  p→data;            // step 2(v)
11:  p = p→right;                // step 2(vi)
12:  }
13:  if (p)
14:  {
15:  st.push(p);                 // step 2(ii)
16:  p = p→left;                 // step 2(i)
17:  }
18:  }
19:  }
```

The following example illustrates non recursive in-order traversal of a binary tree which consists of 7 nodes and root node is 'a'.

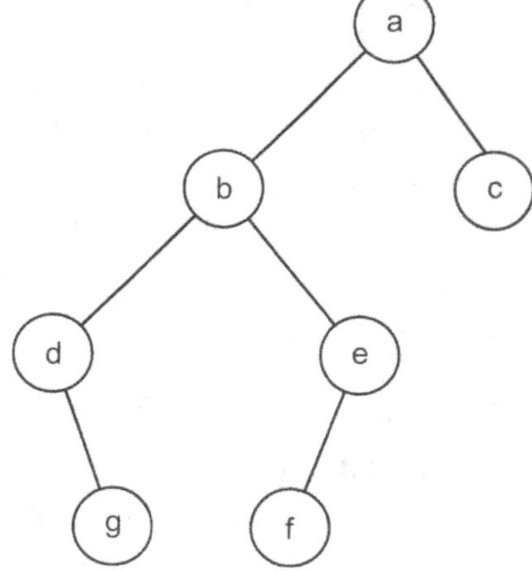

(i)   Initially 'p' points to root i.e., 'a'.

(ii) 'a' is pushed on to stack and 'p' points to b.

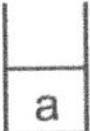

(iii) 'b' is pushed on to stack and 'p' points to 'd'.

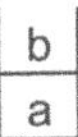

(iv) 'd' is pushed on to stack and 'p' points to NULL. Because there is no left child to 'd'.

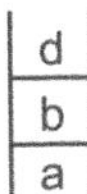

(v)   Since 'p' is NULL and stack is not empty, an element is popped from the stack and stored in 'p'. Now 'p' points to 'd'.

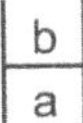

(vi) Display the contents of 'p' i.e., 'd' and 'p' points to 'g' which is right child of 'd'.

Display d

(vii) 'g' is pushed on to stack and 'p' points to NULL. Because there is no left child to 'g'.

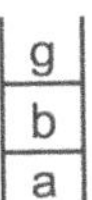

(viii) Since 'p' is NULL and stack is not empty, an element is popped from the stack and stored in 'p'. Now 'p' points to 'g'.

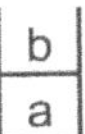

(ix) Display the contents of 'p' i.e., 'g' and 'p' points to NULL. Because there is no right child to 'g'.

Display g

(x)   Since 'p' is NULL and stack is not empty an element is popped from the stack and stored in 'p'. Now 'p' points to b.

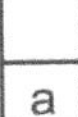

(xi)   Display the contents of 'p' i.e., 'b' and 'p' points to 'e' which is right child of 'b'.

Display b

(xii)   'e' is pushed on to the stack and 'p' points to 'f'.

e
a

(xiii) 'f' is pushed on to the stack and 'p' points to NULL.

f
e
a

(xiv)   Since 'p' is NULL and stack is not empty an element is popped from the stack and stored in 'p'. Now 'p' points to 'f'.

e
a

(xv)   Display the contents of 'p' i.e., 'f' and 'p' points to NULL. Because there is no right child to 'f'.

Display f

(xvi)   Since 'p' is NULL and stack is not empty an element is popped from the stack and stored in 'p'. Now 'p' points to 'e'.

a

(xvii) Display the contents of 'p' i.e., 'e' and 'p' points to NULL. Because there is no right   child to 'e'.

Display e

(xviii) Since 'p' is NULL and stack is not empty an element is popped from the stack and stored in 'p'. Now 'p' points to 'a.'

(xix)   Display the contents of 'p' i.e., 'a' and 'p' points to 'c'.

Display a

(xx)   'c' is pushed on to the stack and 'p' points to NULL, because there is left child to 'c'.

c

(xxi)   Since 'p' is NULL and stack is not empty an element is popped from the stack and stored in 'p'. Now 'p' points to 'c.'

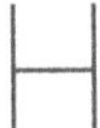

(xxii)   Display the contents of 'p' i.e., 'c' and 'p' points to NULL. Because there is no right child to 'c'.

> Display c

(xxiii)   'p' points to NULL and stack is empty, algorithm terminates.

Inorder traversal is "**d g b f e a c**".

2. Pre-order Traversal of a Binary Tree

(a)   Set the node pointer p to root node of the given binary tree

(b)   Push p pointer onto the stack.

(c)   The following operations are performed until the stack becomes empty.

(i)   Pop the node from the stack and display its data.

(ii)   Push the **right** child pointer onto the stack.

(iii)   Push the left child pointer onto the stack.

Algorithm

```
 1: void preorder(BSTNODE *root)
 2: {
 3: stack st;
 4: BSTNODE *p = root ;          // step 1
 5: if (!p)
 6: return;
 7: st.push(p);                  // step 2
 8: while (!st.empty())          // step 3
 9: {
10: p = st.pop();               // step 3(i)
11: display p→data;
12: if (p→right)
13: s.push(p→right);           // step 3(ii)
14: if (p→left)
15: s.push(p→left);            // step 3(iii)
16: }
17: }
```

The following example illustrates non-recursive pre-order traversal of a binary tree which consists of 7 nodes and root node is 'a'.

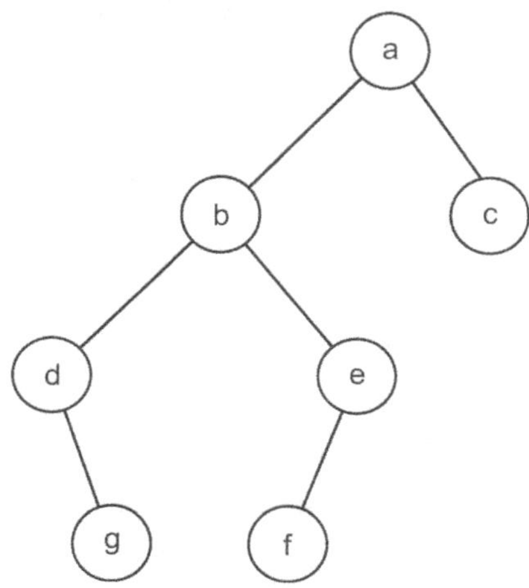

<table>
<tr><td>(i)</td><td>Initially 'p' points to root i.e., 'a'.</td></tr>
<tr><td>(ii)</td><td>'a' is pushed on to stack and 'p' points to b.</td></tr>
<tr><td>(iii)</td><td>An element is popped from the stack and stored in 'p'. Now 'p' points to 'a'.</td></tr>
</table>

(iv)   Display the content of 'p' i.e. 'a'.

Display a

(v)   Right child of 'p' i.e. 'c' is pushed on to stack.

(vi)   Left child of 'p' i.e. 'b' is pushed onto the stack.

(vii)   If stack is not empty, an element is popped from the stack and stored in 'p' i.e. 'p' points to 'b'.

(viii)   Display the contents of 'p'. i.e. 'b'.

Display b

(ix)   Right child of 'p' i.e. 'e' is pushed on to stack.

e
c

(x)   Left child of 'p' i.e. 'd' is pushed on to stack.

d
e
c

(xi)   If stack is not empty, an element is popped from the stack and stored in 'p' i.e. 'p' points to 'd'.

e
c

(xii)   Display the contents of 'p'. i.e. 'd'.

Display d

(xiii)   Right child of 'p' i.e. 'g' is pushed on to stack.

g
e
c

(xiv)   'd' contains no left child.

(xv)   Stack is not empty, an element is popped from the stack and stored in 'p' i.e. 'p' points to 'g'.

e
c

(xvi)   Display the contents of 'p'. i.e. 'g'.

Display g

(xvii)   'g' contains no children.

(xviii) Stack is not empty, an element is popped from the stack and stored in 'p' i.e. 'p' points to 'e'.

e

(xix)   Display the contents of 'p'. i.e., 'e'.

Display e

(xx)   'e' contains no right child.

(xxi)   Left child of 'p' i.e., 'f' is pushed onto the stack

f
c

(xxii)   Stack is not empty, an element is popped from the stack and stored in 'p' i.e., 'p' points to 'f'.

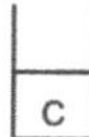

(xxiii)   Display the contents of 'p'. i.e. 'f'.

Display f

(xxiv)   'f' has no children.

(xxv)   Stack is not empty, an element is popped from the stack and stored in 'p' i.e. 'p' points to 'c'.

(xxvi)   Display the contents of 'p'. i.e., 'c'.

Display c

(xxvii)   'c' contains no children.

(xxviii)   Stack is empty and algorithm terminates.

Preorder Traversal is '**a b d g e f c**'.

3. **Post-order Traversal of a Binary Tree:** In non recursive post order binary tree traversal two stacks are used.

(a)   Push root node pointer onto the stack1.

(b)   The following operations are performed until the stack1 becomes empty.

(i)   Pop the node p from the **stack1**.

(ii)   Push the node p onto the **stack2**.

(iii)   Push the left child of p onto the **stack1**.

(iv)   Push the right child of p onto the **stack1**

(c)   The step 2 ensures that the stack1 contains all the nodes in post order. So pop all the nodes from stack2 and display their values.

Algorithm

```
 1:    void postorder(BSTNODE *root)
 2:    {
 3:    BSTNODE *p = root ;
 4:    stack st1, st2 ;
 5:    if (!p)
 6:    return;
 7:    st1.push(p);                        // Step 1
 8:    while (st1.empty( ) != NULL)   // Step 2
 9:    {
10:    p = st1.pop();
11:    st2.push(p);
12:    if (p→left)
13:    st1.push(p→left);
```

```
14:    if (p→right)
15:    st1.push(p→right);
16:    }
17:    while (st2.empty( ) != NULL)     // Step 3
18:    {
19:    p = st2.pop( );
20:    display p→data;
21:    }
22:    }
```

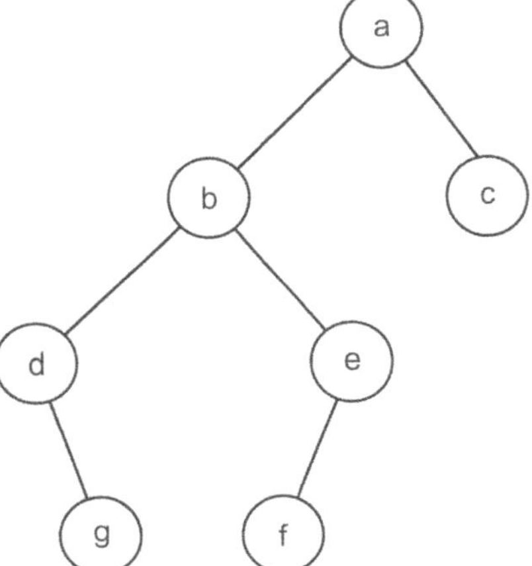

The following example illustrates non recursive preorder traversal of a binary tree which consists of 7 nodes and root node is 'a'.

(i)   Initially 'p' points to root i.e., 'a'.

(ii)   'a' is pushed on to stack1.

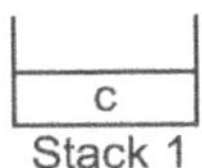

(iii) An element is popped from the stack1 and stored in 'p'. Now 'p' points to 'a'.

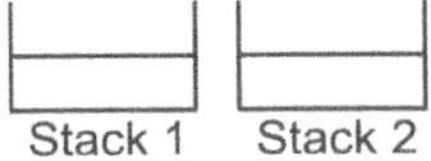

(iv)   'a' is pushed on Stack 2

(v)   'b' is pushed on Stack 1

(vi)   'c' is pushed on Stack 1

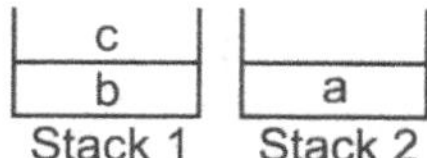

(vii)   An element is popped from the stack1 and stored in 'p'. Now 'p' points to 'c'.

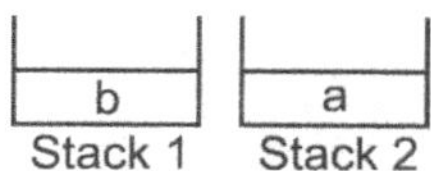

(viii) Push 'c' on Stack 2.

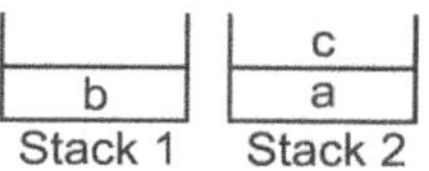

(ix)   An element is popped from the stack 1 and stored in 'p'. Now 'p' points to 'b'. Push 'b' on Stack 2.

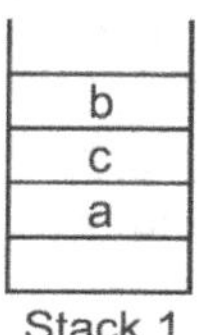

(x)   Push 'd' on Stack 1.

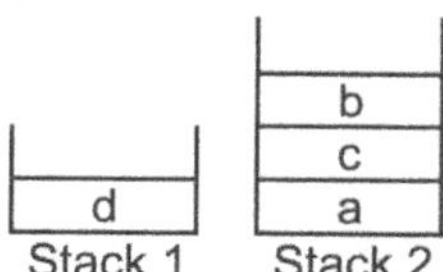

(xi)   Push 'e' on Stack 1.

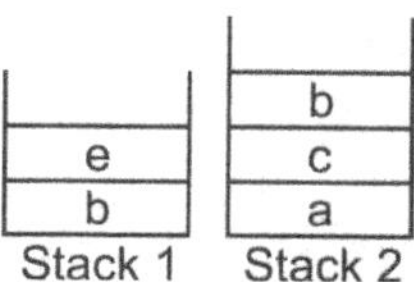

(xii)   An element is popped from the stack1 and stored in 'p'. Now 'p' points to 'e'.

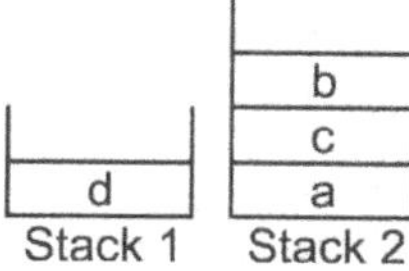

(xiii) Push 'e' on Stack 2.

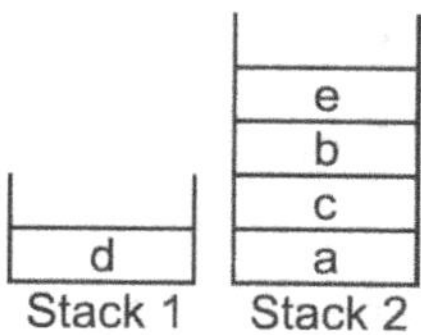

(xiv) Push 'f' on Stack1.

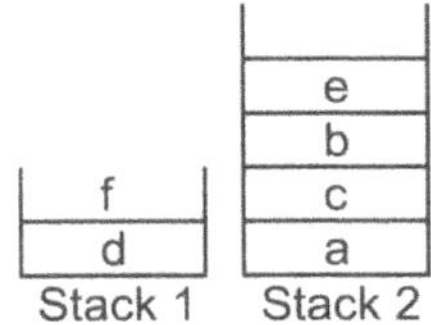

(xv) An element is popped from the stack1 and stored in 'p'. Now 'p' points to 'f'.

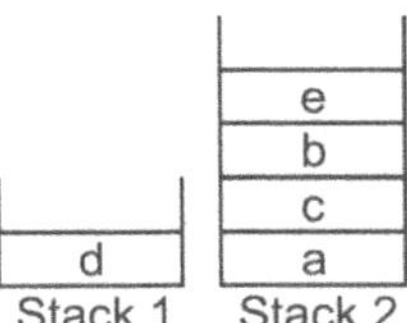

(xvi) Push 'f' on Stack 2.

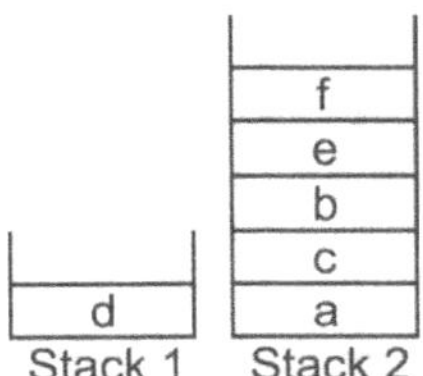

(xvii) An element is popped from the stack1 and stored in 'p'. Now 'p' points to 'd'.

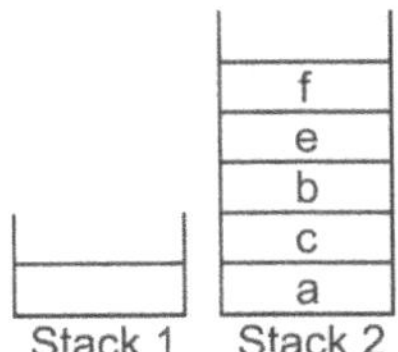

(xviii) Push 'd' on Stack 2.

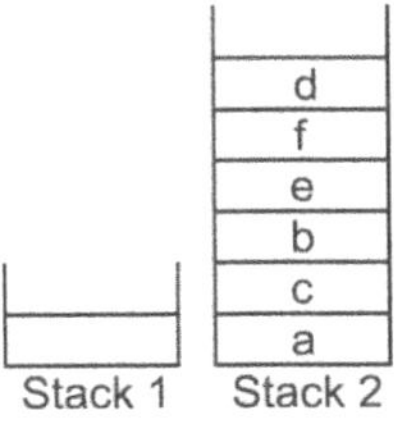

(xix) Push 'g' on Stack 1.

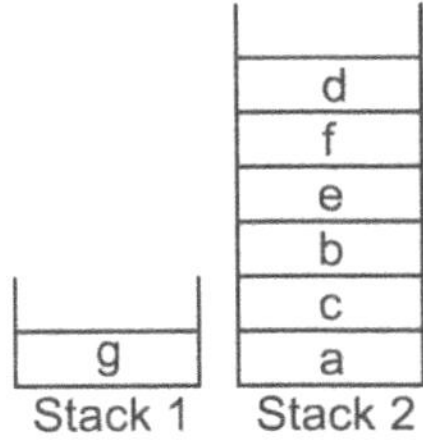

(xx)   An element is popped from the stack1 and stored in 'p'. Now 'p' points to 'g'.

(xxi) Push 'g' on Stack 2.

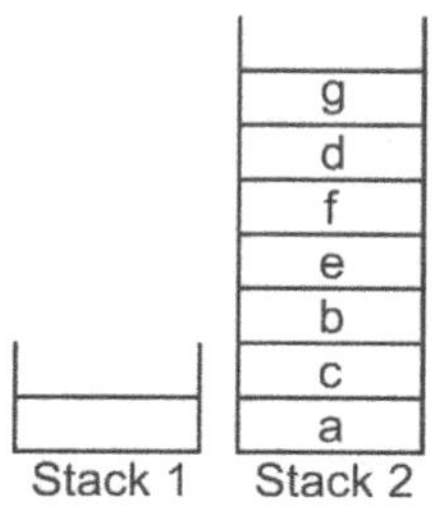

(xxii) Stack 1 is empty. All elements from Stack 2 are popped and displayed.

The order of display is '**g d f e b c a**'.

2.2 SETS AND DISJOINT SET UNION

A set is a collection of ordered elements. It is assumed that the elements that are present in sets are numbers. The represented sets are assumed to be pair-wise disjoint. If S_i and S_j are two sets then these sets must not have any common elements ($S_i \cap s_j = \emptyset$). A partition is a collection of disjoint set. Suppose there are 14 elements, the elements are partitioned into 4 disjoint sets.

$S_1 = \{2, 8, 10, 12\}$, $S_2 = \{1, 3, 5, 7\}$, $S_3 = \{11, 13, 14\}$, $S_4 = \{4, 6, 9\}$
Partition $P = \{S_1, S_2, S_3, S_4\}$

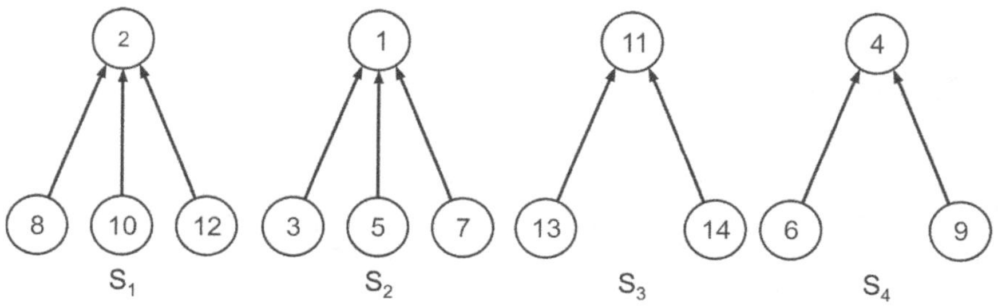

Figure 2.1 Tree representation of Set

Disjoint set Union: When we perform union operation on two disjoint set S_i and S_j, it results in with a new set S_iUS_j which contains all the elements that are present in S_i and S_j. Since all sets are disjoint there are no elements common in both sets. S_i and S_j are replaced with set S_iUS_j.

Union[i, j]: We pass in the two trees with roots *i* and *j* adopting the convention that the first tree becomes the sub-tree of the second. The statement **p[i]:=j** or **p[j]:=i** accomplish the union.

Suppose that we wish to obtain the union of S_1 and S_2. Since we have linked the nodes from children to parent, we simply make one of the trees a sub tree of the other. Thus S_1US_2= {1, 2, 3, 5, 7, 8, 10, 12}. S_1 U S_2 could then have one of the representations of the following Figure 2.2.

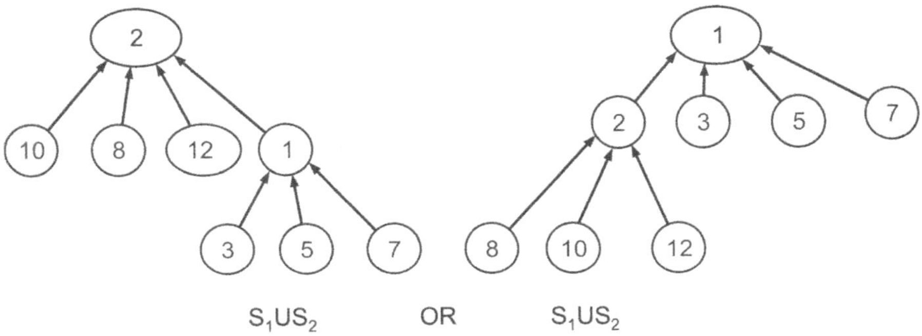

Figure 2.2 Union of sets

Find(*i*). Given the element *i,* find the set containing *i.* Thus, 13 is in set S_3, and 12 is in set S_1.

2.3   REPRESENTATION OF SETS

Sets can be represented in three ways.

1. Tree representation   2.   Data representation

3. Array representation

2.3.1 Tree Representation of Sets

In trees links are given from the parent to the children, but in the implementation of set operation nodes are linked from the children to the parent as shown in Figure 2.1. Union and find are the operations that are performed on these sets.

2.3.2 Data Representation of Sets

The data representation for S_1, S_2, S_3 and S_4 may be of the form as shown in Figure 2.3. Union operation on two sets is accomplished by assigning the parent field of one of the roots to another root. In this two pointers are used, one pointer is with root which points to the set name and another pointer is kept along with each set name which points to the root of the tree.

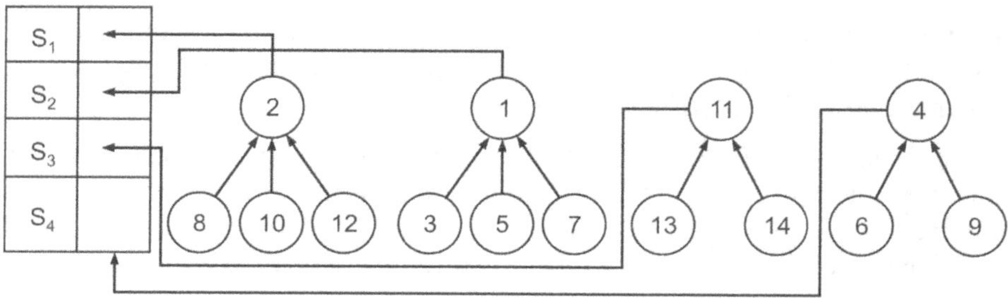

Figure 2.3 Data representation of sets

The following procedure is adopted to find the set name of an element. The elements parent links are followed which leads to the root of the tree and the pointer is used to find the set name. Roots of the trees are used to identifying sets in union and find algorithms.

2.3.3 Array Representation of Sets

This array element gives the present pointer of the corresponding tree node.

i	[1]	[2]	[3]	[4]	[5]	[6]	[7]	[8]	[9]	[10]	[11]	[12]	[13]	[14]
a[i]	−1	−1	1	−1	1	4	1	2	4	2	−1	2	11	11

Figure 2.4 Array representation of sets

The tree nodes are represented using an array a[1..n]. The elements of the set are numbered 1 to n, where 'n' is the maximum number of elements. The element 'k' is represented by k^{th} element of the array which gives the parent node in the corresponding tree. The parent of root nodes is −1.

The root of the tree containing element i is determined in the operation of Find (i) and it is implemented by searching parent value until a node is reached with parent value −1.

Example **1:** Find(8) starts at 8 and then moves to 2 which is 8's parent. Since a[2] is −1, we have reached the root. Hence parent of 8 is 2.

2.4 SIMPLE UNION ALGORITHM

Union (i, j) with roots i and j are joined by the function union(i, j). After union operation root of second tree becomes the root and the first tree becomes its sub tree. The statement x[i]: = j accomplishes the above task.

Algorithm Simple union(i, j)

```
1:   Algorithm Simple union(i, j)
2:   {
3:   X[i]:=j;
```

```
4:  }
5:  Algorithm SimpleFind(i)
6:  {
7:  while(X[i]>0) do i:=X[i];
8:  return i;
9:  }
```

If we have to perform the operations like

Union(1,2), Union(2,3), Union(3,4), Union(4,5),........ Union(n-1,n)

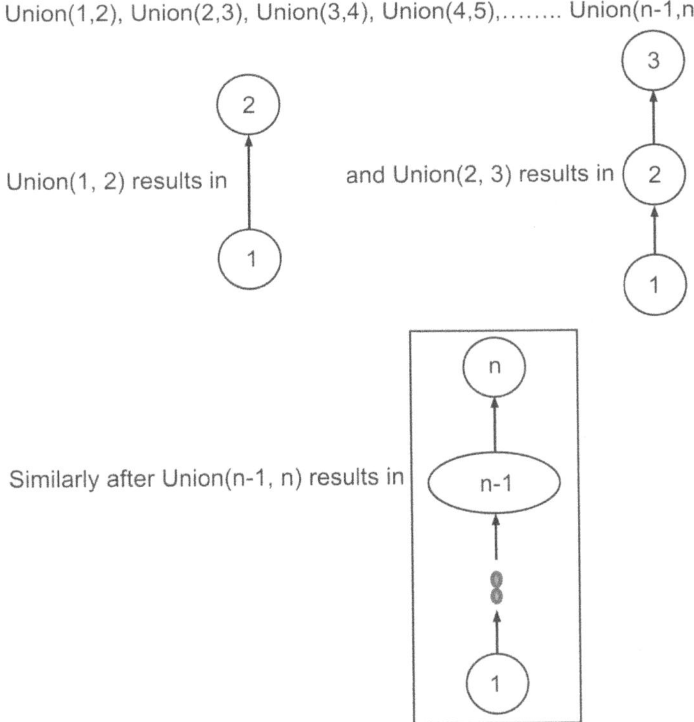

Figure 2.5 Degenerate tree

This sequence will give you Degenerate tree as shown in Figure 2.5.

Analysis: Since the time taken for a union is Constant. The n-1 Unions can be processed in time O(n). Time Complexity = O(n). The time taken for Find operation is O(n).

The sequence of find operations Find(1), Find(2), ... Find(n),

The n Finds can be processed in time $O(\sum_{i=1}^{n} i) = O(n^2)$.

Draw Back: Depth is more to find out the element in degenerate tree.

2.5 WEIGHTED UNION ALGORITHM

We can improve the performance of our union and find algorithms by avoiding the creation of degenerate trees. For that we use Weighting rule for Union (i, j):

Algorithm Weighted Union(i, j):

```
 1: // Union sets with root i and j, i!=j(i not equal
    //to j), using
 2: //  Weighing  rule  X[i]=  -count[i]  and  X[j]= -
    //count[j]
 3: {
 4: Temp:=X[i]+X[j];
 5: if(X[i]>X[j]) then
 6: {  // i has fewer nodes
 7: X[i]:=j;
 8: X[j]:=temp;
 9: }
10: else
11: {  // j has fewer nodes (or) equal nodes
12: X[j]:=i;
13: X[i]:=temp;
14: }
15: }
```

2.5.1 Weighting Rule for Union (i, j)

If the number of nodes in the tree with root i is less than the number in the tree with root j, then make j the parent of i; otherwise make i the parent of j.

Assume that we start with a forest of trees, each having one node. Let T be a tree with m nodes created as a result of a sequence of unions each performed using Weighted Union, The height of T is no greater than $\lfloor \log_2 m \rfloor + 1$.

To implement the weighting rule, we need to know how many nodes there are in every tree. To do this easily, we maintain a *count* field in the root of every tree. If i is a root node, then *count*[i] equals the number of nodes in that tree. Since all nodes other than the roots of trees have a positive number in the p field, we can maintain the count in the p field of the roots as a negative number.

The time to process find is O(log m). Further improvement is still possible in find using collapsing rule.

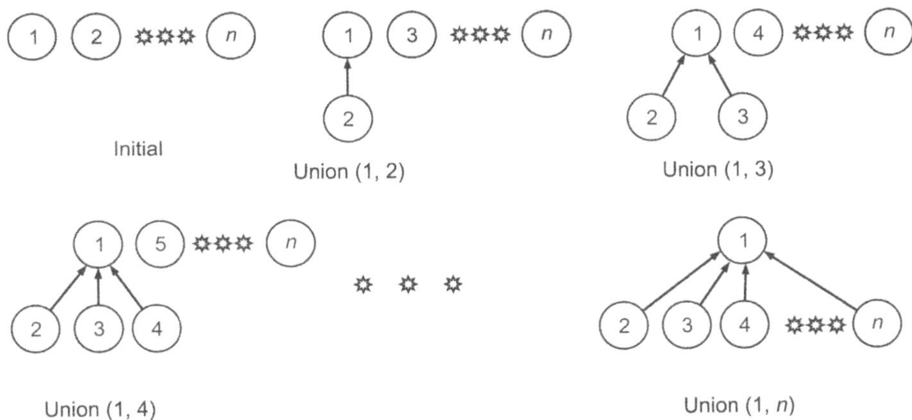

2.5.2 Collapsing Rule

If j is a node on the path from i to its root and $p[i] \neq root[i]$, then set $p[j]$ to *root*[i].

Algorithm for Find with collapsing rule:

```
1:   CollapsingFind(i)
2:   // Find the root of the tree containing element i.
3:   // Use the collapsing rule to collapse all nodes from i to
     //the root.
4:   {
5:   r :=i;
6:   while(p[r] > 0) do r :=p[r];      // Find the root.
7:   while(i≠r) do  // Collapse nodes from i to root r.
8:   {
9:   s :=p[i];      p[i] :=r;      i :=s;
10:  }
11:  return r;
12:  }
```

On time the complexity will become O (1) for any operation.

2.6 GRAPH

Graph is defined as set of vertices and edges i.e., G = (v, e).

There are two types of graph 1. Directed Graph. 2. Undirected Graph. If the edges of the graph are not having direction then it is called undirected graph as shown in Figure 2.6 (a). If the edges of a graph have direction then the graph is called directed graph as shown in Figure 2.6 (b).

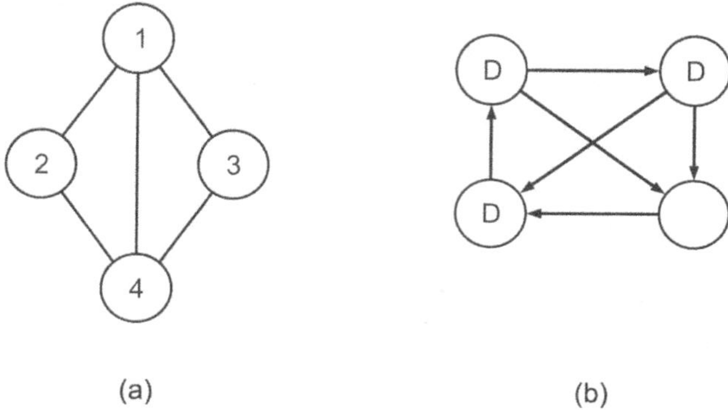

(a)   (b)

Figure 2.6 (a) Undirected graph (b) Directed graph

In a directed graph G two vertices u and v are said to be connected if there is a path in G from u to v and vice versa. An undirected graph is said to be connected if there is a path from u to v in G. Two vertices are said to be adjacent if an edge is present between them. Graphs can be represented in memory by using arrays and linked list. Array representation is called adjacency matrix and linked list representation is called adjacency list.

2.6.1 Adjacency Matrix

A two-dimensional square matrix is used to represent a graph, whose size is n × n where n is the number of vertices in graph. The above graph in Figure 2.6 (a) contains four vertices so the order of the matrix is 4 × 4. The contents of adjacency matrix are 0 and 1, if an edge is present between two vertices then its value is 1 and other contents are 0's. The adjacency matrix for the graph shown in Figure 2.6(a) is given in Figure 2.7.

$$\begin{bmatrix} 0 & 1 & 1 & 1 \\ 1 & 0 & 0 & 1 \\ 1 & 0 & 0 & 1 \\ 1 & 1 & 1 & 0 \end{bmatrix}$$

Figure 2.7 Adjacency matrix of figure 2.6(a)

2.6.2 Adjacency List

Linked lists are used to represent a graph. The number of linked list required are 'n' to represent a graph having 'n' vertices. For the above graph shown in Figure 2.6(a) four linked list are required. For vertex 1, the adjacent vertices are vertex 2, vertex 3, and vertex 4. For vertex 2, the adjacent vertices are vertex 1, and vertex 4. For vertex 3, the adjacent vertices are vertex 1 and vertex 4. For vertex4, the adjacent vertices are vertex 2, vertex 3, and vertex 1. The adjacency list of Figure 2.6(a) is shown in Figure 2.8.

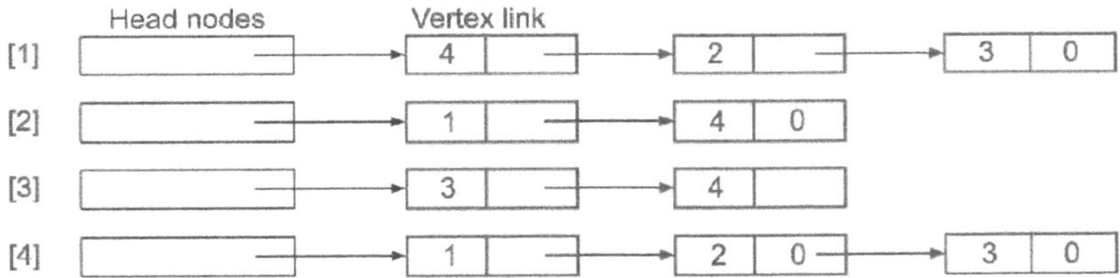

Figure 2.8 Adjacency list of figure 2.6(a)

2.6.3 Graph Traversal Algorithms

Graph traversal algorithms visit the vertices of a graph only once, according to some strategy. There are two basic strategies for the graph traversal:

    1. Breadth first traversal   2. Depth first traversal

2.6.3.1 Breadth First Traversal

If Breadth First Search is used on a graph G which is not connected, then at least one vertex of graph G is not visited. The BFT is an example of a graph traversal algorithm that divides graph G into connected components and traverses each component separately using BFS. By calling BFS algorithm again and again each time with a new unvisited vertex as the starting vertex, a complete traversal of the graph can be prepared. The resulting traversal algorithm is known as Breadth first traversal.

Algorithm for Breadth First Traversal:

```
1:   Algorithm BFT(G, n)
2:   //Breadth first traversal of G.
3:   {
4:   for i := 1 to n do
5:   visited[i] := 0;
6:   for i := 1 to n do
7:   if(visited[i] = 0) then BFS(i);
8:   }
```

Breadth first search of a graph is not unique, many BFS traversals are possible. In breadth first search first starting vertex 'v' is assumed and marks it as the visited vertex. At this time vertex 'v' is unexplored (a vertex is explored when all of its adjacent vertices are visited). Next unvisited adjacent vertices of 'v' are visited. These are the new unexplored vertices, and vertex v has been explored. Exploration continues until no unexplored vertex is left when the list of unexplored vertices operates as a queue.

It traverses the vertices of each component in increasing order of the distances of the vertices from the 'root' of the component, this can be thought of as processing 'wide' and then 'deep'. Multiple BFS are possible. The data structure used in implementation of BFS is queue.

The Idea of the BFS

Visit the vertices from a source vertex v as follows:
1. Visit all vertices at distance 1
2. Visit all vertices at distance 2
3. Visit all vertices at distance 3

etc.

Algorithm for Breadth First Traversal:

```
 1: Algorithm BFS(v)
 2: /* starting vertex v is assumed and BFS of G is
    initiated. For any vertex i, visited[i] =1 if i has
    already been visited. The graph G and array
    visited[ ] are global*/
 3: {
 4: u := v;     // q is a queue of unexplored vertices.
 5: visited[v] :=1;
 6: repeat
 7: {
 8: for all vertices k adjacent to u do
 9: {
10: if(visited[k] = 0) then   // if k is not visited
11: {
12: Add k to q;    // k is unexplored, insert in queue
13: visited[k] := 1;   //mark vertex k as visited
14: }
15: }
16: If q is empty then return; // No unexplored vertex.
17: Delete k from q; // Get first unexplored vertex.
18: }until(false);
19: }
```

The time and space complexity when there are n vertices and e edges are,

$$T(n,e) = \theta(n + e) \qquad S(n,e) = \theta(n)$$

Example: BFS with source vertex as A (Note that the result of a BFS is not unique, one possibility is shown)

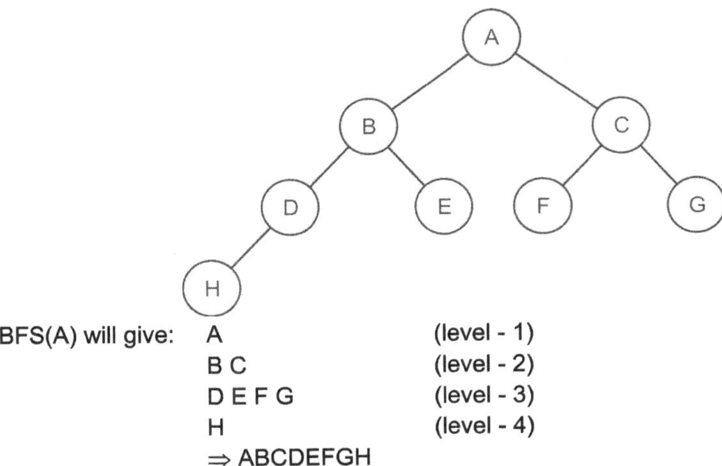

BFS(A) will give: A   (level - 1)
                     B C   (level - 2)
                     D E F G   (level - 3)
                     H   (level - 4)
                     $\Rightarrow$ ABCDEFGH

2.6.3.2 Depth First Traversal

If DFS is used on a graph G which is not connected, then at least one vertex of graph G is not visited. The DFT is an example of a graph traversal algorithm that divides graph G into connected components and traverses each component separately using Depth First Search. By calling DFS algorithm again and again each time with a new unvisited vertex as the starting vertex, a complete traversal of the graph can be prepared. The resulting traversal algorithm is known as Depth first traversal.

A depth first search of a graph differs from a breadth first search in that the exploration of a vertex v is suspended as soon as a new vertex is reached. At this time the exploration of the new vertex u begins. When this new vertex has been explored completely, then the exploration of v continues. The search terminates when all reached vertices have been fully explored. DFS will process the vertices first deep and then wide. After processing a vertex it recursively processes all of its descendants. Multiple DFS are possible. The data structure used in implementation of DFS is stack.

Depth First Traversal: A depth first traversal of a graph is carried out by repeatedly calling DFS, with a new unvisited starting vertex every time till all vertices are visited.

Algorithm for Depth First Traversal:

```
Algorithm DFT(G, n)
//Depth first traversal of G.
{
        for i := 1 to n do
        visited[i] := 0;
        for i := 1 to n do
        if(visited[i] = 0) then DFS(i);

}
```

Algorithm for Depth First Search:

```
DFS(v)
/* starting vertex v is assumed and DFS of G is
initiated with n vertices and an array visited [ ]
initially set to zero, this algorithm visits all
vertices reachable from v for any vertex i,
visited[i] =1 if i has already been visited. The
graph G and array visited [ ] are global*/
{
visited[v] := 1;
for each vertex k adjacent from v do
    {
        if(visited[k] = 0) then   DFS(k);
    }
}
```

The time and space complexity when there are *n* vertices and *e* edges are,

$$T(n,e) = \theta(n + e) \qquad\qquad S(n,e) = \theta(n)$$

Example: DFS with source vertex as *A* (Note that the result of a DFS is not unique, one possibility is shown)

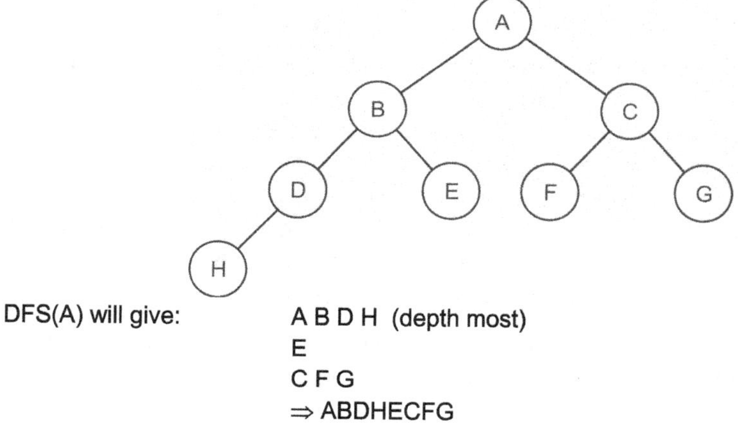

DFS(A) will give: A B D H (depth most)
                           E
                           C F G
                           ⇒ ABDHECFG

Figure 2.9 Example graph

Applications of DFS and BFS

1. Back tracking uses DFS and branch and bound uses BFS for finding optimal and feasible solution.

2. They can be used to find connected and bi-connected components.

3. They can be used to test for the presence of cycles in graph.

4. BFS can be used to find the shortest path from the given vertex to all other remaining vertices when the edges are of unit cost.

5. DFS and BFS are used to check whether graph is connected or not.

6. If non unit cost edges exist, add extra nodes.

Example:

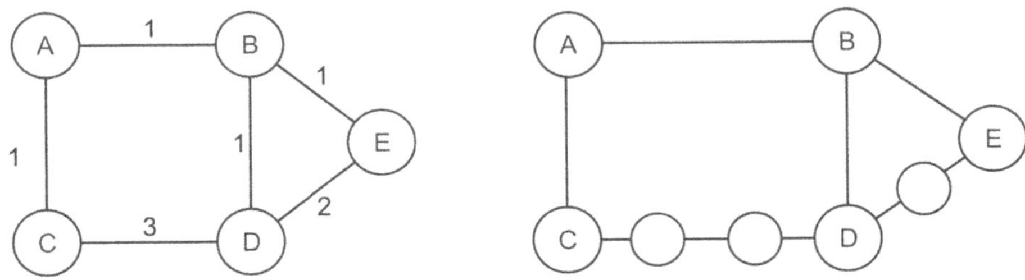

Figure 2.10 Weighted Graph and its equivalent Unitary Graph

2.7 SPANNING TREE

A tree is a connected acyclic Graph. All trees are graphs but all graphs are not trees. A tree is a connected graph without cycles.

Assume there is an undirected graph G, a spanning tree is a sub graph of G, which contain all the vertices of G and subset of edges of graph G. If there are 'n' vertices in graph 'G' then spanning tree contains 'n–1' edges. A spanning tree of a graph 'G' is any tree that includes every vertex in the graph, it is a sub-graph of 'G' containing no circuit.
If spanning tree is constructed using DFS then it is called DFS Spanning tree, if it is constructed using BFS then it is called BFS Spanning trees.

An edge of spanning tree is called a **Branch or tree edge.** An edge in the graph that is not in the spanning tree is called a *Chord.*

Spanning trees are important because of the following reasons:

1. Spanning trees are very important in designing efficient routing algorithm.

2. Spanning trees have wide applications in many areas, such as network design.

The Time Complexity of this algorithm is clearly o(n), where 'n' is the number of edges.

The number of spanning trees in the complete graph kn is n^{n-2}.

The minimum spanning tree as given below:

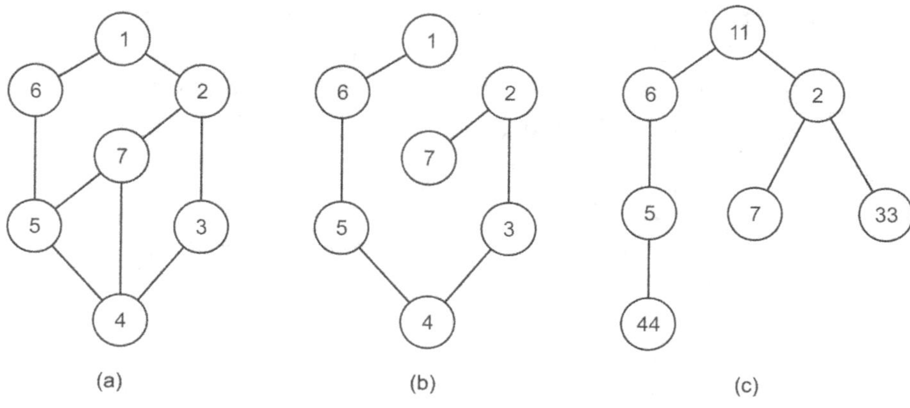

Figure 2.11 (a) Graph (b) DFS Spanning Tree (c) BFS Spanning tree

2.7.1 Types of Edges

Edges of the graph are of four categories:

1. **Tree edge:** It is the edge which is present in spanning tree.

2. **Back edge:** An edge (u, v) which is present in graph but not present in spanning tree and v is an ancestor of u.

3. **Forward edge:** An edge (u, v) which is not in spanning tree and u is ancestor of v.

4. **Cross edge:** An edge (u, v) not in spanning tree and 'v' is neither an ancestor nor a descendant of u.

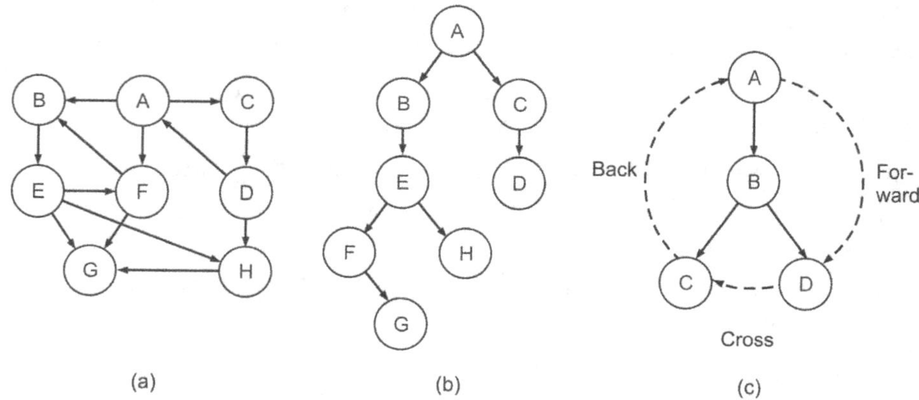

Figure 2.12 (a) Directed Graph (b) DFS (c) Cross and Forward Edges

The graph G shown in Figure 2.12(a) is an undirected graph whose DFS is shown in Figure 2.12(b). The edges that are present in DFS are called tree edges. The Figure 2.12(c) shows edge AD as forward edge, edge CA is back edge and edge DC is cross edge.

2.8 AND-OR GRAPHS

The AND-OR graph are also known as AND-OR trees. A solution to problem can be achieved by decomposing the problem into a set of smaller problems and solving the smaller problems. The above set of problems can be represented by AND-OR graphs as shown in figure 2.13. AND arcs are indicated with a line connecting all the components. In the process of decomposition AND arcs are generated. Many successor nodes can be pointed by an AND arc. To get a solution all successor nodes must be solved. In Figure 2.13 the parent node 'Goal:Acquire Mobile' can be achieved in two ways: 1. Steal Mobile 2. Earn some money and Mobile.

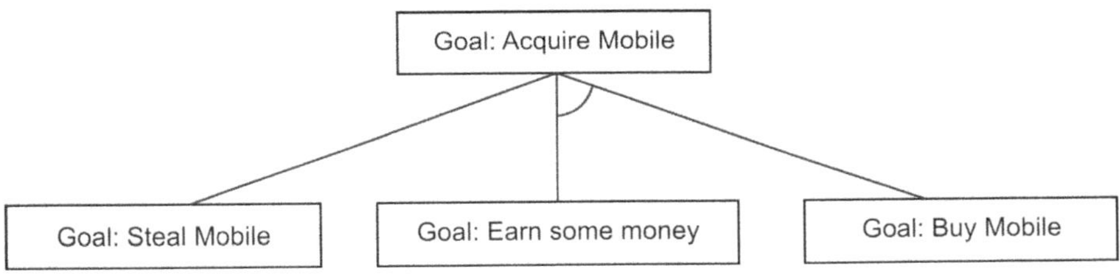

Figure 2.13

In the latter method both successor nodes must be solved to achieve the goal. A path starting from the root node of the graph to a set of nodes representing solution or answer state is found by using AND-OR graph. We can have multiple solution states. In the example shown in Figure 2.14. The root node 'A' has been expanded producing two edges. One leading to B and another are leading to 'C' and 'D'. The above problem has two solutions: (i) B (ii) C & D

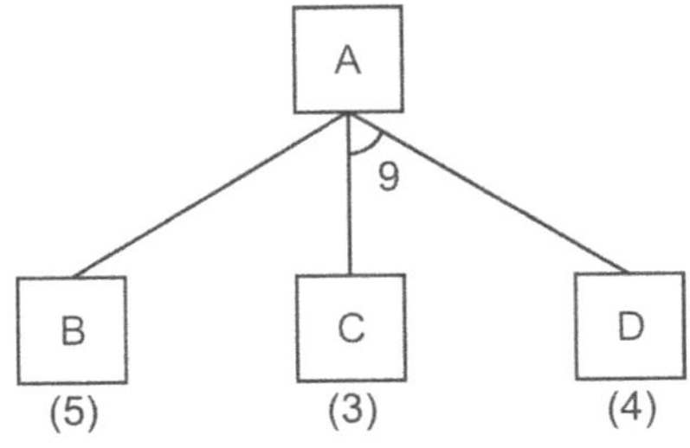

Figure 2.14

The cost incurred to solve a node is represented by its 'F' value. 'F' value of node 'B' is 5, node 'C' is 3 and node 'D' is 4. 'F' value will be these for only terminal nodes. Combination of there terminal nodes gives 'F' value of the parent node. Every operation has a cost, for simplicity, it is assumed that all operation has a uniform cost. Each edge with a single successor has a cost of 1. Nodes having multiple successors have a cost 1 for each of its components.

Whenever a problem has multiple solutions i.e., multiple successor nodes, nodes having lowest 'F' value must be chosen for expansion. According to the example shown in Figure 2.14 node 'C' has lowest 'F' value. If we select 'C' then 'D' also should be selected, because of AND arc then the total cost becomes 9(C + D + 2), we have added 2 because of the operating cost of two nodes. If we go through 'B' the total cost is 6(B + 1). So we have to choose 'B'. 'F' value determines which node to be expanded. Apart from 'F' value of the node we should also consider whether that node is part of the current best path from the initial node. The following example in Figure 2.15 illustrates the above concepts. Among the terminal nodes 'F' value of node 'G' is less which is 3. With AND arc the cost of GH pair is 9(G + H + 2) which is less than EF pair (17) and IJ pair (27). In the next level the path from A through C&D will be 38 where as the path from A through B, to E&F is 18. So node G should not be considered. Either node E or F should be expanded.

Node G is having minimum 'F' value but it is not part of the current best path from the root or initial node.

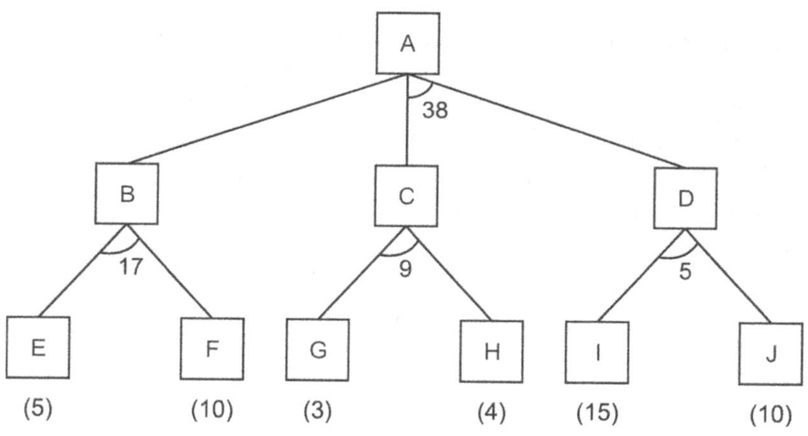

Figure 2.15

2.9 GAME TREES

A game tree is a directed graph whose nodes are positions in a game and whose edges are moves. The complete game tree for a game is the game tree starting at the initial position and containing all possible moves from each position; the complete tree is the same tree as that obtained from the extensive-form game representation. The following examples will provide more detailed explanation on Game-Tree.

2.9.1 The Minimax Search Procedure

The minimax procedure is a Depth First Search process. The set of possible successor position are generated by using the plausible-move generator starting from the current position. Among the above positions the best one is selected after the application of the static evaluation function to those positions. It is assumed that the static evaluation function returns large values to indicate positive situations. The position generated by the best move is as good as the starting position. The goal of the Min-Max Search procedure is to maximize the value of the static evaluation function of the next board position.

The following example in Figure 2.16 illustrates the mini-max search procedure. The static evaluation function returns values ranging from –10 to 10 with 10 indicating a win, –10 indicates a win for the opponent and 0 an even match. From the illustration in Figure K the current position is A. there are three possible moves from A i.e., A to B, A to C and A to D, among these the static evaluation function value of node B is higher than all other nodes. So if we make a move from A to B the possibility of winning is more when compared to moving to C or D from A. This is called as One Ply Search where we considered only one move. As we know that the static evaluation function are not completely accurate. We will try to search further ahead then one ply. In game like chess or tic-tac-toe players think-two-three moves ahead.

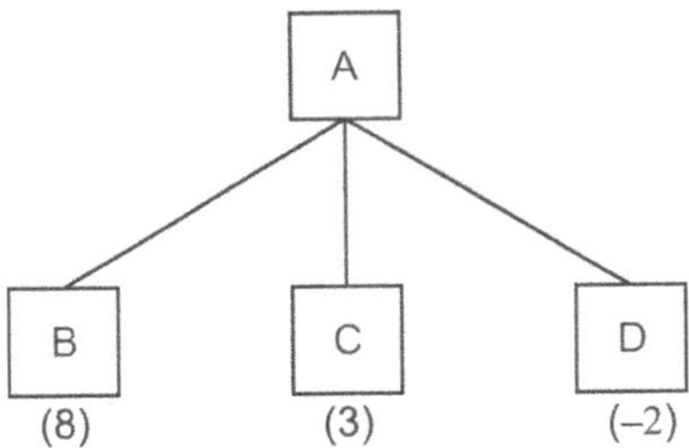

Figure 2.16 One ply search

Now we would like to look ahead and see what will happen to each of the new game position at the next move made by the opponent. To generate the set of successor positions Plausible-move generator is applied.

A Two Ply Search is shown in Figure 2.17. Suppose we made move from A to B, then opponent has three possible moves E, F & G, among these he has to choose one. The goal of the opponent is to minimize the value of evaluating function which increases his chance of winning game. He will choose node F whose value is –6. If we choose node B as our move then after one move one position is very bad because we are in a position where the value of evaluation function is –6 and which is in favor of the opponent. We will be in favorable position if the opponent chooses node E instead of node F. Since the move is made by the opponent we will not get the chance to choose it.

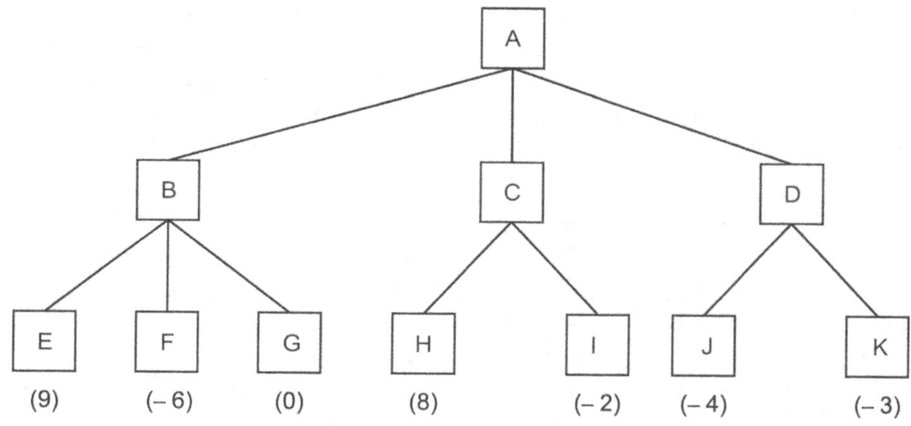

Figure 2.17 Two ply search

In our choice if we select node C instead of node B then the opponent will select node I(minimum evaluation function value) where the value of evaluation function is –2 which is better than –6. The following figure shows the new values that are propagating up the tree.

The minimum value is chosen at the level representing the opponent's choice and moved up. Maximum value was chosen at the level representing our choice.

As shown in the Figure 2.18 the correct move to be made by us is C and the opponent can do nothing but to produce a value of –2.

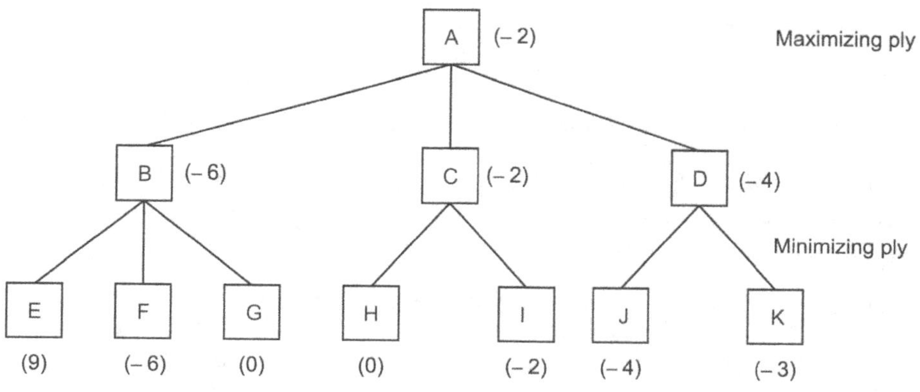

Figure 2.18 Backing up the values of a two ply search

The above process is repeated for more number of ply's and more accurate evaluation are produced to choose the correct move at the top level. The name minimax is derived by the opposing strategies of two players selecting maximum and minimum values at alternate ply's.

Alpha-Beta Cutoffs: Alpha-beta pruning maintains two threshold values, one for a lower bound on the value that a maximizing node may ultimately be assigned (alpha) and another value representing an upper bound, the value that a minimizing node may be assigned (beta). Beta value is used at maximizing levels to determine whether to cutoff the search, and alpha value is used at minimizing levels. At maximizing levels not only beta value, alpha value must also be known to create a minimizing level due to the recursion level of minimax procedure. Similarly at minimizing levels not any alpha value, beta value must also be known. At each level both values must be known, one to use and one to pass down for the next level use.

An example of Alpha-Beta cutoff is shown in Figure 2.19. At node F it is minimizing ply and the value of node F is –5. The value of node C is at most –5. The value of node A can be at least 3 which is achieved by moving to node B. By making any other move which gives a value less than 3 is worse and it can be ignored. After examining node F moving to node C is worst than moving to node B regardless of the value of node G. so it is not required to explore node G at all. Once the value of node F is less than 3 no need to explore the siblings of F, the value of node B is called Alpha cutoff.

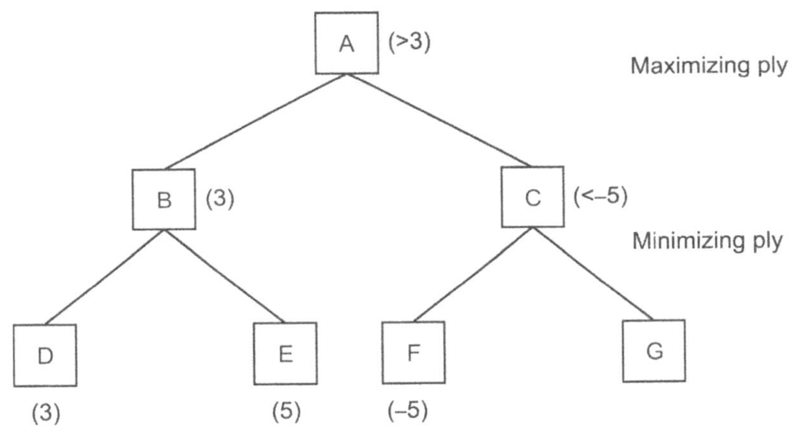

Figure 2.19 An alpha cutoff

While searching the tree given in Figure 2.20, the entire sub tree with root B is searched and it is clear that at node A, a score of at least 3 can be expected.

This is the alpha value and is passed down to node F, by this alpha value exploration of node L can be skipped, which is explained below.

After evaluating node K, node I is guaranteed a maximum score of 0, in turn node F is guaranteed a minimum score of 0, which is less than the alpha value. So there is no need of further exploring of branches of node I i.e., we can skip the exploration of node L. It means that for the maximizing player, it is clear that moving to node C and further to node I will result in getting less score than moving to node B. So he will not choose to move to node C.

After skipping the further exploration of node L, node J is explored whose score is 5, this value is assigned to node F. This is the Beta value at node C. From the Beta value it is clear that Node C is guaranteed to get a score of 5 or less. Next node G is explored. In the exploration of children of node G, first node M is explored whose value is 7, it means that the value of node G is at least 7 and it is more than Beta value. So node G is not considered by the minimizing player at node C which has a minimum value 5 from node F. So it is not required to further explore other branches of node G. so exploration of node N is skipped. From the above example it is inferred that at maximizing level a move can be ruled out if it becomes clear that its value is less than the current threshold, while at minimizing levels, search will be terminated if values that are greater than the current threshold are found.

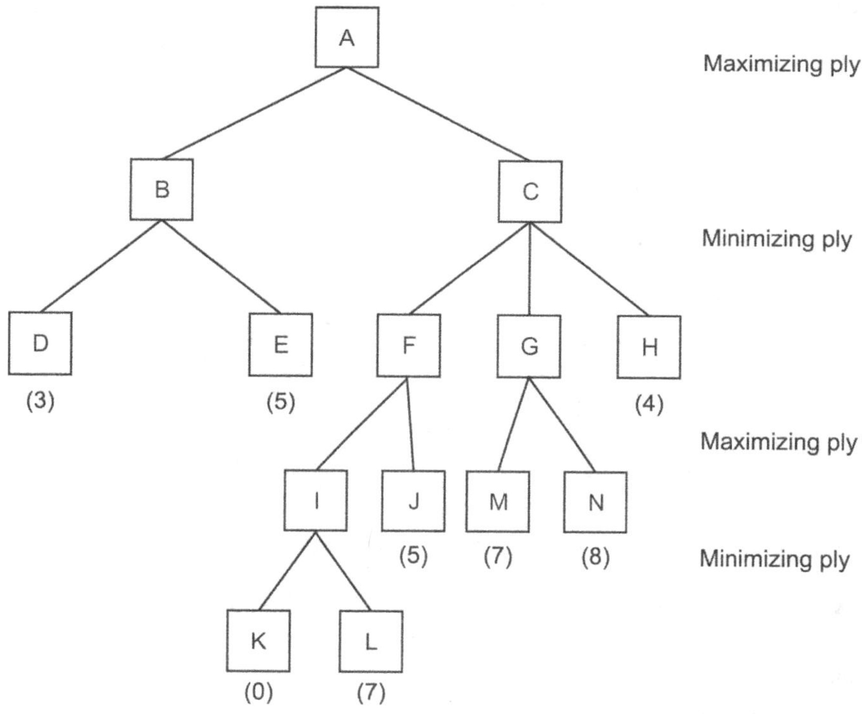

Figure 2.20 Alpha and Beta Cutoffs

2.9.2 NIM Game Tree

Game tree represents all possible instances of a finite game. A game in which if there are no valid sequences of infinite length then that game is called finite game. As an example, let us consider the game of NIM, which is played between two players 'P' and 'Q'. They make moves alternately with P making the first move. A board consisting of a pile of 'n' toothpicks describes the game. From the pile of toothpicks a player can remove either 1, 2 or 3 of the toothpicks which from a legal move. However, a player cannot remove more toothpicks then the existing number of toothpicks on the pile. Loser of the game is the player who picks the last toothpick and the other player wins. The number of toothpicks remaining in the pile describes board configuration. Board configuration and which players have to make the next move describes the game status. In the game of NIM if there are no toothpicks in the pile represents terminal configuration, which means a win for player 'P' if 'Q' made the last move otherwise 'Q' wins. A valid sequence C_1, C_2,....C_m of board configuration with C_m a terminal configuration is an instance of the game.

The NIM game tree for n = 6 is shown in the Figure 2.21 below. Starting configuration is represented by the root node. Move made by players represents transition from are level to the next level. Player P's turn to move are represented by square nodes and it will be in the odd levels where as Q's turn to move are represented by circular nodes and it will be in even levels. The weight of the edge represents number of toothpicks removed by the player. Leaf nodes represents terminal configuration and they have been labeled by the player who wins. In the game of NIM a player can almost remove 3 toothpicks so from any configuration there are at most 3 legal moves and the degree of any node in the game tree of NIM is 3.

Game trees are useful in determine the next move a player should make. The root of Figure 2.21 represents the initial configuration. Game is started by player P. Player P makes the move among three possible moves which maximizes his chance of winning. Evaluation function E(X) is used to decide which move to make this function returns a integer value to the board

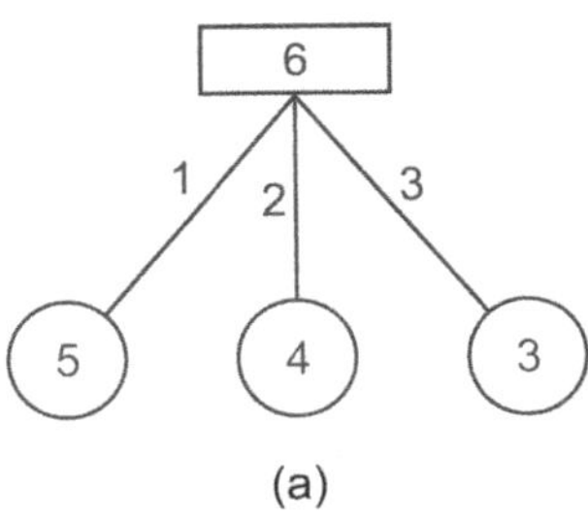

configuration X. High value of E(X) indicates P has a good chance of winning and low value indicating Q has a good chance of winning. If P win's then E(X) value is maximum and in value is minimum if Q wins.

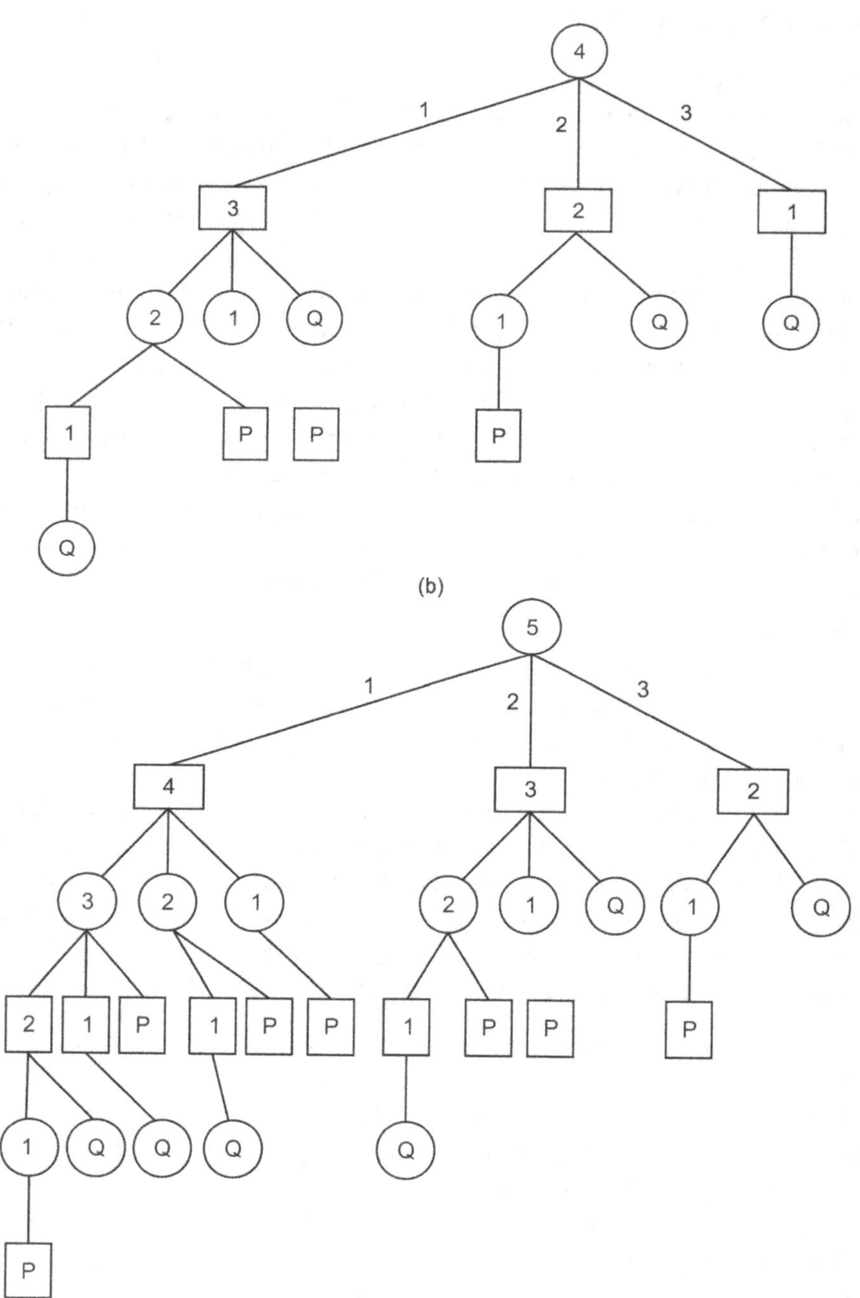

(b)

(c)

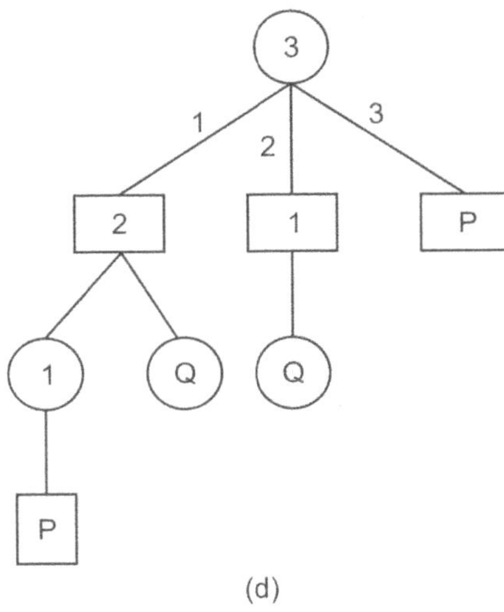

(d)

Figure 2.21(a),(b),(c)&(d)

E(X) = 1 if X is a winning configuration for P

E(X) = –1 if X is a winning configuration for Q

By using the above evaluation function E(X), player P decides which move to make among b, c, d configurations. V(b), V(c) & V(d) is calculated and among these value is maximum player P makes that move, when v(x) is the value of configuration x, for terminal nodes V(x) is equal to E(X) .

For all other nodes

$V(x) = \max\{v(c_i)\}$ if x is square node

$V(x) = \text{mix}\{v(c_i)\}$ if x is circular node

If x is a square node, it is player P's turn and he tries to maximize the evaluation function value. If x is a circular node, it is player Q's turn and he tries to minimize the evaluation function value which minimizes the P's winning chance and increases his chance of winning the game. The above concept is called Minimax procedure.

2.10 CONNECTED COMPONENTS

Connected Graph: A graph is connected if for any two vertices there is a path between them. If a graph G is not connected, its maximal connected sub graphs are called connected components of G. There are two types of connected components namely strongly connected components and Bi-connected components.

2.10.1 Strongly Connected Graph

Connectivity issue for directed graph. Two nodes u and v of a directed graph are connected (if there is a path from u to v and from v to u) i.e., u→v, v→u. This property or relation partitions vertex set v into disjoint sets known as strongly connected components.

2.10.2 Bi-connected Component

Maximal sub graph of the given graph which is bi-connected is said to be bi-connected component of the graph.

A graph is said to be bi-connected if it does not contain articulation point and bridge as shown in Figure 2.21(a). Articulation point is that vertex or node in the graph, the removal of which along with its incident edges partition the graph into two or more non-empty components. Bridge is that edge in the graph, the removal of which partition the graph into two or more non empty components.

Articulation point plays major role in network work communications (It is desirable to design bi-connected graph). Graph can be converted to bi-connected by adding edges. Number of extra edges are less than or equal to number of Articulation Points. Some key observation can be made in regard to bi-connected components of graph.

(a) Two different bi-connect components should not have any common edges.

(b) Two different bi-connected components can have common vertex.

(c) The common vertex which is attained (two or more) bi-connected point of G.

The graph given in Figure 2.22(b) contains two articulation points. Vertex 2 and vertex 3 are articulation points. Result of graph G after deleting vertex 2 is shown in Figure 2.22(c) where the graph has two connected components. A graph is said to be connected if it contains no articulation point. If there exists an articulation point in the given graph then it is an undesirable feature.

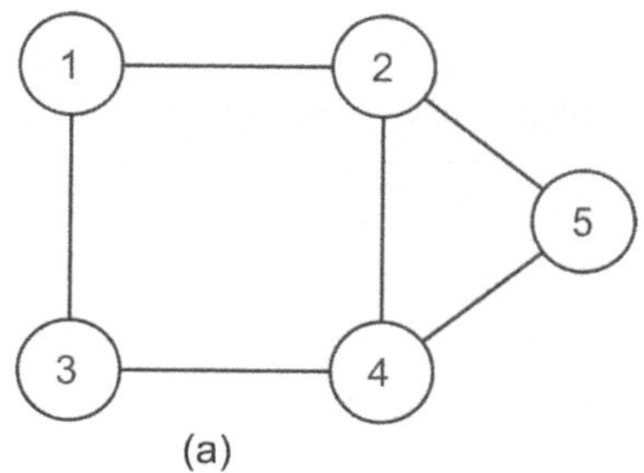

(a)

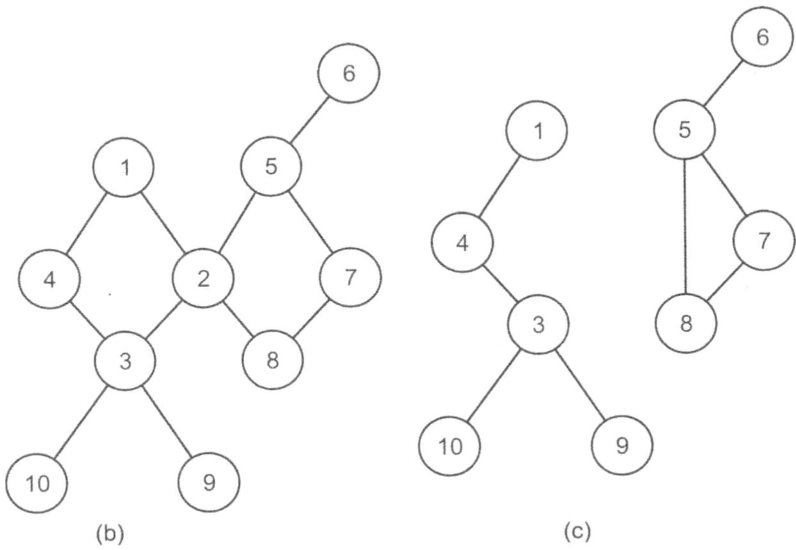

Figure 2.22 (a) Biconnected graph (b) Graph G (c) Result after deleting vertex 2

Identification of Articulation Point: The earliest method is to remove a vertex and its corresponding edges one by one from graph G and test whether the resulting graph is still connected or not complexity $O(v(v + E))$.

Identification of Bi-Connected Components: *Property* 1: Every directed graph is a directed acyclic graph of its strongly connected component. This directed acyclic graph (DAG) is known as meta graph.

Property 2: If c and c' are strongly connected components of graph G and if there is an edge from a node in c to a node in c' then the highest post number (finishing number) in c is always bigger than the highest post number in c'.

Property 3: Let c and c' be distinct strongly connected components of a directed graph G. let u, v $\in$ c and u', v' $\in$ c'. if there is a path from u to u' (u $\rightarrow$ u') in G then there cannot be a path from v' to v in G.

In the above directed graph shown in Figure 2.23(a), edges are present from B to E as well as from E to B. It forms a strongly connected component. Similarly edges are preset from C to F and F to C then C&F forms strongly connected component. Similarly edges I, G, H, K, L, J forms a closed path. Then these edges form a strongly connected component.

Vertex A is a strongly connected component and vertex D is another strongly component. The graph G has 12 vertices and it has five strongly connected components as shown in Figure 2.23(b).

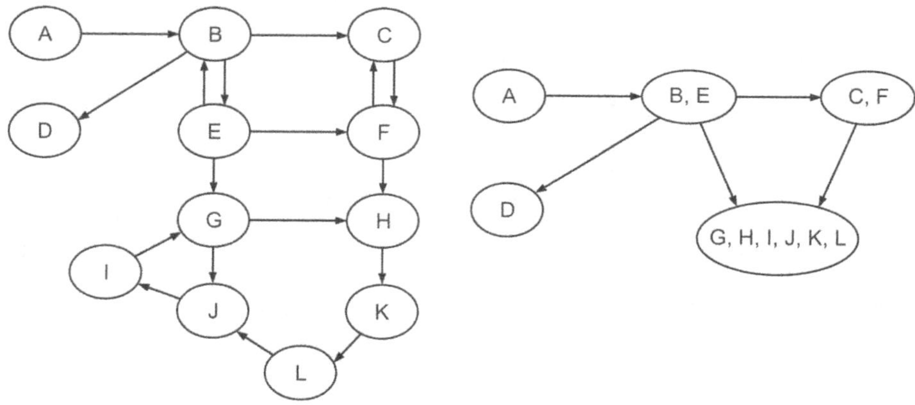

Figure 2.23 (a & b) Graph and its Strong Connected Components

Similarly Graph G2 has 8 vertices and it has four strongly connected components as shown in Figure 2.24.

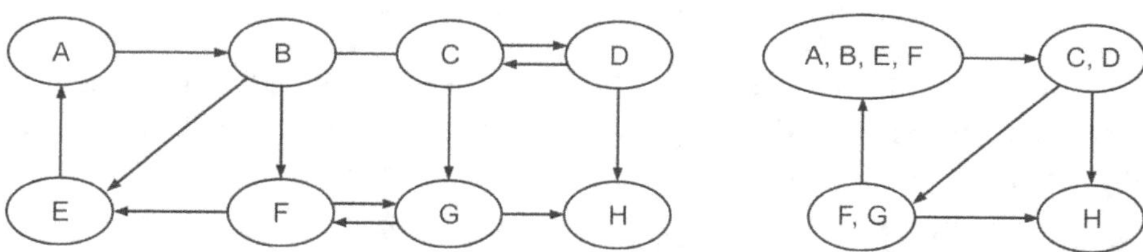

Figure 2.24 Graph and its Strong Connected Components

Objective Question Bank

1. Two biconnected components can have   [   ]
   A.   At most one vertex in common
   B.   At most two vertex in common
   C.   A common vertex
   D.   At most one edge in common

2. A minimum spanning tree of a weighted connected graph is its ....
   with the smallest weight   [   ]
   A.   Ordered tree   B.   Spanning tree
   C.   Forest   D.   Rooted tree

3. A spanning tree is   [   ]
   A.   Undirected tree consisting of only those edges necessary to connect
        all nodes in original graph
   B.   Trees containing more than 2 leaves at every node
   C.   Tree of depth more than n + 1
   D.   All of the above

4. Find (i) returns________________   [   ]
   A. Parent of the node i
   B. Grand Parent of the node i
   C. Root node of the tree that contains i
   D. Returns the position of i

5. Simple Union (i , j) represents   [   ]
   A. p[i] = j   B. p[j] = i
   C. p[i] = j but not p[j] = i   D. p[i] = j or p[j] = i

6. Time taken to perform a simple union operation is   [   ]
   A. O(1)   B. O(log n)
   C. O(nlog n)   D. $O(n^2)$

7. Time required to process a Find for an element at level k is   [   ]
   A. O(1)   B. O(k + 1)
   C. O(k)   D. $O(n^2)$

8. We can increase the performance of simple Union and simple Find algorithms   [   ]
   A. By creating degenerate trees
   B. By avoiding creation of degenerate trees
   C. Either a or b
   D. None

9. If the no. of nodes in the tree with root q is less than the no. of nodes in the tree with root p, then for Weighted Union (p,q) Which one of the following is correct?   [   ]
   A. P[p] = q   B. P[q] = p
   C. P[p] = q or P[q] = p   D. None

10. The numbers declared outside each vertex in depth first spanning tree are called......   [   ]
   A. Depth first numbers (dfns)
   B. breadth first numbers(bfns)
   C. Articulation points
   D. None of these

11. Time taken to perform (n-1) UNIONS is   [   ]
   A. $O(n^2)$ B. $O(n^3)$
   C. O(n)   D. O(1)

12. How many spanning trees does the following graph have?   [   ]
   A. 1   B. 2
   C. 3   D. 4

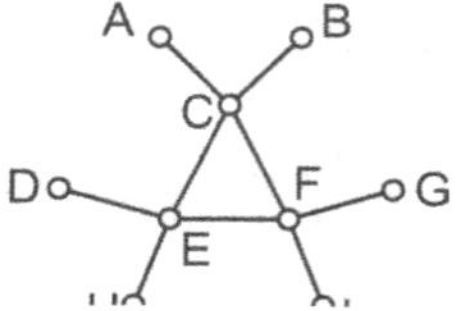

13. Which of the following are disjoint set operations   [   ]
    A. Make-set   B. Union
    C. Find-set   D. All

Fill in the Blanks

1. A graph G is biconnected if and only if it contains no_________________.

2. The operation Find (i) determines the ____________ of the tree containing i.

3. ____________________________is used for testing connected components.

4. Fill in the blanks for the below Algorithms

Algorithm Collapsing Find (i):

```
{
   r:=i;
   while(P[r]>0      do      r:=P[r];
   while(i≠r)        do
   {
      s:= P[i];P[i]=_ _ _ _; i:=s;
   }
   return _ _ _ _;
}
```

5. If there is no common element in both sets then those sets are called as_________________.

6. The operations to perform on disjoint sets are.............................. ,.........................

7. ____________ can be used to determine whether Graph G is connected.

8. The connected components of a graph can be obtained using ______________.

9. If adjacency lists are used, a breadth first traversal will obtain the connected components in ____________ time.

10. Spanning Trees obtained using a breadth first search are called ______________________.

11. A vertex v in a connected graph G is _________________________point iff the deletion of vertex v together with all edges incident to v disconnects the graph into 2 or more non empty components.

12. The Graph G is _________________________iff it contains no articulation points.

13. A maximal biconnected sub graph is a_________________________component.

14. Two biconnected components can have at most one vertex in common and this is an _______________point.

15. The root node of a depth first spanning tree is an articulation point iff it has at least_________children.

16. Broken edges are also called _________________.

17. Trees have a property that is very useful in identifying articulation points and biconnected components.

18. In depth first spanning tree for each vertex u,define $L(u)$ = _________.

19. The Biconnected components of a graph can be obtained using _________________.

20. If adjacency lists are used, a breadth first traversal will obtain the connected components in _______________time.

21. _______________ rule is used for FIND algorithm.

22. _______________ Search is used for testing connected components.

23. A graph G is said to be bi-connected if and only if it contains _________________.

24. Determining the connected components of an undirected graph is an Application of_______________set.

25. The intersection of two biconnected components consists of at most one vertex called an _______________Point.

26. Linked list _______________is an Application of disjoint set.

Review Questions

1. Develop an algorithms for UNION and FIND using weighing rule and collapsing rule respectively.

R09 May 2013

2. (a) Explain set representation using trees and develop algorithms for UNION and FIND using weighing and collapsing rules.

   (b) Define Articulation point. Illustrate with an example.

R09 December 2011

3. Write a Weighted union algorithm. Trace the above algorithm.

   R09 December 2011

4. Draw the complete undirected graphs on one, two, three, four, and Five vertices. Prove that the number of edges in an n-vertex complete graph is n(n–1)/2.

   R09 December 2011

5. (a) Explain about Connected components and Biconnected components.

   (b) Discuss about union and find algorithms.

   R09 November/December 2013

6. (a) What is weighting rule for Union(i, j)? How it improves the performance of union operation? Explain with example.

   (b) What is biconnected graph? How to determine biconnected components of graph?

   R09 June- 2014

7. Explain the usefulness of the following fundamental operations on sets: (i) Find (ii) Delete (iii) Union (iv) Insert.

   R09 April-May, 2012

8. (a) Explain the Disjoint set operations using trees?

   (b) Write Find and Union algorithms?

   R09 April-May, 2012

9. Two sets S1 and S2 are given as below

   S1={1,2,4,6} and S2 ={7,8}

   (a) Draw disjoint sets S1 and S2 using Trees

   (b) Draw disjoint sets S3 using Trees such that S3 = S1 U S2

   (c) Draw disjoint sets S4 using Trees such that S4 = S2 U S1

   (d) Give Pointer representation of S1, S2, S3 and S4.

   R09 April-May, 2012

10. Write and explain the final algorithm for collapse rule with an example.

    R09 April-May, 2012

11. Show that the relation V and W lie in the same biconnected component of G" is not an equivalence relation.

    RA December 2011

12. How we can use spanning tree algorithm to fnd single source shortest path in a given graph G.

    RA December 2011

13. Give an efficient algorithm that takes as input a directed graph
     G = (V,E) and determines whether or not there is a vertex s in V from
     which all other vertices are reachable. Show the time Complexity of
     your algorithm.   **R09 December-January 2011-2012**

14. Given a 2-connected graph G, and two vertices u and v of G, how can
     one find a minimum length cycle through u and v in the graph G? Can
     this be done in polynomial time?

                              R09 December-January 2011-2012

15. Write and explain the algorithms for the following:

     (a) simple union   (b) simple find

16. Write and explain the algorithm for the following:

     (a) weighted union   (b) collapsing find

17. Draw the tree representation of two set union? Explain.

18. (a) Draw the data representation for sets? Explain.

     (b) Explain array representation for sets? Explain.

19. (a) Draw the tree for weighted union?

     (b) Draw the tree for collapsing find?

     (c) Draw the tree for achieving for worst case bound weighted
          union?

20. Write the algorithm for biconnected components?

21. Show that if u unions are performed then no set contains more than
     u + 1 elements?

22. Show that if u unions are performed then at leastmax {n − 2u,0} single
     ton sets remain?

23. Explain Disjoint subsets operations.

24. Explain min, delete, find, union, intersect operations on sets.

25. Write pseudo code for implementation of UNION instruction using
     linked list.

26. Develop UNION and FIND algorithms for disjoint sets using
     weighing and collapsing rules respectively.

27. Explain the properties of strongly connected components.

28. Explain minimum, Delete operations on sets.

29. What is spanning tree? What are its applications?

30. Define biconnected graph. Develop an algorithm that determines a
     connected graph.

31. Define Problem Reduction. Explain in detail about AND-OR Graphs
     with neat example.

32. (a) Define Game Tree. Explain in detail about Minimax Search procedure with neat example.

    (b) Explain about alpha and beta cutoffs with an example.

33. Define Game Tree. Explain in detail about NIM game tree procedure.

3

DIVIDE AND CONQUER

3.1 GENERAL METHOD

Divide and Conquer is a technique which divides the problem into smaller units. After dividing the problem, the technique tries to solve the smaller units. Once the smaller units are solved, the solutions of smaller units are combined to get the final solution of the problem. If input size to a problem is complex, then we say that the problem is large or complex. Small problem is a problem which can be solved with one or two operations.

The Divide and Conquer principle has three steps:

Step 1: Divide: Dividing the given problem into smaller sub problems. Also each of these sub problems is almost of the same size.

Step 2: Conquer: These sub problems are solved independently in a recursive manner.

Step 3: Combine: Combining all the solution of sub problems to get the solution for the original problem.

- If the sub problems are large enough then divide and conquer is reapplied.

- The generated sub problems are usually of same type as the original problem. Hence recursive algorithms are used in divided and conquer strategy.

- A control abstraction (a flow of control of a procedure) for divide and conquer is given below.

Algorithm DC(P)

```
{
if P is very small then return solution of P.
    else
{
Divide(P)and obtain P1,P2,……....PK, k ≥ 1
```

```
Apply DC to each sub problem;
return combine ( DC(P1),D(P2)........DC(PK));
}

}
```

- The computing time of above procedure of divide and conquer is given by the recurrence relation.

$T(n) = h(n)$ n is small

$T(n) = T(n_1) + T(n_2) + \ldots + T(n_k) + f(n)$ where n is sufficiently large

Where h(n) is the time taken by the algorithm to give solution when n is small and T(n) is the time taken by the algorithm DC on any input of size n. f(n) is the time taken by the algorithm for dividing problem P into smaller instances and combining the solutions to sub problems.

The following recurrence relation given the time complexity of problems that come under Divide and Conquer algorithms.

$$T(n) = \begin{cases} T(1)\ldots\ldots\ldots\ldots\ldots\ldots n = 1 \\ aT(n/b) + f(n)\ldots\ldots\ldots n > 1 \end{cases}$$

3.2 BINARY SEARCH

The pre requisite for Binary Search is, elements must be sorted either in non-decreasing or non-increasing order. Let the elements are stored in non-decreasing order, if we want to search for the element say x. Then we first divide the list at mid ((lower bound + upper bound)/2), x is compared with mid element. If x equals to mid element, then search terminates, otherwise two sub lists get created. If x is greater than mid element then right sub list is considered and x is searched in the right sub list. Otherwise i.e., if x is less than mid element then x is searched in the left sub list.

To search the element using binary search method, divide and conquer strategy is used. If we consider that P is the number of elements and if there is only one element then return 1, that means problem P is small enough and cannot be split. If P i.e., number of elements are more than one, then we divide P into two sub lists and try to solve each sub list separately. As soon as the desired element is found in the list, the search terminates successfully. Here actually divide and conquer technique is used and condition for unsuccessful search is low > high.

The non-recursive algorithm is as given below:

```
BinarySearch (A, N, key)
LB←1
UB←N
Found←False
Repeat while(LB≤UB) and (Not Found)
MID←(LB+UB)/2
If (KEY=A[MID])
  Then
        Found←TRUE
  Location←MID
Else
If(KEY<A[MID])
Then
     UB←MID-1
Else
     LB←MID+1
Return
```

Algorithm for Binary Search

Step 1: Set lb = 0 and ub = Number of Items – 1

Step 2: Find the middle of the list as mid = (lb + ub)/2. Take only the integer part, if the result is a real number.

Step 3: Compare the middle item with the searching item. If they are equal then "Item is found" and go to step 8.

Step 4: If the searching item is less than the middle item then the searching item comes before this middle element. So, set ub = mid – 1 and there is no change in the value of first. Go to step 6.

Step 5: Since the above conditions are false the searching elements should be greater than the middle element. So set lb = mid + 1 and there is no change in the value of last. Go to the next step.

Step 6: If lb <= Last then go to Step 2. else go to step 7.

Step 7: Since end of the list is reached, the searching item is "not found" in the list.

Step 8: End of the algorithm.

Example : Assume the list of data to be 18, 32, 35, 48, 62 and 75. Here 18 is the 0th element and 75 is the 5th element.

The above data is sorted. So, Binary Search can be applied.

Case 1: Element to be searched is 35.

The number of elements = 6.

Step 1: lb = 0 and ub = 6 − 1 that is ub = 5. The list looks like this.

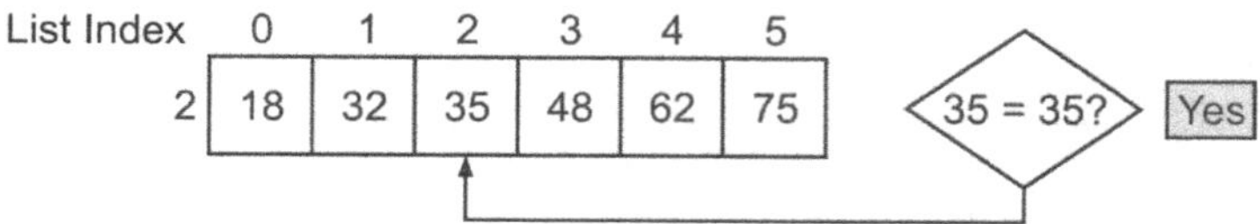

Step 2: Mid = (0 + 5)/2. That is, Mid = 2 (Only integer part is taken).

Step 3: Compare the middle item (second element which is 35) with the searching item. The searching item is also 35. So, the **"Item is found"** and stop the searching process.

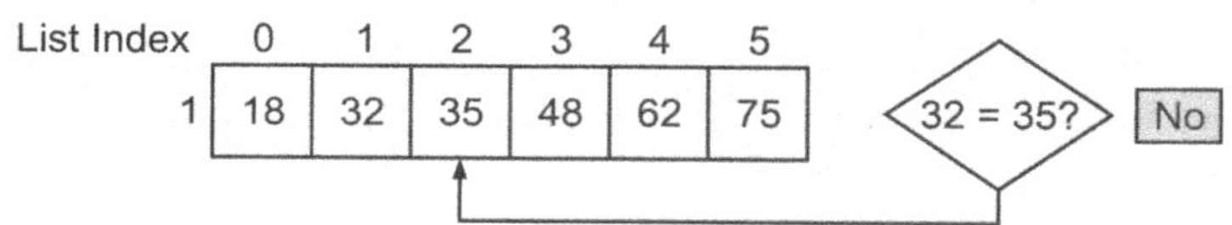

Case 2: Element to be searched is 32.

Step 1: lb = 0 and ub = 5.

Step 2: Mid = (0 + 5)/2. That is, Mid = 2 (Only integer part is taken).

Step 3: Compare the middle item 35 with the searching item. The searching item is 32 is not equal to 35. So proceed to next step.

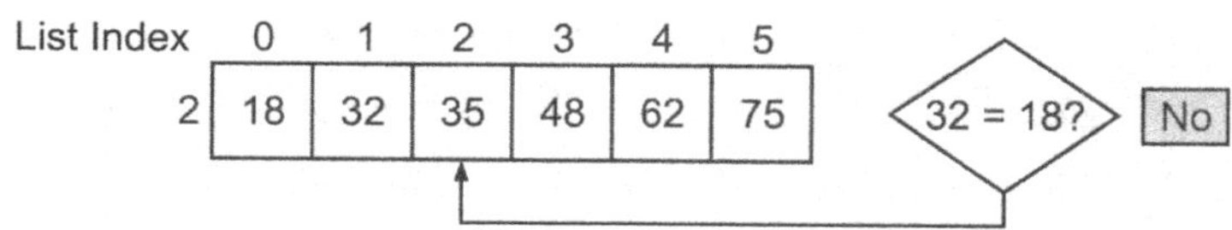

Step 4: The searching item 32 is less than 35. So it should appear before 35. Now lb = 0 and ub = mid − 1. that is ub = 2-1. So ub = 1.

Step 5: Compute Mid = (0 + 1)/2 that is Mid = 0 (integer part).

Step 6: Compare 0th item with 32. That is compare 18 and 32. Since they are not equal proceed to next step.

Step 7: Since the searching item 32 is greater than 18, the searching item comes after 18. lb = mid + 1. That is lb = 0 + 1. So, lb = 1 and ub =1. Now Mid = (1 + 1)/2 = 1.

Step 8: Compare 32 with the item in position 1. That is also 32. So, the **"Item is found"** and stop the searching process.

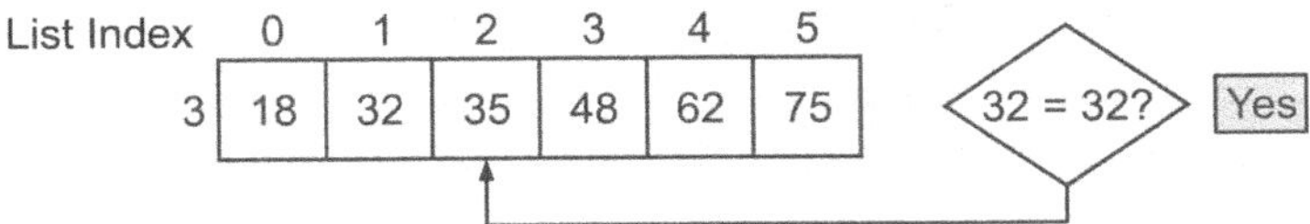

Case 3: Unsuccessful Search

Element to be searched is 50.

Step 1: lb = 0 and ub = 5.

Step 2: Mid = (0 + 5)/2. That is, Mid = 2 (Only integer part is taken).

Step 3: Compare the middle item 35 with the searching item. The searching item is 50 is not equal to 35. So proceed to next step.

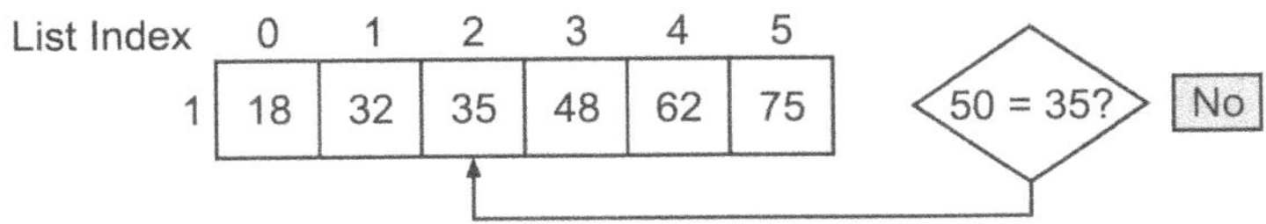

Step 4: The searching item 32 is greater than 35. So it should appear after 35. Now lb is modified i.e., lb = mid + 1 = 3, ub = 5.

Step 5: Compute Mid = (3 + 5)/2 that is Mid = 4 (integer part).

Step 6: Compare 4th item with 50. That is compare 62 and 50. Since they are not equal proceed to next step.

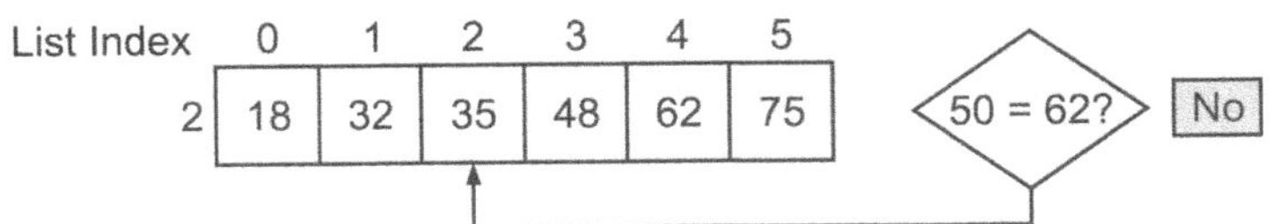

Step 7: Since the searching item 50 is less than 62, so it should appear before 62. Now ub is modified.

$$ub = mid - 1 = 3, lb = 3 \text{ and } Mid = (3 + 3)/2 = 3.$$

Step 8: Compare 3rd element with 50. That is compare 48 with 50. Since they are not equal, proceed to next step.

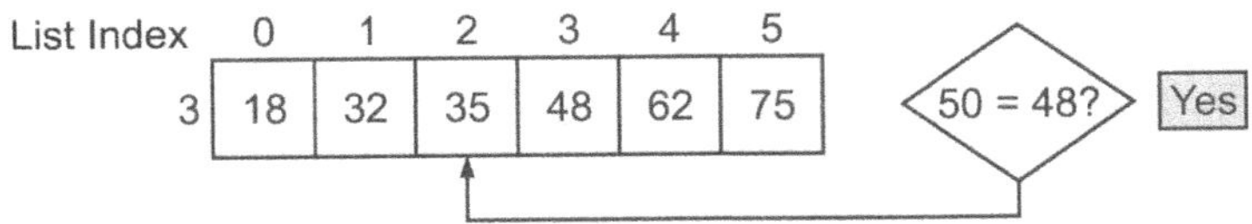

Step 9: The searching item 50 is greater than 48. So it should appear after 48. Now lb is modified i.e., lb = mid + 1 = 3 + 1 = 4, ub = 3.

Now lb <= ub, condition is not satisfied. Now the search element is not found in the list. Search is unsuccessful.

3.2.1 Recursive Algorithm for Binary Search

Let a_i, $1 < i < n$, be a list of elements that are sorted in non decreasing order. Consider the problem of determining whether a given element x is present in the list. If x is present, we are to determine a value j such that $a_j = x$. If x is not in the list, then j is to be set to -1. Let $P = (n, a_i, ..., a_l, x)$ denote an arbitrary instance of this search problem (n is the number of elements in the list, $a_i, ..., a_l$ is the list of elements, and x is the element searched for). Divide-and-conquer can be used to solve this problem.

```
 1:  Algorithm RBinSrch(a, lb, ub, x)
 2:  //Given an array a[i : l] of elements in non
     //decreasing order, 1< i < l, determine whether x
     //is present, and if so, //return j  such that x =
     //a[j]; else return 0.
 3:  {
 4:  if(lb = ub)   then       // If Small(P)
 5:  {
 6:  if(x = a[lb]) then return i;
 7:  else return -1;
 8:  }
 9:  else
10:  {               //Reduce P into a smaller subproblem
11:  mid:= [lb+ub)/2];
12:  if(x = a[mid]) then return mid;
13:  else if (x < a[mid]) then
14:  return BinSrch(a,lb,mid-1,x);
15:  else return BinSrch(a,mid+1,ub,x);
16:  }
17:  }
```

The recurrence relation for Binary Search is:

$$T(n) = T(n/2) + b \qquad n > 1$$

$$T(n) = a \qquad n = 1$$

For $n = 1$, we have only one comparison i.e., constant time $T(n) = a$, $n = 1$.

For $n > 1$, mid is calculated and element to be searched is compared with mid. After that array is divided into two equal half's and search will take place only one half depending on the condition. To calculate mid we require constant time i.e., 'b'.

$$T(n) = T(n/2) + b.$$

The time complexity for this algorithm is

	Best	Average	Worst
Successful search	O(1)	O(log n)	O(log n)
Unsuccessful search	O(log n)	O(log n)	O(log n)

3.3 MAXIMUM AND MINIMUM

In this problem we have to find the maximum and minimum element in an array of 'n' elements. Our focus is on the number of comparisons made while analyzing the time complexity of the problem. The main goal of the algorithm is to store maximum element in variable max and minimum element in variable min. We have two versions of max-min problem.

1. Iterative max-min
2. Recursive max-min

3.3.1 Iterative Maximum and Minimum Algorithm

Initially max and min contains first element. Comparison starts from second element to the last element.

```
 1:  Algorithm Iter_MaxMin(x,n,max,min)
 2:  // set max to the maximum & min to the minimum of
     // x[1:n]
 3:  {
 4:  max:=min:=x[1];
 5:  for i:=2 to n do
 6:  {
 7:  if(x[i]>max) then max:=x[i];
 8:  else if(x[i]<min) then min:=x[i];
 9:  }
10:  }
```

Algorithm: Iterative Maximum & Minimum

- Now the best case occurs when the elements are in increasing order.

  → The no. of element comparison is (n − 1).

- The worst case occurs when the elements are in decreasing order.

  → The no. of elements comparison is 2(n − 1)

- The average no. of element comparison is < than 2(n − 1)

- On the average x[i] is > than max half the time, and so, the average number of comparison is 3n/2 − 1.

Analysis:

Case study 1: 70, 65, 62, 50, 45, 40, 10, 8

Min = 70

Max = 70

i = 2   if x[i] > max i.e., 65>max condition is false

if x[i] < min i.e., 65<70 condition is true

The variable min is modified and the new min = 65.

In the above iteration two comparisons are made and min is modified. Similarly for all the remaining iterations we make two comparisons and variable min is modified in each iteration. When elements are stored in non-increasing order the above algorithm falls in worst case and number of comparisons are 2(n – 1).

Case study 2: 8, 10, 40, 45, 50, 62, 65, 70

min = 8

max = 8

i = 2   if x[i] > max i.e., 10>max condition is true. The variable max is modified and new max = 10. We are not checking x[i] < min condition.

In the above iteration only one comparison is made and variable max is modified. Similarly for all the iterations we make only one comparison and max is modified in each iteration. As the loop is starting from second element, the numbers of comparisons are n – 1. When the elements are stored in ascending order, the above algorithm falls in best case and the numbers of comparisons are n – 1.

3.3.2 Recursive Maximum and Minimum Algorithm

A divide and conquer algorithm for maximum and minimum problem is to find the maximum and minimum element of the list. An arbitrary instance of the problem P is represented by (n, x[i],......,x[j]) where 'n' is the no. of elements in the list (x[i],....,x[j]). P has to be divided into two smaller instances P_1 and P_2 of approximately same size if the list has more than two elements where P_1 = ([n/2], x[1],........x[n/2]) & P_2 = (n – [n/2], x[[n/2] + 1], ..., x[n]). P_1 and P_2 are solved recursively invoking the same divide-and-conquer algorithm. Then the solutions of P_1 and P_2 are combined by storing maximum of max(P_1) and max(P_2) in max(P) and minimum of min(P_1) and min(P_2) in min(P).

Algorithm: Recursively Finding the Maximum & Minimum

```
1:   Algorithm RecurMaxMin(i,j,max,min)
2:   //x[1:n] is a global array, parameters i & j
3:   //are integers, 1<=i<=j<=n.
4:   {
5:   if(i=j) then max:= min:= X[i];    // small(P) if
     //array has one element
```

```
 6:   else if (i=j-1) then // Another case of small(p) if
      //array has two elements
 7:   {
 8:   if (X[i]<X[j]) then
 9:   {
10:   max:=X[j];
11:   min:=X[i];
12:   }
13:   else
14:   {
15:   max:=X[i];
16:   min:=X[j];
17:   }
18:   }
19:   else
20:   {
21:   // if P is not small, divide P into subproblems.
22:   // find where to split the set mid:=[(i+j)/2];
23:   //solve the subproblems
24:   MaxMin(i, mid, max, min);
25:   MaxMin(mid+1,j,max1,min1);
26:   //combine the solution
27:   if (max<max1) then max=max1;
28:   if(min>min1) then min = min1;
29:   }
30:   }
```

- The procedure is initially invoked by the statement,

  MaxMin(1,n,x,y)

- Suppose we simulate MaxMin on the following 10 elements

Recursive Max – Min:

1	2	3	4	5	6	7	8	9	10
12	15	8	13	4	17	14	19	21	16

```
                    | 1 | 10 | 21 | 4 |

        | 1 | 5 | 13 | 4 |              | 6 | 10 | 14 | 21 |

  | 1 | 3 | 15 | 8 |  | 4 | 5 | 13 | 4 |    | 6 | 8 | 19 | 14 |  | 9 | 10 | 16 | 21 |

| 1 | 2 | 15 | 12 |  | 3 | 3 | 8 | 8 |    | 6 | 7 | 17 | 14 |  | 8 | 8 | 19 | 19 |
```

By the above figure we see that the root node contains (1, 10, max, min) as the values of (i, j, max, min) corresponding to the initial call to MaxMin, max & min values are computed at last. This execution produces two new calls to MaxMin, two nodes are created with 5 elements each and they are (1, 5, max, min) and (6, 10, max, min) thus split the set into 2 subsets of approximately the same size. Node (1, 5, max, min) is split into two subsets of approximately the same size and they are (1, 3, max, min) and (4, 5, max, min). Node (1, 3, max, min) is split into two subsets of approximately the same size and they are (1, 2, max, min) and (3, 3, max, min). Node (1, 2, max, min) has two elements so maximum and minimum are found because these is a small problem. Node (3, 3, max, min) has one element so maximum and minimum are found because these is a small problems. Node (6, 10, max, min) is split into two subsets of approximately the same size and they are (6, 8, max, min) and (9, 10, max, min). Node (6, 8, max, min) is split into two subsets of approximately the same size and they are (6, 7, max, min) and (8, 8, max, min). Node (6, 7, max, min) has two elements so maximum and minimum are found because these is a small problem. Node (8, 8, max, min) has one element so maximum and minimum are found because these is a small problems.

Now the values to max and min are assigned. The numbers included in the upper left corner of each node represent the order in which max & min are assigned values.

- From the tree, we can immediately see the maximum depth of recursion is 4. (including the 1st call)

  No. of element Comparison:

- If T(n) represents this no., then the resulting recurrence relations is

  $T(n) = \{$ $T([n/2] + T[n/2] + 2$ $\quad\quad n > 2$

  1 $\quad\quad\quad\quad\quad\quad\quad\quad\quad\quad n = 2$

  0 $\quad\quad\quad\quad\quad\quad\quad\quad\quad\quad n = 1$

  $\rightarrow$ When 'n' is a power of 2, n = 2^k for some +ve integer 'k', then

  $T(n) \quad = 2T(n/2) + 2$

  $\quad\quad\quad = 2(2T(n/4) + 2) + 2$

  $\quad\quad\quad = 4T(n/4) + 4 + 2$

  $\quad\quad\quad *$

  $\quad\quad\quad *$

  $\quad\quad\quad = 2^{k-1} \, T(2) +$

  $\quad\quad\quad = 2^{k-1} + 2^{k-2}$

  $\quad\quad\quad = 2^{k}/2 + 2^{k-2}$

  $\quad\quad\quad = n/2 + n - 2$

  $\quad\quad\quad = (n + 2n)/2 - 2$

  $\quad\quad\textbf{T(n) = (3n/2) - 2}$

*Note that (3n/2) – 2 is the best-average, and worst-case no. of comparisons when 'n' is a power of 2.

3.4 QUICK SORT

Quick sort is a sorting algorithm that uses the divide and conquer strategy. The three steps of quick sort are as follows:

Divide: Rearrange the elements and split the array into two sub arrays based on pivot element. Each element in the left sub array is less than or equal to the pivot element and each element in the right sub array is greater than or equal to the element.

Conquer: Recursively sort the two sub arrays. They are further divided until the sub array is of size 1.

Combine: Combine all the sorted elements in a group to form a sorted list.

This is also called "Partition Exchange Sort". First element is called Pivot or Key. Array is divided into two parts based on Pivot element. Here the elements are rearranged such that left side of key elements is less than key and right side of key elements is greater than key.

3.4.1 Quick Sort Algorithm

```
1:   Read N
2:   Repeat for I=1,2,….,N
3:   Read(X[I])
4:   Call Quick(X,1,N)
5:   Repeat for I=1,2,…..,N
6:   Write(X[I])
7:   Exit
Procedure Quick(X,LB,UB)
      // The elements stored in array X[1,n] are in not
      // sorted initially.
      // n is total number of elements
      // LB is initially at index 1 and UB is at index n
      // of an array X
      // By this recursive algorithm the array will be
      // sorted in ascending order.
      If(LB<UB)
      then

                  // partition is used to divide the
                  // array into two sub arrays and k
                  // is the position of partitioning
                  // element.
            Call partition(X, LB, UB, POSITION);
                        // recursively sort the sub arrays
            Call Quick (X, LB, POSITION-1);
            Call Quick (X, POSITION+1, UB);
      }
}
```

```
procedure partition(X, LB, UB, pos)
// first element of the sub array is assumed to be pivot
   1:   Pivot:=X[LB];
   2:   I←LB+1
   3:   J←UB
   4:   Repeat While(I<J){
   5:   Repeat While(X[I]≤pivot) and (I<UB)
         I←I+1
   6:   Repeat While(X[J]>pivot)
         J←J-1
   7:   if(I<J) then
         {
         T←X[I]
         X[I]←X[J]
         X[J]←T
         }
   8:   X[IB]←X[J]
   9:   X[J]←pivot
  10:   POSITION←J
  11:   Return
```

The partition function is called to arrange the elements such that all the elements that are less than pivot are at the left side of pivot and all the elements that are greater than pivot are all at the right of pivot. In other words pivot is occupying its proper position and the partitioned list is obtained in an ordered manner. This procedure is continued by repeatedly partitioned the list.

Example: Consider the list of unsorted elements as:

62, 71, 72, 80, 82, 60, 52, 51, 42. We will consider pivot = X[LB] i.e., 62 where LB = 1, UB = 9, i = LB + 1 = 2, j = UB = 9.

1	2	3	4	5	6	7	8	9
62	71	72	80	82	60	52	51	42

Pivot   i   j

We check while(X[i]<=pivot) i.e., 71<=62 condition is false, loop terminates at i value 2. While(X[j]>pivot) i.e., 42>62 condition is false, loop terminates at j value 9. Now i<j condition is satisfied. X[i] and X[j] elements are swapped. i<j condition is true, the same loop is continued. while(X[i]<=pivot) i.e., 42<=62 condition is true i value increments. Next we check 72<=62 condition is false, loop terminates at i value 3. while(X[j]>pivot) i.e., 71>62 condition is false, loop terminates at j value 8.

1	2	3	4	5	6	7	8	9
62	42	72	80	82	60	52	51	71

                     i   j

Now i<j i.e., 3<8 condition is true, then X[i] and X[j] are swapped i.e., elements 51 and 72 are swapped. As i<j condition is true the same loop is continued.

While(X[i]<=pivot) i.e., 51<=62 condition is true, i value increments to 4. Next we check 80<=62 condition is checked it is false, loop terminates at i value 4.

While(X[j]>pivot) i.e. 72>62 condition is true j value decrements to 7, next 52>62 condition is checked it is false, loop terminates at j value 7.

1	2	3	4	5	6	7	8	9
62	42	51	80	82	60	52	72	71

(i at position 4, j at position 7)

As i<j i.e., 4<7 condition is true then X[i] and X[j] are swapped. As i<j condition is true, the same loop is continued. while(X[i]<=pivot) i.e., 52<=62 condition is true, then i value increments to 5. Next 82<=62 condition is checked, it is false, loop terminates at i value 5. while(X[j]>pivot) i.e., 80>62 condition is true, then j value decrements to 6. Next 60>62 condition is checked, it is false, then loop terminates at j value 6.

1	2	3	4	5	6	7	8	9
62	42	51	52	82	60	80	72	71

(i at position 5, j at position 6)

As i<j condition is true then X[i] and X[j] are swapped i.e., elements 82 and 60 are swapped. As i<j condition is true, the same loop is continued. while(X[i]<=pivot) i.e., 60<=62 condition is true, then i value increments to 6. Next 82<=62 condition is checked, it is false, loop terminates at i value 6. While (X[j]>pivot) i.e., 82>62 condition is true then j value decrements to 5. Next 60>62 condition is checked, it is false, then loop terminates at j value 5.

1	2	3	4	5	6	7	8	9
62	42	51	52	60	82	80	72	71

(j at position 5, i at position 6)

As i<j condition is false then X[j] and key are swapped i.e., elements 62 and 60 are swapped. Now the given list is divided at pivot into two sub-lists. The left sub-list is called sub-list 1 and it contains elements that are less than pivot (62), and the right sub-list is called sub-list 2, it contains elements that are greater than pivot (62). This is called first partition and after first partition the pivot element (62) is placed in its proper position. Now we apply algorithm quick on sub-list 1 and sub-list 2.

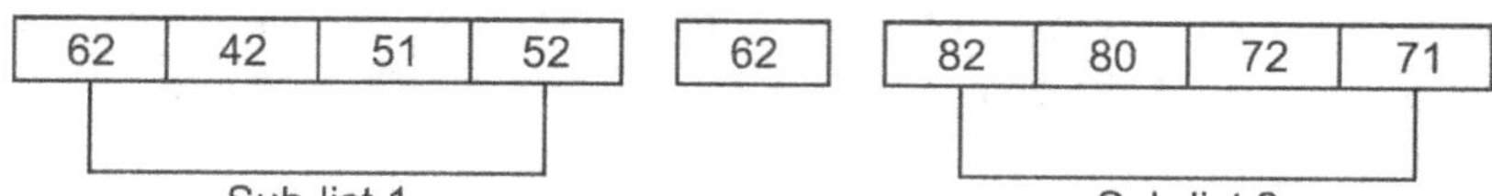

Now we will consider 60 as pivot for sublist 1 and repeat above steps to place pivot at proper position. Proper position of pivot means all the elements that are less than pivot should be left side of pivot and all the elements that are greater than pivot are at right side of pivot. Hence we get.

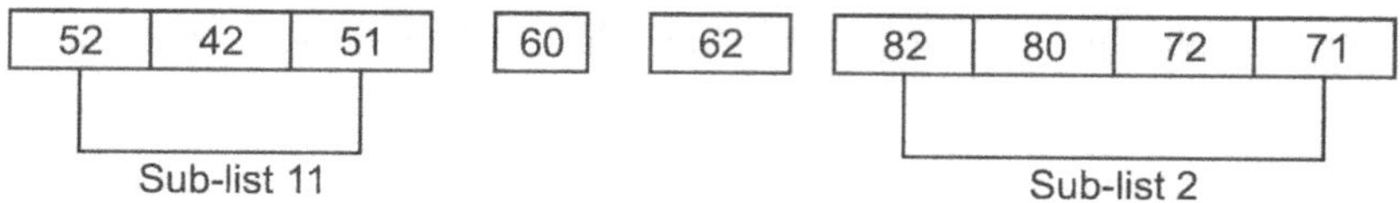

Now the sub-list 1 is further divided into two sub-lists sub-list 11 and sub-list 12. Sub-list 11 has three elements and sub-list 12 has zero elements because in sub-list 1 there are no elements greater than 60. Now we will consider 52 as pivot for sublist 11 and repeat above steps to place pivot at proper position. Hence we get.

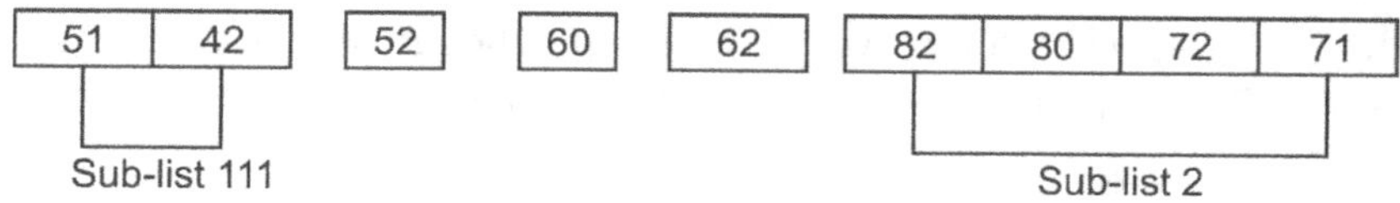

Now the sub-list 11 is further divided into two sub-lists sub-list 111 and sub-list 112. Sub-list 111 has two elements and sub-list 112 has zero elements because in sub-list 11 there are no elements greater than 52. Now we will consider 51 as pivot for sub-list 111 and repeat above steps to place pivot at proper position. Hence we get.

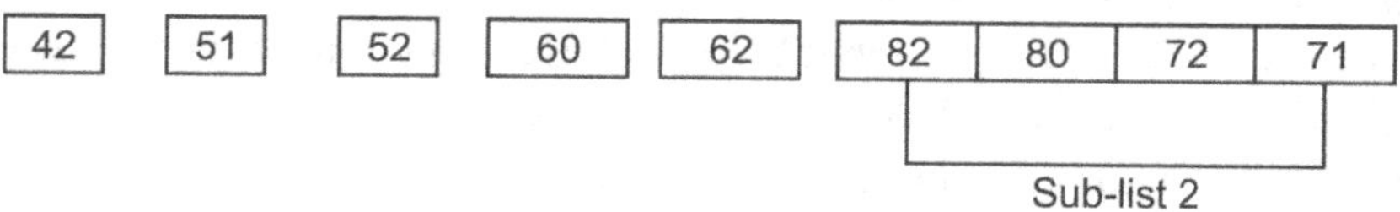

After partition left sub-list 111 has only one element so it is not further sub divided. Now the same procedure is applied on sub-list 2 with 82 as pivot and repeat above steps to place pivot at proper position. Hence we get.

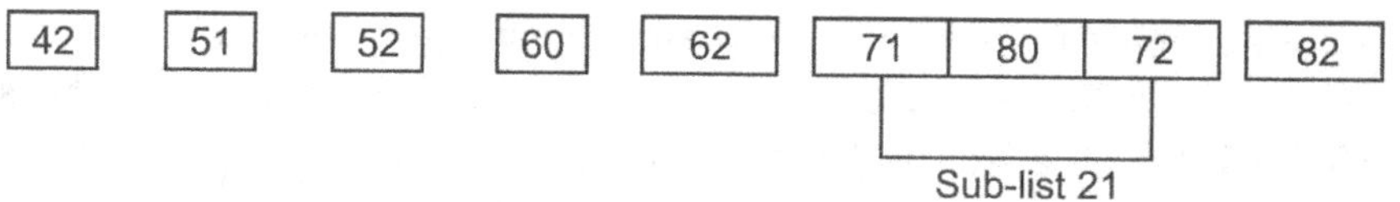

Now the sub-list 2 is further divided into two sub-lists sub-list 21 and sub-list 22. Sub-list 21 has three elements and sub-list 22 has zero elements because in sub-list 22 there are no elements greater than 82. Now we will consider 71 as pivot for sublist 21 and repeat above steps to place pivot at proper position. Hence we get.

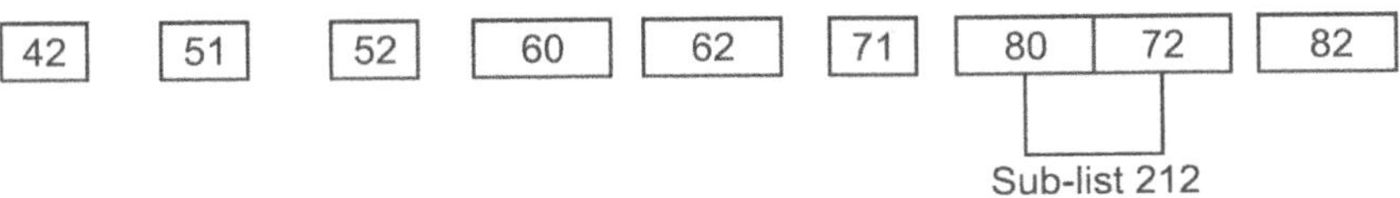

Now the sub-list 21 is further divided into two sub-lists sub-list 211 and sub-list 212. Sub-list 211 has zero elements because in sub-list 21 there are no elements less than 71 and Sub-list 212 has two elements. Now we will consider 80 as pivot for sublist 212 and repeat above steps to place pivot at proper position. Hence we get.

42	51	52	60	62	71	72	80	82

Thus 80 is placed at its proper position and we get a sorted list.

Analysis of algorithm: The running time of quick sort depends on whether partition is balanced or unbalanced, which in turn depends on which elements of an array to be sorted are used for partitioning. A very good partition splits an array up into two equal sized arrays. A bad partition, on other hand, splits an array up into two arrays of very different sizes. The worst partition puts only one element in one array and all other elements in the other array. If the partitioning is balanced, the quick sort runs faster. On the other hand, if partitioning is unbalanced, the quick sort runs very slow.

3.4.2 Best Case Time Complexity

The best case of quick sort will happen if each partitioning stage divides the array exactly in half. In other words, the best to be a median of the keys in X[low......high] every time procedure 'partition' is called. The procedure 'partition' always split the array to be sorted into two approximately equal sized arrays. Pivot is placed in its proper position, to divide the array number of comparisons required is n − 1.

If the procedure 'partition, produces two sub arrays of size n/2, the recurrence relation is then

$$T(n) = T(n/2) + T(n/2) + (n - 1)$$

$$= 2T(n/2) + (n - 1) \qquad n > 1$$

$$= 1, \qquad\qquad \text{if } n = 1$$

$$\text{Otherwise} \quad T(n) = 2[2T(n/4) + (n/2 - 1)] + (n - 1)$$

$$= 4\,T(n/4) + 2n - 3$$

Simplifying this recurrence in a similar manner, we get,

$$T(n) = 2^k T(n/2^k) + kn - (2^k - 1)$$

The base condition for the recurrence is $T(1)$. So in this case we have

$$n/2^k = 1 \implies 2^k = n \implies k = \log n.$$

Substituting for k we get,

$$T(n) = nT(1) + n \log (n) - (n - 1)$$
$$= n\log n + 1$$
$$= O(n\log n)$$

3.4.3 Worst Case Time Complexity

The worst case for Quick sort can arise when the partition algorithm divides the array in such a way that either the left sub array or the right sub array is empty.

In this case the problem size is reduced from n to $n - 1$ after first partition.

The recurrence relation for the worst case is as follows.

$$T(n) = T(n - 1) + (n - 1) \quad \text{if } n > 1$$
$$= 0, \text{ if } n \leq 1.$$

Simplify this we get, $T(n) = (n - 1) + (n - 2) + \text{--------} + 2 + 1 = ((n - 1)n)/2 = O(n^2)$.

$$T(n) = O(n^2)$$

Example: Apply quick sort to the following elements:

10	20	30	40	50	60	70
pivot	i					j

10	20	30	40	50	60	70
	pivot	i				j

10	20	30	40	50	60	70
		pivot	i			j

10	20	30	40	50	60	70
			pivot	i		j

10	20	30	40	50	60	70
				pivot	i	j

10	20	30	40	50	60	70
					pivot	i j

10	20	30	40	50	60	70

Here we are getting $n - 1$ partitions and each partition has n comparisons.

3.4.4 Average Case Time Complexity

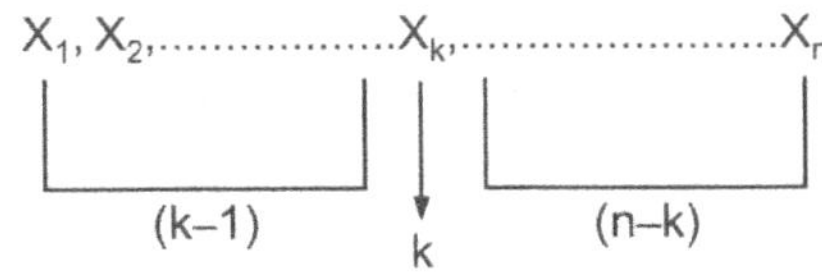

$$C_a(n) = (n + 1) + C_a(k - 1) + C_a(n - k)$$

$$C_a(n) = (n + 1) + 1/n \sum_{k=1 \text{ to } n} [C_a(k - 1) + C_a(n - k)]$$

Here $C_a(0) = 0$

$C_a(1) = 0$ no elements

$K = 1,2,3,.....n$

$$nC_a(n) = n(n + 1) + [C_a(0) + C_a(n - 1)$$
$$+ C_a(1) + C_a(n - 2) + ... + C_a(n - 1) + C_a(0)]$$
$$n.C_a(n) = n(n + 1) + 2[C_a(0) + C_a(1) + ... + C_a(n - 1)] \quad .....(3.1)$$

Replacing 'n' by $(n - 1)$

$$(n - 1)C_a(n - 1) = n(n - 1) + 2[C_a(0) + ... + C_a(n - 2)] \quad .....(3.2)$$

Subtracting 3.2 from 3.1

$$n.C_a(n) - (n - 1)C_a(n - 1) = n^2 + n - n^2 + n + 2C_a(n - 1)$$
$$= 2n + 2C_a(n - 1)$$
$$nC_a(n) = 2n + 2C_a(n - 1) + (n - 1)C_a(n - 1)$$
$$= 2n + C_a(n - 1)[2 + n - 1]$$
$$= 2n + C_a(n - 1)(n + 1) \qquad .....(3.3)$$

Divide 3 with $n(n + 1)$

$$C_a(n)/(n + 1) = 2/(n + 1) + C_a(n - 1)/n$$

Repeatedly using this equation to substitute for

$$C_a(n - 1), C_a(n - 2), ...$$
$$= 2/(n + 1) + 2/n + C_a(n - 2)/(n - 1)$$

//Substitute $n = n - 1$.

$$= 2/(n + 1) + 2/n + 2/(n - 1) + C_a(n - 3)/(n - 2)$$

$$C_a(n)/(n + 1) = 2\sum_{k=3}^{n+1} 1/k + C_a(1)/2$$

$$= 2[\log x]_{2 \text{ to } n + 1}$$

$$C_a(n)/(n + 1) = 2[\log(n + 1) - \log 2]$$

$$C_a(n) = 2(n + 1)[\log(n + 1) - \log(2)]$$
$$= n \log n$$
$$= O(n \log n)$$

Time Complexity of Quick sort in all cases are:

Best case	Average case	Worst case
O(n log n)	O(n log n)	$O(n^2)$

3.5 MERGE SORT

The merge sort is a sorting algorithm that uses the divide and conquers strategy. In this method division is dynamically carried out.

Merge sort on an input array with n elements consists of three steps.

Divide: Partition array into two sub lists S1 and S2 with n/2 elements each.

Conquer: Recursively sort S1 and S2.

Combine: Merge S1 and S2 into a unique sorted group.

Merge sort has two algorithms mergesort and merge. Mergesort divides the array into two equal halfs irrespective of elements. This procedure continues until sub array is of size 1. Initially there are n elements in an array which are not sorted. After division we are having n sorted sub arrays of size 1, because array of size 1 is a sorted array. Now we have to combine these sorted arrays.

Algorithm merge will merge two sorted sub arrays into one sorted array. In merge sort we are not sorting elements, by the virtue of division of elements sub array becomes sorted. Here sorting takes place while combining the arrays.

3.5.1 Recursive Merge Sort Algorithm

```
1:   Read N
2:   Repeat for I=1,2……..N
3:   Read [X(I)]
4:   Call MERGESORT(X,L,N)
5:   Exit
Procedure MERGESORT(X,lb,ub)
 2:  If (lb<ub)
       Then
           MID <--- [(lb+ub)/2]
            Call MERGESORT(X, lb, mid)
        Call MERGESORT(X,mid+1,ub)
        Call MERGE(X,lb,mid,ub)
3. Return
        Procedure MERGE(X,lb,mid,ub)
```

```
1:  I  ← Lb.
2:  J  ← Mid+1
3:  K ← Ub
4:  Repeat while(I≤mid)and(J≤ub)
5:  If[(X[I])≤X[J]]
Then
    B[k]← X[I]
    I ← I+1
    k ← k+1
Else
    B[k] ← X[J]
    J ← J+1
    k ← k+1
6:  Repeat while (I≤mid)
    B[k] ← X[I]
    I ← I+1
    K ← k+1
7:  Repeat while (J≤ub)
    B[k] ←  X[J]
    J ← J+1
    K ← k+1
8:  Repeat for k ← Lb,Lb+1,……….ub
    X[k] ← B[k]
9:   Return
```

Example: Let us assume there are 11 elements to be sorted using merge sort technique where low = 1 and high = 11. Now the array is divided into two equal half's at mid value 6, left sub array has low = 1, high = mid = 6 and right sub array has low = mid + 1 = 7, high = 11. The left sub array and right sub array are further divided into equal half's until sub array of size 1. The following tree diagram shows the partition of the array done by the procedure merge sort.

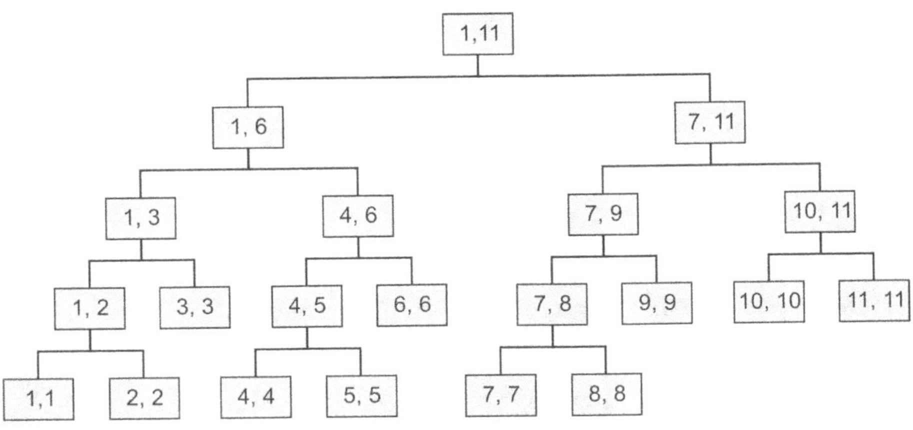

Initially we have an array of size n after partition we have n sub arrays of size one as shown in figure below.

| 1 | 2 | 3 | 4 | 5 | 6 | 7 | 8 | 9 | 10 | 11 |

Now all sorted sub arrays are merged using merge algorithm. The tree of calls for merge algorithm is shown in the figure below. The order of splitting is remembered and in the similar fashion elements are merged. Recursion remembers the order of splitting. First sub array 1 and sub array 2 are merged to form a sorted sub array represented by (1,1,2) where the first parameter is lb, second parameter is mid and third parameter is ub, next this array is merged with sub array 3 to form a sorted sub array represented by (1,2,3). Next sub array 4 and sub array 5 are merged to form a sorted sub array represented by (4,4,5), next this array is merged with sub array 6 to form a sorted sub array represented by (4,5,6). Now the sorted sub array (1,2,3) and sorted sub array (4,5,6) are merged to form sorted sub array (1,3,6). Similarly sorted sub arrays 7, 8, 9, 10, 11 are merged to form sorted sub array (7, 9, 11). Finally two sorted sub arrays (1, 3, 6) and (7, 9, 11) are merged to form sorted array(1, 6, 11).

Tree of calls of Merge:

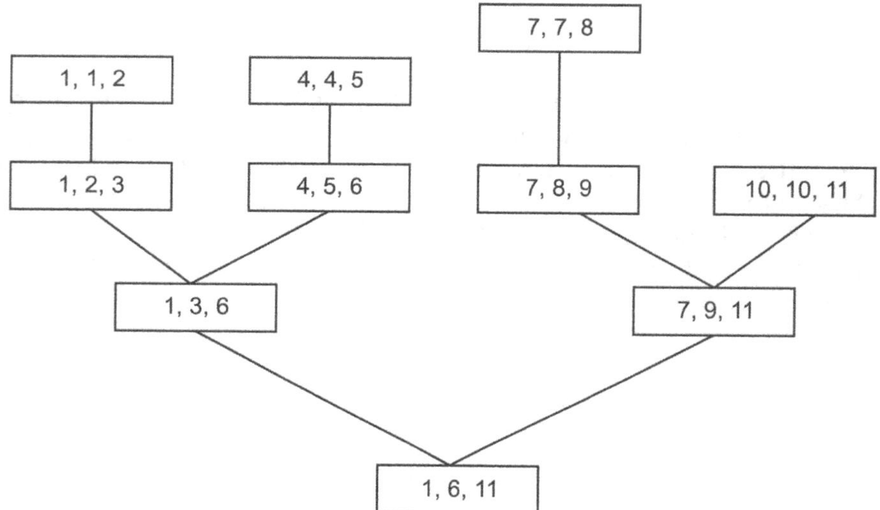

Example: Sort 9, 2, 8, 6, 5 using merge sort.

From the above example lb = 1, ub = 5 and mid = 3. As lb < ub condition is true, implies that an array has more than one element. Merge sort will split the array into two parts, first sub array consists of elements (9, 2, 8) and second sub array consists of elements (6, 5). First sub array is further split into two parts they are (9, 2) & (8). The sub array (9, 2) is again split into (9) & (2). In sub array (9) & sub array (2), lb < ub condition fails because lb = ub as they have only one element. Now we have two sub arrays of size 1 which are sorted and they contain (9) & (2). They are merged using merge algorithm and sub array (2, 9) is formed. After combining these two sub arrays into one sub array (2, 9), third sub array containing (8) is checked. As it has only one element no further splitting taken place. Now sub array containing (2, 9) & sub array containing (8) are merged using merge algorithm and sub array formed is (2, 8, 9).

After completing the left sub array, right sub array (6, 5) starts splitting. Sub array (6, 5) is split into sub array (6) & sub array (5). They are not further divided because they contain only one element. Sub array (6) and sub array (5) are merged to form sub array (5, 6). Now sub array (2, 8, 9) & sub array (5, 6) are merged to form sorted array (2, 5, 6, 8, 9).

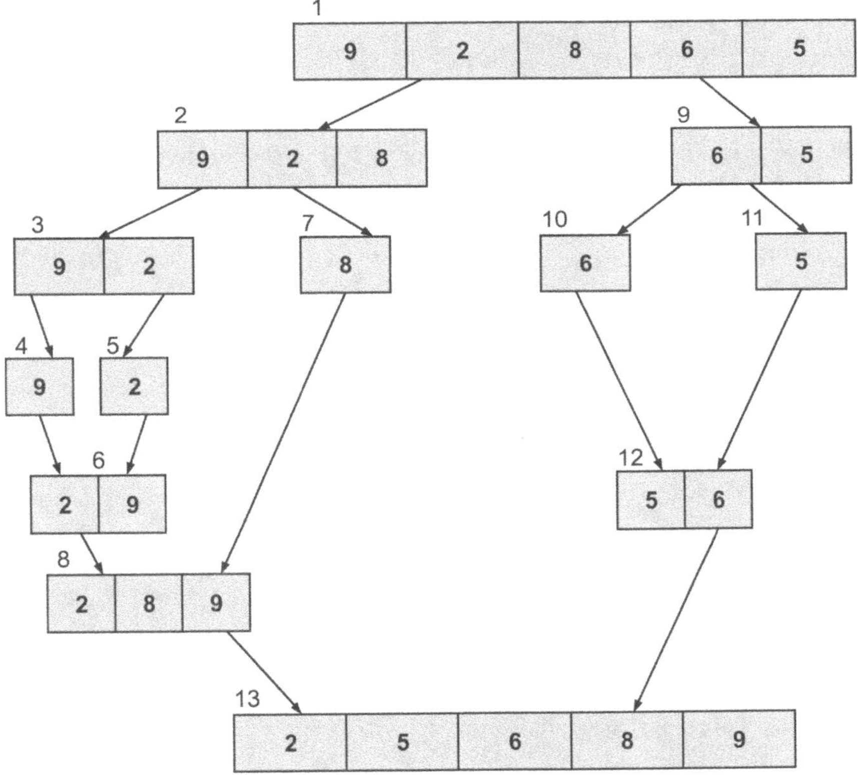

The following figure shows the process of split and merges for the above problem. The number above the array indicates the sequence of operation.

Note: The tree of calls of merge and merge sort shows that first we split and after the completion of splitting, the process of merging starts. Actual process of split and merge is bit different from the above procedure and it is as follows. If we trace the algorithm first array is split into left sub array and right sub array then left sub array is further splitting into two sub arrays, after combining these two sub arrays the right sub array starts splitting. If we analyze the above example, initially array contains (9, 2, 8, 6, 5) first it is divided into (9, 2, 8) & (6, 5). Sub array (9, 2, 8) is divided into (9, 2) & (8). Array (9, 2) is further divided into (9) & (2). Now (9) & (2) are merged to form (2, 9). The splitting of right sub array takes place after merging (2, 9). Now (2, 9) & (8) are merged to form (2, 8, 9). After this merging sub array (6, 5) starts splitting.

3.5.2 Time Complexity of Merge Sort

Here array is divided into two equal half's which is independent of elements. Because of the above reason Best case, Worst case and Average case are same.

Recurrence relation for merge sort is:

$$T(n) = a \qquad\qquad n = 1$$

$$T(n) = 2T(n/2) + cn \qquad n > 1$$

When $n = 1$ algorithm terminates. For $n > 1$ array is divided into two equal parts $(2T(n/2))$. To merge two sub arrays of size $n/2$, the time complexity is α to n (cn).

$$T(n) = \begin{cases} a & n = 1,\ a\ \text{is constant} \\ 2T\left(\dfrac{n}{2}\right) + C.n & n > 1, C\ \text{is constant} \end{cases}$$

By using substitution procedure i.e., $n = n/2$.

$$T(n) = 2T(n/2) + C.n$$

Sub $n = n/2$

$$= 2[2T(n/4) + C.n/2] + C.n$$

$$n = n/4 \implies 4[2T(n/8) + C.n/4] + 2C.n$$

$$= 8T(n/8) + 3.C.n$$

$$= 2^3 T(n/2^3) + 3C.n$$

$$= 2^k T(1) + k.C.n$$

$$= n.a + C.\log_2 n.n$$

$$= an + C.n.\log_2 n$$

If $2^k < n <= 2^{k+1}$, then

$$T(n) \leq T(2^{k+1})$$

Therefore $T(n) = O(n \log_2 n)$

3.5.3 Space Complexity

Merge sort requires 2n locations. The additional n locations are required for merging two sorted sub lists. Stack space required by the merge sort for the use of recursion. Since merge sort splits each array into two equal sized sub arrays. The maximum depth of stack is 'log n'. The additional space required is 'n + log n', n for auxiliary array and log n stack space.

3.5.4 Two Way Merge Sort

In this algorithm an array of size 'n' is treated as 'n' sub arrays on size 1. Array of size 1 is a sorted array. Now two sorted arrays are combined into a single array which is sorted in the same order. In pass 1 two adjacent sorted sub arrays of size 1 are combined to form a sub array of size 2 which are also sorted in the same order. Before pass 1 there are 'n' sub arrays of size 1. After pass1 there are n/2 sub arrays of size 2. In pass 2 two adjacent sorted arrays of size 2 are combined to form a sub array of size 4. After pass 2 there are n/4 sub array of size 4. Totally we will have 'log n' passes. In each pass there are 'n' comparisons. Total number of comparisons are (n log n).

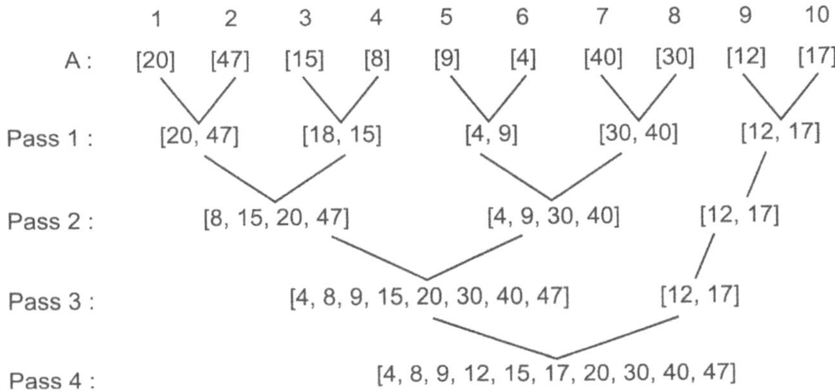

3.6 MATRIX MULTIPLICATION

Let A and B be the 2 n*n Matrix. The product matrix C=AB is calculated by using the formula, C (i, j)=   A(i,k) B(k,j) for all 'i' and and j between 1 and n.

The time complexity for the matrix Multiplication is $O(n^3)$. Divide and conquer method suggest another way to compute the product of n*n matrix. To apply divide and conquer N must be power of 2, otherwise enough rows and columns of zero can be added to both A and B. So that the resulting dimension are the powers of two. This process is called Padding of Zeros. If n = 2 then the following algorithm is used to compute matrix multiplication operation for the elements of A & B.

```
Algorithm Mat_Mul (A,B,C,n)
{
        for i:=1 to n do
        for j:= 1 to n do
                            C[i,j] :=0;
                                for  k:=1 to n do

        C[i,j]:=C[i,j]+A[i,k] ×B[k,j];
}
```

If n > 2, then the elements are partitioned into sub matrix n/2*n/2. Since 'n' is a power of 2 these product can be recursively computed using the same formula. This Algorithm will continue applying itself to smaller sub matrix until 'N" become suitable small (n = 2) so that the product is computed directly .

- The formula are

$$C11 = A11\ B11 + A12\ B21$$

$$C12 = A11\ B12 + A12\ B22$$

$$C21 = A21\ B11 + A22\ B21$$

$$C22 = A21\ B12 + A22\ B22$$

To compute AB using the equation we need to perform 8 multiplication of n/2*n/2 matrix and from 4 addition of n/2*n/2 matrix.

Since n/2 × n/2 matrix can be can be added in Cn^2 for some constant C, The overall computing time T(n) of the resulting divide and conquer algorithm is given by the sequence.

$$T(n) = b \qquad\qquad n <= 2\ \text{a \&b are}$$

$$T(n) = 8T(n/2) + cn^2 \qquad n > 2\ \text{constant}$$

That is $T(n) = O(n^3)$

Example: Multiply Matrix A and Matrix B using Divide and Conquer

$$A = \begin{bmatrix} 2 & 2 & 2 & 2 \\ 2 & 2 & 2 & 2 \\ 2 & 2 & 2 & 2 \\ 2 & 2 & 2 & 2 \end{bmatrix} B = \begin{bmatrix} 1 & 1 & 1 & 1 \\ 1 & 1 & 1 & 1 \\ 1 & 1 & 1 & 1 \\ 1 & 1 & 1 & 1 \end{bmatrix}$$

$$C = A \times B$$

$$C = \begin{bmatrix} 2 & 2 & 2 & 2 \\ 2 & 2 & 2 & 2 \\ 2 & 2 & 2 & 2 \\ 2 & 2 & 2 & 2 \end{bmatrix} X = \begin{bmatrix} 1 & 1 & 1 & 1 \\ 1 & 1 & 1 & 1 \\ 1 & 1 & 1 & 1 \\ 1 & 1 & 1 & 1 \end{bmatrix}$$

Matrix A and B are partitioned into two sub matrices of size N/2 × N/2

$$A = \begin{bmatrix} A_{11} & A_{12} \\ A_{21} & A_{22} \end{bmatrix} B = \begin{bmatrix} B_{11} & B_{12} \\ B_{21} & B_{22} \end{bmatrix}$$

Matrix A dimension is 4 × 4 which is divided into four sub matrices of size 2 × 2.

Matrix B dimension is 4 × 4 which is divided into four sub matrices of size 2 × 2.

$$A_{11} = \begin{bmatrix} 2 & 2 \\ 2 & 2 \end{bmatrix} A_{12} = \begin{bmatrix} 2 & 2 \\ 2 & 2 \end{bmatrix} A_{21} = \begin{bmatrix} 2 & 2 \\ 2 & 2 \end{bmatrix} A_{22} = \begin{bmatrix} 2 & 2 \\ 2 & 2 \end{bmatrix}$$

$$B_{11} = \begin{bmatrix} 1 & 1 \\ 1 & 1 \end{bmatrix} B_{12} = \begin{bmatrix} 1 & 1 \\ 1 & 1 \end{bmatrix} B_{21} = \begin{bmatrix} 1 & 1 \\ 1 & 1 \end{bmatrix} B_{22} = \begin{bmatrix} 1 & 1 \\ 1 & 1 \end{bmatrix}$$

$$A = \begin{bmatrix} \begin{array}{cc|cc} 2 & 2 & 2 & 2 \\ 2 & 2 & 2 & 2 \\ \hline 2 & 2 & 2 & 2 \\ 2 & 2 & 2 & 2 \end{array} \end{bmatrix} B = \begin{bmatrix} \begin{array}{cc|cc} 1 & 1 & 1 & 1 \\ 1 & 1 & 1 & 1 \\ \hline 1 & 1 & 1 & 1 \\ 1 & 1 & 1 & 1 \end{array} \end{bmatrix}$$

$$C = A \times B$$

$$C = \begin{bmatrix} \begin{array}{cc|cc} 2 & 2 & 2 & 2 \\ 2 & 2 & 2 & 2 \\ \hline 2 & 2 & 2 & 2 \\ 2 & 2 & 2 & 2 \end{array} \end{bmatrix} \times \begin{bmatrix} \begin{array}{cc|cc} 1 & 1 & 1 & 1 \\ 1 & 1 & 1 & 1 \\ \hline 1 & 1 & 1 & 1 \\ 1 & 1 & 1 & 1 \end{array} \end{bmatrix}$$

$$C = \begin{bmatrix} A_{11} & A_{12} \\ A_{21} & A_{22} \end{bmatrix} \times \begin{bmatrix} B_{11} & B_{12} \\ B_{21} & B_{22} \end{bmatrix} = \begin{bmatrix} C_{11} & C_{12} \\ C_{21} & C_{22} \end{bmatrix}$$

$$C = \begin{bmatrix} C_{11} & C_{12} \\ C_{21} & C_{22} \end{bmatrix}$$

where

$$C_{11} = A_{11} B_{11} + A_{12} B_{21}$$

$$C_{12} = A_{11} B_{12} + A_{12} B_{22}$$

$$C_{21} = A_{21}\,B_{11} + A_{22}\,B_{21}$$

$$C_{22} = A_{21}\,B_{12} + A_{22}\,B_{22}$$

$$C_{11} = \begin{bmatrix} 2 & 2 \\ 2 & 2 \end{bmatrix} \times \begin{bmatrix} 1 & 1 \\ 1 & 1 \end{bmatrix} + \begin{bmatrix} 2 & 2 \\ 2 & 2 \end{bmatrix} \times \begin{bmatrix} 1 & 1 \\ 1 & 1 \end{bmatrix}$$

Similarly C_{12}, C_{21} and C_{22}

$$C = \begin{bmatrix} 8 & 8 & 8 & 8 \\ 8 & 8 & 8 & 8 \\ 8 & 8 & 8 & 8 \\ 8 & 8 & 8 & 8 \end{bmatrix}$$

3.6.1 Strassen's Matrix Multiplication

Matrix multiplication are more expensive then the matrix addition $O(n^3)$. We can attempt to reformulate the equation for C_{ij} so as to have fewer multiplication and possibly more addition.

Strassen showed that 2×2 matrix multiplication can be accomplished in 7 multiplication and 18 addition or subtractions.

The divide and conquer approach can be used for implementing Strassen's matrix multiplication.

- **Divide:** Divide matrices into sub-matrices:A_0, A_1, A_2 etc.

- **Conquer:** Use a group of matrix multiply equations.

- **Combine:** Recursively multiply sub-matrices and get the final result of multiplication after performing required additions or subtractions.

$$\begin{bmatrix} C_{11} & C_{12} \\ C_{21} & C_{22} \end{bmatrix} = \begin{bmatrix} A_{11} & A_{12} \\ A_{21} & A_{22} \end{bmatrix} \times \begin{bmatrix} B_{11} & B_{12} \\ B_{21} & B_{22} \end{bmatrix}$$

$$S_1 = (A_{11} + A_{22})(B_{11} + B_{22})$$

$$S_2 = (A_{21} + A_{22}) \times B_{11}$$

$$S_3 = A_{11} \times (B_{12} - B_{22})$$

$$S_4 = A_{22} \times (B_{21} - B_{11})$$

$$S_5 = (A_{11} + A_{12}) \times B_{22}$$

$$S_6 = (A_{21} - A_{11}) \times (B_{11} + B_{12})$$

$$S_7 = (A_{12} - A_{22}) \times (B_{21} + B_{22})$$

$$C_{11} = S_1 + S_4 - S_5 + S_7$$

$$C_{12} = S_3 + S_5$$

$$C_{21} = S_2 + S_4$$

$$C_{22} = S_1 + S_3 - S_2 + S_6$$

Now we will compare the actual our traditional matrix multiplication procedure with strassen's procedure. In strassen's multiplication

$$C_{11} = S_1 + S_4 - S_5 + S_7$$

$$= (A_{11} + A_{22})(B_{11} + B_{22}) + A_{22}(B_{21} - B_{11}) - (A_{11} + A_{12})$$

$$\times B_{22} + (A_{12} - A_{22}) \times (B_{21} + B_{22})$$

$$= A_{11} B_{11} + A_{11}B_{22} + A_{22}B_{11} + A_{22}B_{22}$$

$$+ A_{22}B_{21} - A_{22}B_{11} - A_{11}B_{22} - A_{12}B_{22}$$

$$+ A_{12}B_{21} + A_{12}B_{22} - A_{22}B_{21} - A_{22}B_{22}$$

$$= A_{11}B_{11} + A_{12}B_{21}$$

3.6.2 Strassen's Algorithm

Here we are dividing matrices in sub-matrices and recursively multiplying sub-matrices.

Algorithm st_ Mul(int *A, int *B, int *C, int n)

```
{
    if(n== 1)then
    {
    (*C) = (*C) + (*A) * (*B);
    }
    else
    {
        St_Mul(A,B,C,n/4);
        St_Mul(A,B+(n/4), C+(n/4),n/4);
        St_Mul(A+2 *(n/4), B, C+2 *(n/4), n/4);
        St_Mul(A+2 *(n/4), B+(n/4), C+3 *(n/4),n/4);
        St_Mul(A+(n/4), B+2 *(n/4),C, n/4);
        St_Mul(A+(n/4), B+3 *(n/4), C+(n/4), n/4);
        St_Mul(A+3 *(n/4), B+2*(n/4), C+2*(n/4),n/4);
        St_Mul(A+3*(n/4), B+3*(n/4),C+3*(n/4),n/4);
    }
}
```

3.6.3 Time Complexity of Strassen's Algorithm

Recurrence Relation $\quad T(n) = b \qquad\qquad n \leq 2$

$$T(n) = 7T(n/2) + an^2 \qquad n > 2$$

Where a and b are constants working with this formula we get.

$$
\begin{aligned}
T(n) &= 7T(n/2) + an^2 \\
&= 7[7T(n/4) + a(n/2)^2] + an^2 \\
&= 7^2[7T(n/8) + a(n/4)^2] + 7an^2/4 + an^2 \\
&= 7^3 T(n/8) + an^2(7/4)^2 + 7an^2/4 + an^2 \\
&= 7^3 T(n/8) + an^2[1 + 7/4 + (7/4)^2 + \ldots\ldots + (7/4)^{k-1}] \\
&= 7^k T(n/2^k) + an^2 \sum_{x=0}^{k-1} (7/4)^k \\
&= 7^k T(n/2^k) + an^2 (7/4)^k \\
&= 7^{\log_2 n} T(n/n) + an^2 (7/4)^{\log_2 n} \\
&= 7^{\log_2 n} b + an^2 . 7^{\log_2 n}/(4^{\log_2 n}) \\
&= 7^{\log_2 n} b + an^2 . 7^{\log_2 n}/n^2 \\
&= (b + a) 7\log 2n \\
&= n^{\log_2 7} \\
&= n^{2.81} \\
&= O(n^{2.81})
\end{aligned}
$$

Thus divide and conquer is an algorithmic strategy having with the principle idea of dividing the problem into sub problems. Then solution to these sub problems is obtained in order to get the final solution for the given problem.

Recurrence Relations and Time Complexities:

	Recurrence Relation	Time Complexity
MAX-MIN	$T(n) = 2T(n/2) + 2$	$O(n)$
Merge Sort	$2T(n/2) + n$	$O(n \log n)$
Binary Search	$T(n) = 2T(n/2) + c$	$O(\log n)$
Matrix Multiplication	$8T(n/2) + n^2$	$O(n^3)$
Strassen's Matrix multiplication	$7T(n/2) + n^2$	$O(n^{2.81})$

Previous Gate Questions and Answers

1. Consider the Quick sort algorithm. Suppose there is a procedure for finding a pivot element which splits the list into sub-lists each of which contains at least one-fifth of the elements. Let T(n) be the number of comparisons required to sort n elements. Then

    (a) $T(n) \leq 2T(n/5) + n$

    (b) $T(n) \leq T(n/5) + T(4n/5) + n$

    (c) $T(n) \leq 2T(4n/5) + n$
    (d) $T(n) \leq 2T(n/2) + n$

Answer: (b)

Solution:

If we want to sort n elements with the help of quick sort algorithm. If pivot elements which split the lists into two sub lists each in which one list contains one-fifth element or n/5 and other list contains 4n/5 and balancing takes n so

$$T(n) \leq T(n/5) \leq T(4n/5)+n$$

$$[\textbf{Note: } n - n/5 = 5n - n/5 = 4n/5]$$

Objective Question Bank

1. For the quick sort algorithm, what is the time complexity of the best/worst case?   [   ]
    A. best case: $O(n)$ worst case: $O(n*n)$
    B. best case: $O(n)$ worst case: $O(n*\log(n))$
    C. best case: $O(n*\log(n))$ worst case: $O(n*\log(n))$
    D. best case: $O(n*\log(n))$ worst case: $O(n*n)$

2. The complexity of Binary search algorithm is   [   ]
    A. $O(n)$ B. $O(\log n)$ C. $O(n^2)$ D. $O(n \log n)$

3. The complexity of merge sort algorithm is   [   ]
    A. $O(n)$ B. $O(\log n)$ C. $O(n^2)$ D. $O(n \log n)$

4. Which of the following is not the required condition for binary search algorithm?   [   ]
    A. The list must be sorted
    B. There should be the direct access to the middle element in any sublist
    C. There must be mechanism to delete and/or insert elements in list
    D. None of above

5. Which of the following is not a limitation of binary search algorithm?   [   ]

    A. Must use a sorted array
    B. Requirement of sorted array is expensive when a lot of insertion and deletions are needed
    C. There must be a mechanism to access middle element directly
    D. Binary search algorithm is not efficient when the data elements are more than 1000.

6. Binary search algorithm cannot be applied to   [   ]
   A. Sorted linked list   B.   Sorted binary trees
   C. Sorted linear array   D.   Pointer array

7. _______ algorithm searches a given value or element in an already sorted array by Repeatedly dividing the search interval into half

                                                                          [   ]
   A. Binary   B.   Binary search
   C. Sorting   D.   Merge

8. _______ is a sorting algorithm based on the divide and conquer technique   [   ]
   A. Merge sort   B.   Integer
   C. Greedy   D.   Recursive

9. Which of the following sorting algorithm is of divide-and-conquer type?   [   ]
   A. Bubble sort   B.   Insertion sort
   C. Quick sort   D.   All of above

10. The computing time of binary search of best case for successful search is   [   ]
   A. $O(1)$ B. $O(\log n)$
   C. $O(n)$ D. $O(n \log n)$

11. The computing time of binary search of average case for successful search is   [   ]
   A. $O(1)$ B. $O(\log n)$
   C. $O(n)$ D. $O(n \log n)$

12. The computing time of binary search of worst case for successful search is   [   ]
   A. $O(1)$ B. $O(\log n)$
   C. $O(n)$ D. $O(n \log n)$

13. The computing time of binary search of best case for unsuccessful searches is   [   ]
   A. $O(1)$ B. $O(\log n)$
   C. $O(n)$ D. $O(n \log n)$

14. The computing time of binary search of average case for unsuccessful searches is   [   ]
   A. $O(1)$ B. $O(\log n)$
   C. $O(n)$ D. $O(n \log n)$

15. Which of the following sorting algorithms has the lowest worst case
    complexity?   [   ]
    A. Merge sort   B.   Quick sort
    C. Selection sort.   D.   Insertion sort

16. A sort which relatively passes through a list to exchange the first
    element with any element less than it and then repeats with a new first
    element is called   [   ]
    A. Heap sort   B.   Quick sort
    C. Selection sort.   D.   Insertion sort

17. The sorting technique where array to be sorted is partitioned again and
    again in such a way that all elements less than or equal to partitioning
    element appear before it and those which are greater appear after it, is
    called   [   ]
    A. Merge sort   B.   Quick sort
    C. Selection sort.   D.   None of these

18. In Worst case Quick Sort has order   [   ]
    A. O(nlogn)   B. $O(n^2/2)$
    C. O (log n)   D. $O(n^2/4)$

19. Which of the following is the best sorting algorithm   [   ]
    A. Merge Sort   B.   Heap Sort
    C. Bubble Sort   D.   Quick Sort

20. Which of the following sorting technique have same O (nlogn)
    complexity in all the cases?   [   ]
    A. Insertion Sort   B.   Quick Sort
    C. Merge Sort   D.   Selection sort

21. The running time of quick sort depends heavily on the selection
    of   [   ]
    A. No of inputs
    B. Arrangement of elements in array
    C. Size of elements
    D. Pivot element

22. Average and worst case complexity of Binary search is   [   ]
    A. O(log n)   B.   O(n)
    C. O(2n)   D. $O(n^2)$

23. The ______ step count is the maximum number of steps that can be
    executed for the given parameters   [   ]
    A. Worst-Case   B.   Average-Case
    C. Best-Case   D.   None

24. Which of the following is the best sorting algorithm   [   ]
    A. Merge Sort   B.   Heap Sort
    C. Bubble Sort   D.   Quick Sort

25. Which of the following sorting technique have same O (nlogn) complexity in all the cases?   [   ]
    A. Insertion Sort   B.   Quick Sort
    C. Merge Sort   D.   Selection sort

26. The running time of quick sort depends heavily on the selection of   [   ]
    A. No of inputs
    B. Arrangement of elements in array
    C. Size of elements
    D. Pivot element

Fill in the Blanks

1. Merge sort splits each set into two approximately equal-sized subsets, the maximum depth of the stack is proportional to ____________

2. Quick sort is a sorting algorithm that uses the ____________________ strategy

3. Merge sort is a sorting algorithm that uses the ______________strategy

4. The______________________________approach   can   be   used   for implementing Stassen's Matrix Multiplication

5. The______________________________is   an   algorithmic   strategy   having with the principle idea of dividing the problem into sub problems

6. The time complexity of Stassen's matrix multiplication is__________

7. The   time   complexity   for   general   matrix   multiplication   is ______________.

8. Merging 4 sorted files containing 50, 10, 25 and 15 records will take__________time

9. The complexity of Binary search algorithm is ____________________

10. The computing time of binary search of worst case for unsuccessful searches is __________

11. Sorting a ____________________is an application of Merge sort

12. Binary search Works only on ____________________list.

13. ____________________also called partition exchange sort.

14. The complexity of Binary search algorithm is ____________.

15. Merging 4 sorted files containing 50, 10, 25 and 15 records will take_____time.

Review Questions

1. (a) Write a pseudo code for a divide and conquer algorithm for finding values of both the largest and the smallest elements in an array of n numbers.

   (b) Apply quick sort algorithm to sort the list E,X,A,M,P,L,E in alphabetical order. Draw the tree of the recursive calls made.

   R09 set no 2 December-January, 2011-2012

2. (a) Give the partition algorithm for Quick sort.

   (b) Modify the above algorithm to get the selection sort algorithm. Explain the transition.

   R09 set no 4 December-January, 2011-2012

3. (a) Explain the divide and conquer strategy. How it can be useful in the problem solving.

   (b) Assuming that quick sort uses the first item in the list as the pivot item:

   (i) Give a list of n items (for example, an array of 10 integers) representing the worst-case scenario.

   (ii) Give a list of n items (for example, an array of 10 integers) representing in the best-case scenario.

   R09 set no 1 December-January, 2011-2012

4. The kth quantiles of an n-element set are the (k-1) elements from the set that divide the sorted set into k equal sized sets. Give an algorithm to list the kth quantiles of a set.

   R09 set no 4 December-January, 2011-2012

5. (a) Write and explain the control abstraction for Divide and conquer and give the time complexity.

   (b) Discuss Strassen's matrix multiplication and derive the time complexity.

   R09 May2013

6. (a) Compute 2101*1130 by applying Divide and Conquer method.

   (b) Applying Divide and Conquer strategy, write a recursive algorithm for finding the maximum and the minimum elements from a list.

   R09 December 2011

7. Define Divide and conquer Technique. Explain Binary Search using this method. Derive its time complexity.

R09 November/December-2013

8. (a) Apply divide and conquer strategy to the following input values for searching 112 and –14 by showing the values of low, mid, high for each search. –15, –6, 0, 7, 9, 23, 54, 82, 101, 112, 125, 131, 142, 151

   (b) Why Strassen's matrix multiplication method is efficient? Explain with suitable example.

R09 June-2014

9. Compute the product of the following matrices of 4 × 4 size, using Strassen's matrix multiplication method.

$$A = \begin{bmatrix} 1 & 2 & 3 & 4 \\ 5 & 1 & 3 & 2 \\ 2 & 1 & 2 & 3 \\ 1 & 4 & 6 & 2 \end{bmatrix} \quad B = \begin{bmatrix} 2 & 9 & 3 & 2 \\ 3 & 1 & 5 & 4 \\ 7 & 8 & 3 & 1 \\ 3 & 3 & 4 & 5 \end{bmatrix}$$

R09 April-May 2012

10. Solve the average case recurrence relation for quick sort.

December 2011

11. (a) Write and explain the control abstraction for Divide and Conquer.

    (b) Write Quick sort algorithm and analyze the time complexity in Average case. [8 + 7]

12. (a) Define Divide and conquer Technique. Explain Binary Search using this method. Derive its time complexity.

    (b) Explain about Strassen's matrix multiplication. Derive its time complexity. [8 + 7]

13. (a) Write and explain the control abstraction for Divide and Conquer.

    (b) Briefly explain Merge Sort Algorithm with suitable example and Derive its Time Complexity. [8 + 8]

14. (a) Show how quick sort sorts the following sequences of keys in ascending order.

    12, 25, 35, 43, 48, 59, 77, 85, 86, 94?

    (b) Discuss the time complexity of the quick sort algorithm for the above case? [15]

15. (a) Show how Merge sort sorts the following sequences of keys in ascending order.

    12, 22, 33, 44, 48, 56, 57, 65, 76, 84 with a neat diagram representing sequence of recursion calls?

    (b) Discuss the time complexity of Merge sort?

4

THE GREEDY METHOD

4.1 THE GREEDY METHOD

The Greedy method is the most simple design technique. It is an optimization problem which has numerous applications. Optimization problems are ones where in there is a need to find the best among all possible solutions. In other words it is required to find the solution which has the optimal (maximum or minimum) value satisfying the given constraints.

Most of the problems have **n** inputs and require us to obtain a subset that satisfies some constraints which is called a feasible solution. The feasible solution that either maximizes or minimizes a given objective function is called an optimal solution. A problem may have any number of feasible solutions but there will be only one optimal solution. Optimal solution is one of the feasible solution for which either the cost is minimum or profit is maximum. There are two types of problems in greedy method they are subset paradigm and ordering paradigm.

As the name suggest they are short sighted in their approach taking decision on the basis of the information immediately at the hand without worrying about the effect these decision may have in the future.

The Greedy method algorithm generally works in stages. In the greedy approach, each stage is chosen has to satisfy the constraints given in the problem and it forms feasible solution, if it is the best option among all possible choices that are available, and then it will be included in the optimal solution. The choice of a stage once made cannot be changed in subsequent stages. This version of Greedy technique is called subset paradigm. The name greedy technique is given to this method because each stage of the technique has to satisfy the constraints while not to give up anything at each point.

4.1.1 Functions of Greedy Algorithms

To construct the solution in an optimal way, algorithm maintains two sets. One contains chosen items and the other contains rejected items. The following four functions are available in greedy algorithm:

1. A function that checks whether chosen set of items provide a solution.
2. A function that checks the feasibility of a set.
3. The selection function tells which of the candidates is the most promising.
4. An objective function, which does not appear explicitly, gives the value of a solution.

The "greedy-choice property" and "optimal substructure" are two components in the problem that provide to a greedy strategy.

Greedy-choice property: A globally optimal solution can be arrived at by making a locally optimal choice. In other words, when we are considering which choice to make, we make the choice that looks best in the current problem, without considering results from sub problems.

Optimal substructure: A problem exhibits optimal substructure if an optimal solution to the problem contains within it optimal solutions to sub problems.

An input 'a' is selected from the array X by the function SELECT and the function FEASIBLE determines if 'a' can be included into the optimum solution vector. The function UNION actually combines 'a' with partial solution and updates the objective function. Procedure GREEDY describes that, once a particular problem is chosen and the procedures SELECT, FEASIBLE and UNION are properly implemented.

Greedy method control abstraction for the subset paradigm:

```
Procedure GREEDY(X,n)    //X(1:n) contains the n inputs
     optimum-solution <- ø //initialize the optimum-
                             //solution to empty
     for  i<-1 to n do
          a <--SELECT(X)
          if FEASIBLE(optimum-solution, a)
               then optimum-solution<-UNION(optimum-
solution, a)
          end if
     repeat
     return(solution)
     end GREEDY.
```

4.2 KNAPSACKS PROBLEM

Given a set of objects, each with a weight and a profit, it is to be determined the number of each object to include in a collection so that the total weight is less than or equal to a given limit and the total profit is as large as possible.

Given n objects and a knapsack or bag with a capacity M, the problem is to place 'n' objects in knapsack or bag. A weight and profit are associated with each object, object 'i' has a weight w_i and profit p_i. The profit $p_i x_i$ is earned if a fraction x_i, $0 <= x_i <= 1$, of object 'i' is placed into the knapsack and the object with weight $w_i x_i$ is stored in the knapsack. The total weight of all chosen objects can be at most M which is the knapsack capacity. The main objective of the knapsack problem is to maximize the total profit earned by filling the knapsack with the objects. Greedy method is used to solve the knapsack problem.

Formally, the problem can be stated as

maximize $\Sigma_{1 \leq i \leq n} P_i X_i$

Subject to $\Sigma_{1 \leq i \leq n} W_i X_i \leq M$ and $0 \leq x_i \leq 1, 1 \leq i \leq n$

$\Sigma_{(1 \leq i \leq n)} W_i X_i \leq M$ is the objective function

All inputs are not considered for the solution set in a knapsack problem, a subset of inputs is selected hence this problem will fall under subset paradigm. Further if a selected object doesn't fit into the knapsack, then a fraction of it is added to fill the knapsack.

Example: Consider the following instance of the knapsack problem:

n = 3, m = 20, $(p_1, p_2, p_3) = (25, 24, 15)$ and $(w_1, w_2, w_3) = (18, 15, 10)$.

Four feasible solutions are:

	(p_1)	(p_2)	(p_3)	
Profit (p_i)->	25	24	15	bag capacity=20(weight)
i->	1	2	3	
Weights (w_i)->18	15	10		
	(w_1)	(w_2)	(w_3)	

Any solution that satisfies the objective function is called feasible solution

$$\Sigma_{(1 \leq i \leq n)} W_i X_i \leq M.$$

Four feasible solutions which satisfy the objective function are considered. In first feasible solution we randomly choose the fractions x_1, x_2, x_3 as 1/2, 1/3, 1/4 and their corresponding weights and profits are calculated.

In the second feasible solution objects are chosen with decreasing order of profits and their corresponding weights and profits are calculated. In the third feasible solution objects are chosen with increasing order of weights and their corresponding weights and profits are calculated. The above feasible solution doesn't give optimal profit. Optimal profit is obtained if the objects are placed with decreasing order of p/w ratio, which is the fourth feasible solution.

S.No	$X_i \rightarrow (x_1, x_2, x_3)$	$\sum w_i x_i$	$\sum p_i x_i$
1.	(1/2, 1/3, 1/4)	18(1/2) + 15(1/3) + 10(1/4) = 9 + 5 + 2.5 =16.5	25(1/2) + 24(1/3) + 15(1/4) = 12.5 + 8 + 3.75 = 24.25
2.	(1, 2/15, 0)	18(1) + 15(2/15) + 0 = 18 + 2 = 20	25(1) + 24(2/15) + 0 = 28.2
3.	(0, 2/3, 1)	0 + 15(2/3) + 10 = 20	0 + 24(2/8) + 15(1) = 3
4.	(0, 1, 1/2)	0 + 15(1) + 10(1/2) = 20	0 + 24(1) + 15(1/2) = 31.5

➡ ① ② ③ ④ are called feasible solutions and

④ is called optimal solution

The maximum /optimal profit is 31.5.

There are so many ways to solve this problem, which will give many feasible solutions for which we have to find the optimal solution. But in this algorithm, it will generate only one solution which is going to be feasible as well as optimal. First, we find the profit & weight ratios of each and every object and sort it according to the descending order of the ratios. Select an object with highest p/w ratio and check whether its weight is lesser than the capacity of the bag, if so place 1 unit of the first object and decrement the capacity of the bag by the weight of the object you have placed. Repeat the above steps until the capacity of the bag becomes less than the weight of the object you have selected in this case place a fraction of the object and come out of the loop.

An optimal solution is obtained by selecting a solution having optimum value among all possible feasible solutions. Greedy approach directly produces an optimal solution, in knapsack problem one can get optimal solution directly by selecting the objects in the decreasing order of p/w ratio.

Time Complexity   = Time Complexity to find p_i/w_i vector.

+ Time complexity to sort the objects such that

$p[i]/w[i] >= p[i + 1]/w[i + 1]$.

+ Time Complexity of Greedy Knapsack.

$= C_1 * n + C_2 * n \log n + C_3 * n = O(n \log n)$.

4.3 JOB SEQUENCING WITH DEADLINES

There are 'n' jobs, each job has a deadline 'd' and a profit 'p', each job will take one unit of machine time for its completion. There is only one machine for processing jobs, since one job can be processed in a single machine the other job has to be in its waiting state until the job is completed and the machine becomes free. If the job 'i' is completed before its deadline 'd_i' then a profit p_i is earned. The feasible solution for the above problem is to find a subset of jobs S such that all the jobs in the subset 'S' has to be completed before their respective deadlines. The sum of the profits of the jobs in S is the value of feasible solution S. An optimal solution is a feasible solution with maximum value. All inputs are not considered for the solution set in this problem, a subset of inputs is selected hence this problem will fall under subset paradigm.

Given 'n' jobs, associated with each job a deadline d and a profit p. For any job 'i' the profit p_i is earned if and only if the job is completed by its deadline d_i. To complete a job, one has to process the job on a machine for one unit of time. Only one machine is available for processing jobs. Since one job can be processed in a single machine. The other job has to be in its waiting state until the job is completed and the machine becomes free. A feasible solution for this problem is a subset J of jobs such that each job in this subset can be completed by its deadline.

The value of feasible solution J is the sum of the profits of the jobs in J. An optimal solution is a feasible solution with maximum value. Since the problem involves the identification of a subset, it fits the subset paradigm.

The problem is given the number of jobs, their profit and deadlines, it is required to find a sequence of jobs, which will be completed before its deadlines, and it should yield a maximum profit. So the waiting time and the processing time should be less than or equal to the dead line of the job.

Example:

Let n = 4, Profits (p_1, p_2, p_3, p_4) = (100,10,15,27) and Deadlines (d_1, d_2, d_3, d_4) = (2,1,2,1).

Maximum deadline of the jobs is 2. It means that at most we can do two jobs only among four jobs. A feasible solution contains all possibilities of execution of two jobs and one job.

The feasible solutions and their values are:

S.No.	Feasible solution	Solution sequence	Value (Profit)
1.	(1, 2)	2,1	110
2.	(1, 3)	1,3 or 3,1	115
3.	(1, 4)	4,1	127
4.	(2,3)	3,2	25

Contd...

S.No.	Feasible solution	Solution sequence	Value (Profit)
5.	(3,4)	4,3	42
6.	(1)	1	100
7.	(2)	2	10
8.	(3)	3	15
9	(4)	4	27

Solution 3 is optimal. In this solution only jobs 1 and 4 are processed and the value is 127.

These jobs must be processed in the order job 4 followed by job 1. Thus the processing of job 4 begins at zero and that of job 1 is completed at time 2.

An optimal solution is obtained by selecting a solution having optimum value among all possible feasible solutions. Greedy approach directly produces an optimal solution, in this problem one can get optimal solution directly by selecting the jobs in the non increasing order and checking whether they can be completed before deadline.

A General Algorithm for Job Sequencing with Deadlines:

```
Algorithm Greedy job(d,J,n)
{
        J :={1};
          for  i :=2 to  n   do
            {
                If (all jobs in J U{ i } can be completed
by their deadlines) then J := J U{ i };
            }
   }
```

A Greedy Algorithm for job sequencing with deadlines and profits:

```
Algorithm JS(d, j, n)
  {
              d[0] :=J[0] :=0;
              J[1] :=1;
              k  := 1;
              for  i :=2 to n   do
              {
                        r  :=k;
                        while((d[J[r]]>d[ i ]) and
                            (d[J[r]]!=r)) do r :=r - 1 ;
                        if((d[J[r]]<=d[z]) and
                            (d[k]>r)) then
                          {
for  q :=k  to (r+1) step -1 do J[g+1]  := J[g];
```

```
J[r+1] :=1 ;    k := k+1;
                              }

                    }
    return   k;
}
```

- There are two possible parameters for JS Algorithm in terms of which its complexity can be measured. These are n, the number of jobs, and s, the number of jobs included in the solution J.
- Each iteration takes $O(1)$ time.
- The computing time of JS can be reduced from $O(n^2)$ to nearly $O(n)$.

A spanning tree of a graph is an undirected tree consisting of only those edges that are necessary to connect all the vertices in the original graph. A Spanning tree has a property that for any pair of vertices there exist only one path between them and the insertion of an edge to a spanning tree form a unique cycle.

4.4 MINIMUM COST SPANNING TREE

The cost of a spanning tree is the sum of cost of the edges in that tree. Determine the spanning tree whose cost is minimum. There are two methods to determine minimum cost spanning trees are

1. Prim's Algorithm.
2. Kruskal's Algorithm

Spanning trees are important because of the following reasons:

1. Spanning trees are very important in designing efficient routing algorithm.
2. Spanning trees have wide applications in many areas, such as network design.

The Time Complexity of this algorithm is clearly $o(n)$, where 'n' is the number of edges.

The number of spanning trees in the complete graph kn is n^{n-2}.

4.4.1 Prim's Algorithm

Let us understand the Prim's algorithm with the help of some example:

Now, we will consider all the vertices first. Then we will select an edge with minimum weight. The algorithm proceeds by selecting adjacent edges with minimum weight. Care should be taken for not forming circuit.

Given Graph:

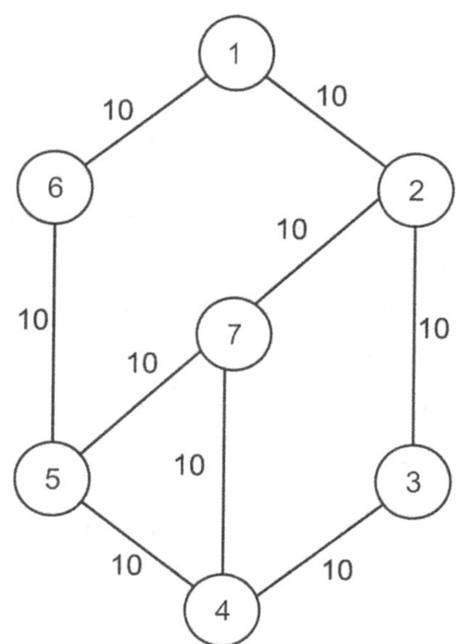

Edge	Cost	Spanning Tree
Step 1:		
(1,6)	10	
Step 2:		
(6,5)	25	

Step 3:

(5,4)   22

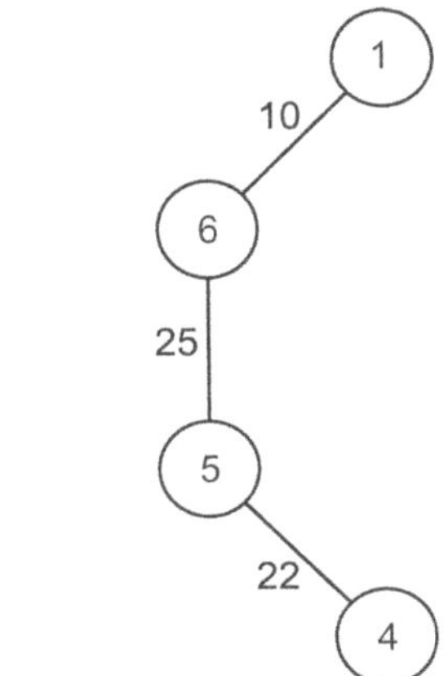

Step 4:

(4,3)   12

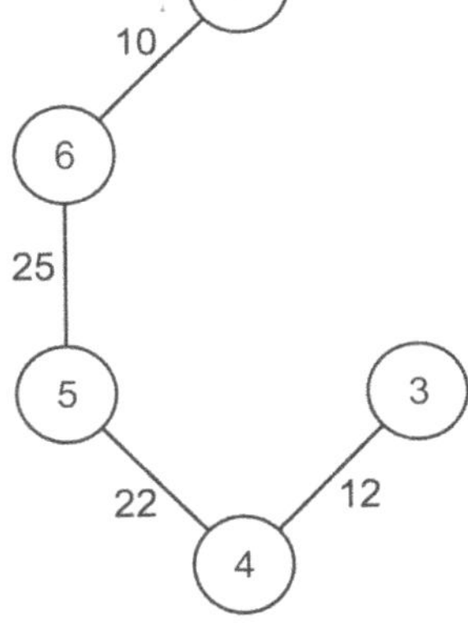

Step 5:

(3,2)   16

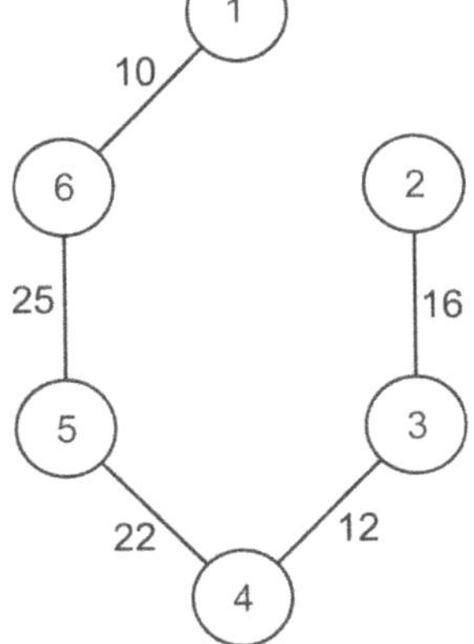

Step 6:

(2,7)   14

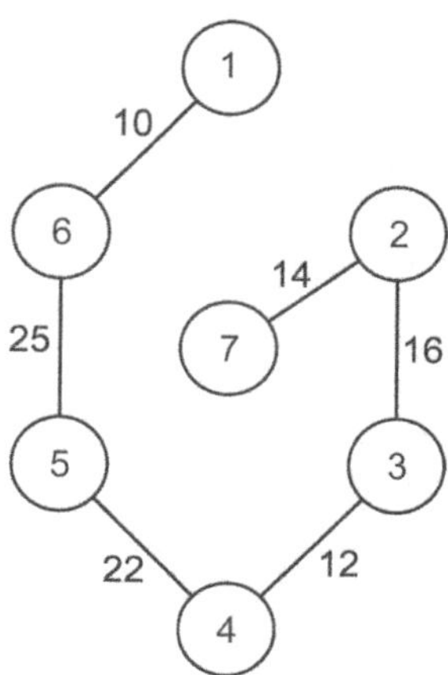

Total Cost = 99

No. of Vertices = 7

No. of Edges = 6

- It has Time Complexity of **O(n²)**, where n = number of Vertices

Prim's Algorithm:

```
Algorithm Prim-MST(G, cost, n, tree)
    // G is an array that stores all the edges of the
    //graph.
    // PCost is an array storing the cost of each
    //edge.
    // The cost can be positive value of an edge.
    // Store ∞ when there is no edge between two
    //vertices.
    {
            min:=cost[p,q];

    // initially we store the starting in array tree

            tree[i,j]:=p;
            tree[1,2]:=q;
            for i:=1 to n do
    // finding minimum cost edge from neighbouring
        // vertices
            if(cost[i,q]<cost[i,p])
                    optimum[i]:=q;
            else
                    optimum[i]:=p;
    // after visiting vertex p or q put 0 in array.
        // optimum at pᵗʰ and qᵗʰ index
```

```
                optimum[p]:=optimum[q]:=0;
          for i:=2 to n-1
            {
              // find remaining n-2 edges from the
              // graph for building tree. let j be the
              // index such that optimum [j]1=0;
              // also the cost [j, optimum[j] is
                //minimum we will store vertex
              //j at optimum distance and
                // Neighboring of j in array tree
                Tree[i,1]: = j;
                Tree [i,2]: = optimum[j];
              // obtain the total minimum of spanning
                //tree
                  Min: = min + cost[j], optimum [j];
                  Optimum [j]: =0 ;
                for k:= 1 to n do
                if (optimum [k]!= 0) AND (cost  (k,
    optimum(k))>cost[k, j])then
            }
    return min; // returning total minimum
    // cost of spanning tree
```

Analysis: The algorithm spends most of its time in finding the smallest edge. so, time of the algorithm basically depends on how do we search this edge. Therefore prism's algorithm runs in $O(n^2)$ time.

4.4.2 Krushkal's Algorithm

In krushkal's algorithm always the minimum cost edge has to be selected. It is not necessary that selected optimum edge is adjacent.

E.g.,: consider the graph give below:

First we select all the vertices then an edge with optimum weight is selected from heap. Even though it is not adjacent to previously selected edge, care should be taken for not forming circuit.

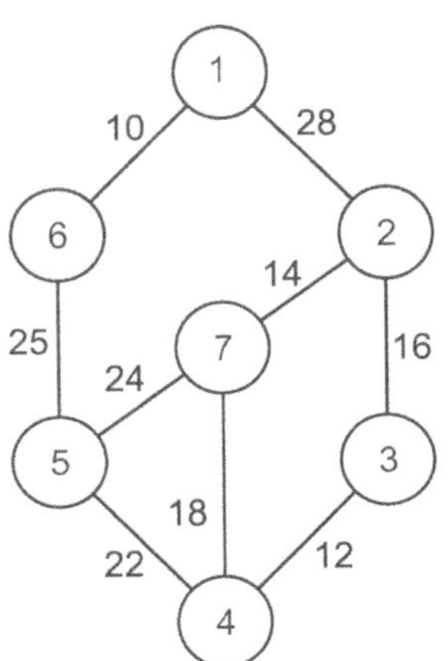

Edge	Cost	Spanning Tree
Step 1:		
(1,6)	10	
Step 2:		
(4,3)	12	
Step 3:		
(2,7)	14	
Step 4:		
(2,3)	16	
Step 5:		
(7,4)	18	*REJECT Because it forms a circuit.*
Step 6:		
(5,4)	22	

STEP-7:

(5,6)   25

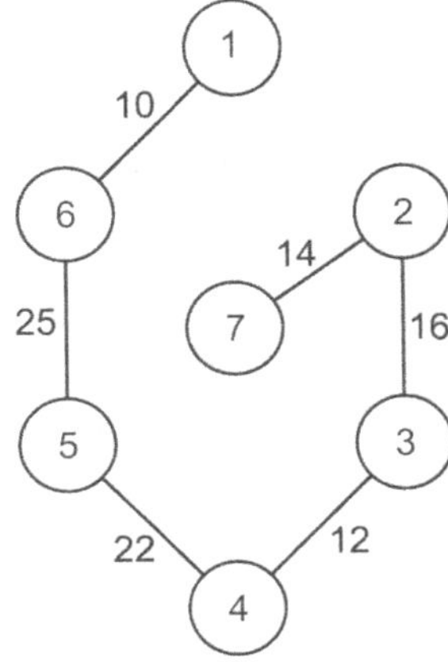

Algorithm

```
    Algorithm krushkal (g, cost, n, tree)
    //G be an array  of  edge of the given graph
    // there is an array storing edge (p, q)
    // tree contains the edges of minimum cost
    //spanning tree-min holds the minimum cost
    //of sparing tree
    {
    delete minimum cost edge (p, q) from heap and
    reheap/
    S:= find(p);
    T:= find (q); //finds the minimum cost edge
    If (s!=t) then// checks whether it creates cycle
    or not
    {
    i=i++;
    tree[I,1]: =p;
    tree[I, 2]: =q     ;
    min:= min+cost[p, q];
    union (s, t);// merge s and t
    }
    Return min ; // returning min cost spanning tree//
```

4.5 OPTIMAL STORAGE ON TAPES

The programs stored on computer tape are retrieved sequentially. The retrieval time of a program is proportional to the length of the program. There are **n** programs that are to be stored on a tape of length **L**. The length of the program i is a length l_i. All 'n' programs can be stored on the tape if and only if the sum of the lengths of the programs is at most

$L \sum_{k=1}^{n} l_{ik} \le L$. The tape is initially positioned at the front. Whenever a program X is to be retrieved from this tape, first we have to retrieve all programs that are stored before X and then X is retrieved. If there are two programs before X then the time taken to retrieve X is equal to the retrieval time of first two programs and retrieval time of X.

If the programs are stored on the tape are arranged in the order $I = i_1, i_2, i_3 .....i_n$ the time t_p required to retrieve program i_p is proportional to $\sum_{k=1}^{p} l_{ik}$.

If all programs are retrieved equally, then the expected or mean retrieval time (MRT) is $(1/n) \sum_{i=1}^{n} t_i$.

In the optimal storage on the tape problem, we are required to find a permutation for the n programs, so that when they are stored on the tape in this order the MRT is minimized.

All inputs are considered for the solution set in this problem, number of feasible solutions is equal to the number of permutations of input optimal solution is the solution for which the mean retrieval time is minimum. The order of selection of inputs decides the optimal solution hence this problem will fall under the ordering paradigm.

Example: Let n = 3 and $(l_1, l_2, l_3) = (5, 10, 3)$. There are n! = 6 possible orderings and their respective MRT values are;

Ordering i	MRT(i)
1,2,3	$(5) + (5 + 10) + (5 + 10 + 3) = 38$
1,3,2	$(5) + (5 + 3) + (10 + 5 + 3) = 31$
2,1,3	$(10) + (10 + 5) + (10 + 5 + 3) = 43$
2,3,1	$(10) + (10 + 3) + (10 + 3 + 5) = 41$
3,1,2	$\mathbf{(3) + (3 + 5) + (3 + 5 + 10) = 29}$
3,2,1	$(3) + (3 + 10) + (3 + 10 + 5) = 34$

The Optimal ordering is **3, 1, 2 and the MRT is 29.**

The greedy method simply requires us to store the programs in non-descending order of their length. This ordering can be carried out in $O(n \log(n))$ time using an efficient sorting algorithm.

4.6 OPTIMAL MERGE PATTERNS

Two sorted files A, B having n_1 and n_2 records respectively can be merged into single file and the time complexity to accomplish the above task is

$O(n_1 + n_2)$. Merging of more than two sorted files is accomplished by repeatedly merging sorted files in pairs. Given n sorted files, pair wise merging of n sorted files into a single sorted file is accomplished in many different ways. Different pairings require differing amounts of computing time. Hence this problem is in the ordering paradigm.

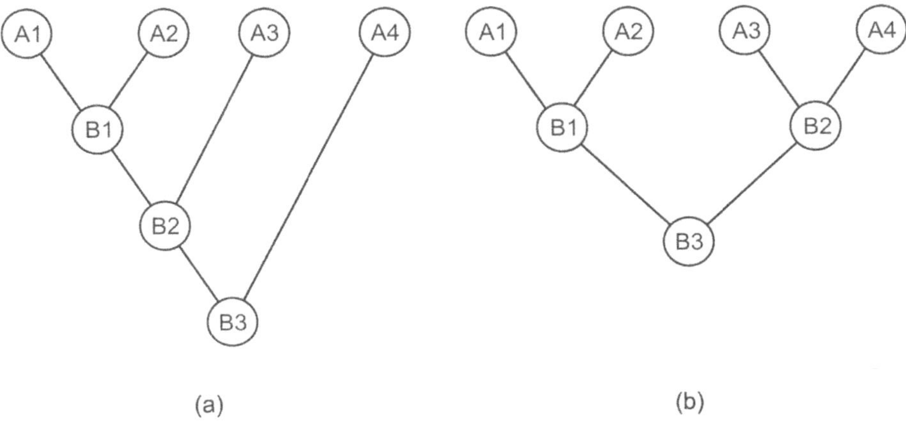

(a)   (b)

Figure 4.1

Given, 'n' Sorted files of some order are to be merged. The Optimal Merge Pattern follows the procedure. Let the given set of files A1, A2, A3 and A4 are to be merge, we first merge A1 and A2 to get a file B1. Then we could merge B1 and A3 to get B2. Finally, we could merge B2 and A4 to get the desired sorted file B3 as shown in Figure 4.1.a. Another way of merging is to merge A1 and A2 to get B1, then merge A3 and A4 and get B2. Finally merge B1 and B2 and get the desired sorted file B3 as shown in Figure 4.1.b. Total there are twelve feasible solutions two feasible solutions are shown in Figure 4.1a & Figure 4.1b, another five feasible solutions are shown in Figure 4.2.

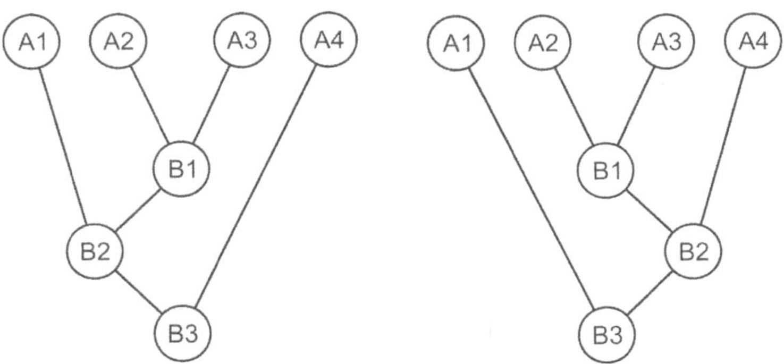

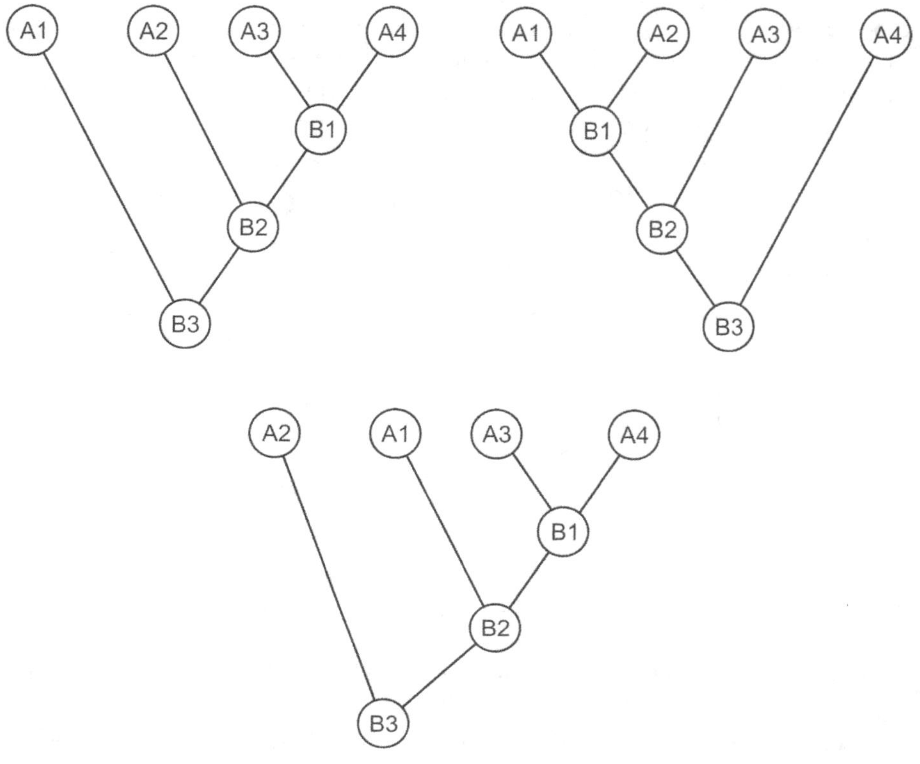

Figure 4.2

Among all feasible solutions, optimal solution is one whose cost is minimal. Greedy approach says at each step, merge the two smallest size files.

Example 1: Consider the following files (x1, ..., x5) with sizes (25, 11, 20, 6, 32) the greedy method generate the following merge pattern.

Greedy approach says at each step, merge the two smallest size files.

First sort all the files: 6, 11, 20, 25, 32

Merge two smallest files (6 &11) and again sort, the resultant files are given below

    17, 20, 25, 32

Merge two smallest files (17&20) and again sort, the resultant files are given below

    25, 32, 37

Merge two smallest files (25&32) and again sort, the resultant files are given below 37, 57 these two files are merged into a single file of size 94

Merge x4 and x2 to get z1 ($|z1|$ = 17), merge z1 and x3 to get z2 (z2 = 37), merge x1 and x5 to get z3(z3 = 57) merge z2 and z3 to get z4(z4 = 94).

The total number of records moved = $17 + 37 + 57 + 94 = 205$

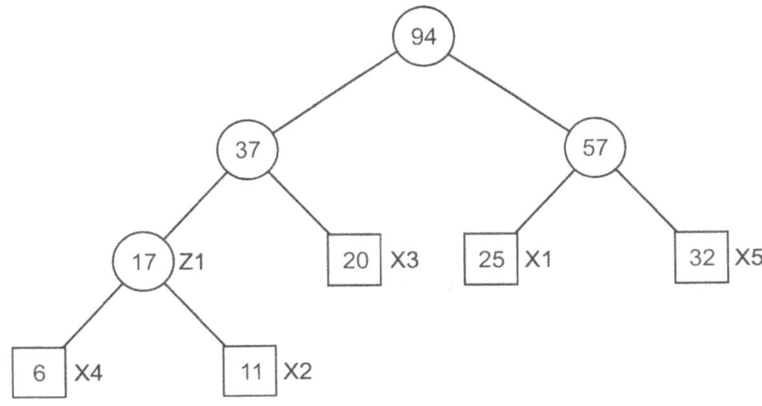

Figure 4.3 Binary merge tree representing a merge pattern

In two-way merge pattern each merge step involves the merging of two files. The Two-way merge patterns can be represented by binary merge trees. The greedy method to generate merge trees also works for the case of k-ary merging. The greedy rule to generate optimal merge trees is at each step choosing k sub-trees with least length for merging. Similarly we can have three way merge pattern in which each merge step involves the merging of three files except for the last merge. External nodes or leaf nodes are drawn as squares and represent the given input files. Each internal node has exactly two children, and it represents the file obtained by merging the files represented by its two children. The number in each node is the number of records present in the file represented by that node.

Algorithm to generate a two-way merge tree:

```
treenode = record {
            treenode*lchild; treenode*rchild;
            integer weight;
};
Algorithm Tree(n)
{
        for I;=1 to n-1 do
        {
                Pt:=new treenode; //Get a new treenode.
                (pt->Ichild):=Least(list)I //Merge two trees
```

```
                                             //with
        (pt->rchild):=Least(list);  //smallest
                                             //lengths.
        (pt -t weight):=((pt->Lchild)->weight)
              +((pt->rchild)->weight)
        Insert(list, pt);
    }
    return  Least(list); //Tree left in first is the
//merge tree.
}
```

4.7 SINGLE SOURCE SHORTEST PATHS

Graphs can be used to represent the highway structure of a state or country with vertices representing cities, edges representing sections of highway and weights of the edges may be distance between two cities or time taken to travel or cost incurred for travelling. A traveler wishing to drive from city A to B would like to know whether there a path from A to B, if multiple paths are available from A to B ? Which is the shortest path?

Given a directed graph $G = (V, E)$, where V is the set of Vertices and E is the set of Edges, a weighting function cost for the edges of G, and a source vertex V_0. The problem of Single-Source Shortest Paths is to determine the shortest paths from V_0 to all the remaining vertices of G. It is assumed that all the weights are positive. Since the shortest path between V_0 and some other node v is an ordering among a subset of the edges. Hence this problem is in the ordering paradigm.

To formulate a greedy-based algorithm to generate the shortest paths, we must conceive of a multistage solution to the problem and also of an optimization measure. One possibility is to build the shortest paths one by one. As an optimization measure we can use the sum of the lengths of all paths so far generated. For this measure to be minimized, each individual path must be of minimum length. If we have already constructed t shortest paths, then using this optimization measure, the next path to be constructed should be the next shortest minimum length path. The greedy way to generate the shortest paths from V_0 to the remaining vertices is to generate these paths in non-decreasing order of path length. First, a shortest path to the nearest vertex is generated. Then a shortest path to the second nearest vertex is generated, and so on.

Example: Consider the following graph G:

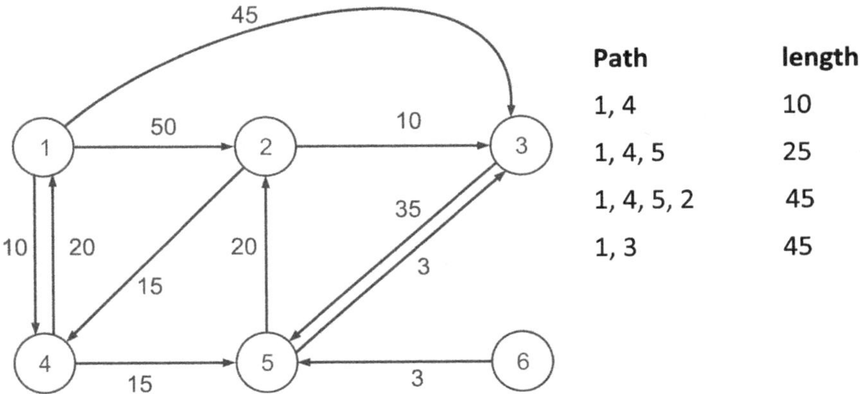

For the graph G shown above the nearest vertex to $V_o=1$ is 4(cost[1,4]=10). Therefore the path 1, 4 is the first path generated. The second nearest vertex to node 1 is 5 and the distance between 1 and 5 is 25. The path 1, 4, 5 is the next path generated. In order to generate the shortest paths n this order, we need to be able to determine (1) the next vertex to which a shortest path must be generated and (2) a shortest path to this vertex.

Greedy algorithm to generate shortest paths:

```
Algorithm Shortest Paths(v, cost, dist, n)
{
        for i :=1 to n do
        {//initialize S.
             S[i]:= false; dist[i] :=cost[v, i];
        }
        S[v] :=true; dist[v]:=0.0; //put v  in S.
        for num := 2 to n-1 do
        {
             Choose u from among those vertices not in
             S such that dist[u] is minimum;
             S[u] := true: //put u in S.
             for (each w adjacent to u with S[w]=false)
do
             //Update distances.
                  If {dist[w]>dist[u]+cost[u, w]} then
                       dist[w]:=dist[u]+cost[u,w];
        }
}
```

Analysis of shortest path algorithm: Any shortest path algorithm must examine each edge in the graph at least once since any of the edges could be in a shortest path. Hence, the minimum possible time for such an algorithm would be $\Omega(|E|)$. Since cost adjacency matrices were used to represent the graph, it takes $O(n^2)$ time just to determine which edges are in G, and so any shortest path algorithm using this representation must take $\Omega(n^2)$ time. The overall run time is $O((n+|E|) \log n)$.

Objective Question Bank

1. The essence of each greedy algorithm is the _________ policy   [   ]
   - A. Iteration
   - B. Backtracking
   - C. Selection
   - D. Looping

2. Greedy algorithms chiefly solve _____ problems   [   ]
   - A. Optimization
   - B. Vector
   - C. Sorting
   - D. Intractable

3. In mathematical optimization, greedy algorithms solve combinatorial problems having the properties of matroids.   [   ]
   - A. Trees
   - B. Vectors
   - C. Binary Search Tree
   - D. Matroids

4. Optimization problems are often solved efficiently by expanding a partial solution until the problem is solved, using _____ algorithms   [   ]
   - A. Divide-and-conquer
   - B. Brute-force
   - C. Greedy
   - D. Dynamic-programming

5. Greedy algorithms can be characterized as being, and also as.   [   ]
   - A. Long sighted, non-recoverable
   - B. Short sighted,non-recoverable
   - C. Long sighted, recoverable
   - D. None of the above

6. Arrange the greedy algorithm components in an order   [   ]
   1. Selection function
   2. Objective function
   3. Candidate set
   4. Solution function
   5. Feasibility function
   - A. 2-3-1-5-4
   - B. 2-3-1-4-5
   - C. 3-1-5-2-4
   - D. 3-1-2-5-4

7. Kruskal's algorithm is a greedy algorithm in graph theory that finds a minimum spanning tree for a _______, _____________graph   [   ]
   A. Connected, non-weighted
   B. Not connected weighted graph
   C. Connected weighted graph
   D. All of the above.

8. Time complexity of kruskals algorithm is ___________   [   ]
   A. O(E)   B.   O(logE)
   C. O(E log V)   D.   O(log V)

9. Optimal merge patterns, the total time complexity is   [   ]
   A. O(n log n)   B.   O(logn)
   C. O(n)   D.   O(nm)

10. Using optimal merge patterns find the total cost of (5,10, 20, 30, 30) = (F4, F3, F1, F2, F5)   [   ]
    A. 210   B.   213
    C. 208   D.   207

11. Order profit-weight ratios of all objects   [   ]
    A. $p_i/w_i \geq (p_i + 1)/(w_i + 1)$ for $1 \leq i \leq n - 1$
    B. $p_i/w_i \leq (p_i + 1)/(w_i + 1)$ for $1 \leq i \leq n - 1$
    C. $p_i/w_i \geq (p_i + 1)/(w_i + 1)$ for $1 \geq i \leq n - 1$
    D. $p_i/w_i \leq (p_i + 1)/(w_i + 1)$ for $1 \ i \geq n$

12. Using Largest profit-weight ratio strategy: $(w_1,w_2,w_3) = (18,15,10)$, $(p_1,p_2,p_3) = (25,24,15)$, what is the feasible solution for the above knapsack problem   [   ]
    A. 30   B.   31
    C. 31.5   D.   32

13. Time complexity of prim's algorithm   [   ]
    A. $O(n^2)$ B.   O(n)
    C. O(log n)   D.   O(m n)

Fill in the Blanks

1. Two activities are ___________if their intervals don't overlap.

2. _____subset of edges(E) that connects all vertices of G.

3. Edge is ______if it can be added to set without destroying this invariant.

4. Kruskal's algorithm _______into one by choosing a light edge that connects them.

5. _______Scans the set of edges in monotonically increasing order by weight.

6. Kruskal's algorithm uses a _______to determine whether an edge connects vertices in different components.

7. Prim's algorithm compulsory builds always _____ no. of trees.

8. In Prim's at each step, adds a _____crossing cut $(V_A, V - V_A)$ to A. V_A = vertices that A is incident on.

9. Prim's uses _________ to find light edge quickly.

10. Time complexity of prim's algorithm using binary heaps____.

11. Time complexity of prim's algorithm using Fibonacci heaps___.

12. _______ a spanning tree with the smallest total weight.

13. How do we check if a cycle is formed when a new edge is added in MST____.

14. A tree in the forest is used to represent a ______.

15. If $(u, v) \in E$ and $u \in S_1$, $v \in S_2$, then perform ___of S_1 and S_2 in MST.

16. Time complexity of MST is_____.

17. Time complexity of Dijkstra's algorithm____.

18. AOE means_________.

19. The longest path (critical path) problem can be solved by the ______.

20. Extended Binary Tree Representing in a ________Merge.

21. To minimize the transmission and decoding costs, we may use short strings to represent more frequently used messages but this can be solved by using an____ problem.

22. If all programs are retrieved equally often, then the mean retrieval time (MRT) is______ in Optimal Storage on Tapes.

23. Total time of Optimal Merge Patterns is ______.

24. Time Complexity of the SSSP algorithm______ time.

25. A path from s to a node x outside Y is called special if every intermediary node on the path belongs to Y called_____ problem.

Review Questions

1. (a) Let F(I) be the value of the solution generated on problem instance I by Greedy Knapsack when the objects are input in non decreasing order of the W_i (weights). Let E(I) be the value of an optimal solution for this instance. How large can the ratio E(I)/F(I)get?

   (b) Find an Greedy optimal placement for 13 programs on three tapes T0, T1 and T2 where the programs are of lengths 12, 5, 8, 32, 7, 5, 18, 26, 4, 3, 11, 10 and 6.

R09 December 2011

2. Explain the problem of Single Source Shortest Path Problem and write its algorithm using Greedy approach. Prove that it works with a numerical example.

R09 December 2011

3. (a) Define Spanning Tree. Write and explain the Prim's algorithm.

   (b) Applying the Prim's algorithm, construct a minimal spanning tree for graph given bellow:

R09 November / December-2013

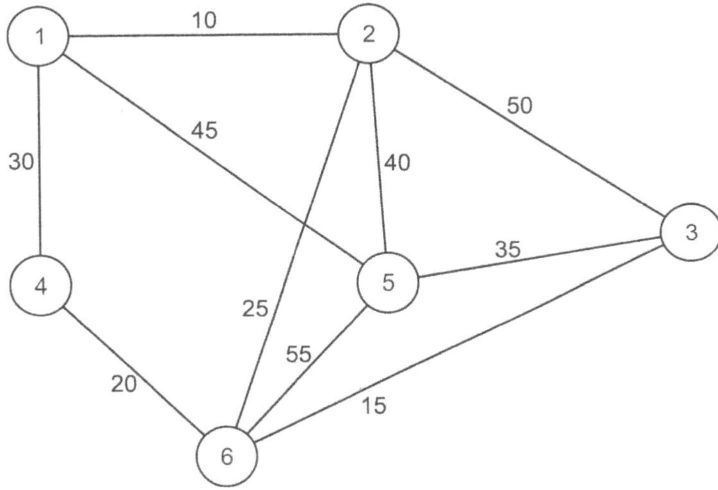

4. What is job sequencing with deadlines problem? Let $n = 5$, $(p_1, p_2, \ldots, p_5) = (10, 3, 33, 11, 40)$ and $(d_1, d_2, \ldots, d_5) = (3, 1, 1, 2, 2)$. Find the optimal solution using greedy algorithm.

R09 June-2014

5. (a) What is the solution generated by the function Job sequencing when $N = 7$, $(P_1, P_2, \ldots P_7) = (3, 5, 20, 18, 1, 6, 30)$ and $(d_1, d_2, \ldots d_7) = (1, 3, 4, 3, 2, 1, 2)$

   (b) What is Greedy method and discuss its applications.

R09 May-2013

6. (a) Write the control abstraction for the Greedy method.

   (b) Compare Kruskhal's and Prim's algorithm. Give their time complexities.

R09 April-May, 2012

7. (a) Explain the 0/1 Knapsack problem.

   (b) Find an optimal solution to the Knapsack instance $n = 7$, $m = 15$, and $(P_1, P_2, \ldots P_7) = (10,5,15,7,6,18,3)$ and $(W_1, W_2, \ldots W_7) = (2,3,5,7,1,4,1)$.

R09 April-May, 2012

8. (a) Find the feasible solution for job sequencing with deadlines for the instance n = 5, $(P_1,...,P_5)$ = (20, 15, 10, 5, 1) and $(d_1,...,d_5)$ = (2,2,1,3,3).

   (b) Explain the 0/1 knapsack problem algorithm with Greedy concept.

R09 April-May, 2012

9. (a) Explain the control abstraction of Greedy method compare this with Dynamic programming.

   (b) Write Kruskals algorithm that generates minimum spanning tree for every connected undirected graph.

R09 April-May, 2012

10. (a) Let G(V,E) be any weighted connected graph. If C is any cycle of G then show that the heaviest edge of C can not belong to any minimum-cost spanning tree of G.

    (b) Give an example set of denominations of coins so that a greedy change making algorithm will not use the minimum number of coins.

RA December 2011

11. How many comparisons of edge weights will be done by the minimum spanning tree algorithm, in total, if the input is a complete undirected graph with n vertices and vi is the start vertex.

12. (a) Compute the time complexity of deriving minimum spanning tree from the weighted connected graph using Kruskal's algorithm.

    (b) Prove that if $p_1/w_1 >= p_2/w_2 >= .... >= p_n/w_n$, then Fractional Greedy Knapsack algorithm generates an optimal solution to the given instance of the fractional Knapsack problem.

R09 December-January, 2011-2012

13. (a) Explain the Prim's algorithm with the appropriate example.

    (b) Write the Prim's algorithm to find the minimum spanning tree.

R09 December-January, 2011-2012

14. Consider the problem of scheduling n jobs of known durations t_1, t_2, .., t_n for execution by a single processor. The jobs can be executed in any order, one job at a time. You want to find a schedule that minimizes the total time spent by all the jobs in the system.

    (a) Design a greedy algorithm for this problem.

    (b) Does the greedy algorithm always yield an optimal solution.

R09-December-January, 2011-2012

15. (a)   Describe the Knapsack problem using greedy method.

    (b)   Explain about Single source shortest path problem.

16. (a)   Explain the terms feasible solution, optimal solution and objective function.

    (b)   Explain the Knapsack problem. Find an optimal solution to the Knapsack instance $n = 7$, $m = 15$, $(p_1, p_2, p_3 \ldots p_7) = (10,5,15,7,6,18,3)$ and $(w_1, w_2, w_3, \ldots w_7) = (2, 3, 5, 7, 1, 4, 1)$.

5

DYNAMIC PROGRAMMING

5.1   THE GENERAL METHODS

An algorithm design method that has a sequence of decisions in its solution to a problem is called Dynamic programming. Decisions are made one at a time leading to optimal sequence of decisions. In taking each individual decision 'The Principle of Optimality' should be followed. There are some problems for which it is not possible to make optimal decision sequence from sequence of stepwise decisions, one way to solve the above problems is to try all possible decision sequences. All decision sequences are enumerated, among them the best one is selected. Normally time complexities of problems solved using dynamic programming are very high, because all possible solutions have to be explored and among them best one is selected. Dynamic programming reduces complexity by the elimination of many enumerations which won't follow the principle of optimality.

The idea of dynamic programming is thus quite simple, avoid calculating the same thing twice, usually by keeping a table of known result that fills up a sub instances are solved. Dynamic programming uses bottom-up technique. We usually start with the smallest and hence the simplest sub-instances. By combining their solutions, we obtain the answers to sub-instances of increasing size, until finally we arrive at the solution of the original instances. The essential difference between the greedy method and dynamic programming is that the greedy method only one decision sequence is ever generated, where as in dynamic programming, many decision sequences may be generated. However, sequences containing sub-optimal sub-sequences can not be optimal and so will not be generated.

The Principle of Optimality: It states that an optimal sequence of decisions has the property that whatever the initial state and decision are, the remaining decisions must constitute an optimal decision sequence with regard to the state resulting from the first decision.

5.2 MULTISTAGE GRAPHS

A graph G is a set of vertices and edges. Graphs are of two types – directed graph and undirected graphs. A multistage graph G is a directed graph in which the vertices are partitioned into two or more stages. A stage is a disjoint set of vertices. Each stage consists of some vertices such that there is no edge between them. In the multistage graph an edge is present between two vertices which are present in adjacent stages only. Let 's' and 't' be the source and destination respectively. The cost of a path from source (s) to destination (t) is the sum of the costs of the edges on the path. The MULTISTAGE GRAPH problem is to find a minimum cost path from 's' to 't'. Each set V_i defines a stage in the graph. Every path from 's' to 't' starts in stage-1, goes to stage-2 then to stage-3, then to stage-4, and so on, and terminates in stage-k. This MULISTAGE GRAPH problem can be solved using two ways they are i) Forward Method ii) Backward Method.

5.2.1 Forward Method

Assume that there are 'k' stages in a graph. In this FORWARD approach, we will find out the cost of each and every node starting from the kth stage to the 1st stage. We will find out the path (i.e.,) minimum cost path from source to the destination (i.e.,) [Stage-1 to Stage-k]. A cost matrix cost (n) which stores the distance from any vertex to the destination. If a vertex is having more than one path, then we have to choose the minimum distance path and the intermediate vertex, which gives the minimum distance path, will be stored in the distance array 'D'. In this way we will find out the minimum cost path from each and every vertex. Finally cost (1) will give the shortest distance from source to destination. For finding the path, start from vertex-1 then the distance array D(1) will give the minimum cost neighbor vertex which in turn give the next nearest vertex and proceed in this way till we reach the Destination. For a 'k' stage graph, there will be 'k' vertex in the path. In the above graph $V_1...V_5$ represent the stages. This five stage graph can be solved by using forward approach as follows:

Procedure: k>= 2 disjoint sets V_i, 1<= i <= k. In addition, if <u,v> is an edge in E, then u∈ V_i and v ∈ V_{i+1} for some i, 1 <= i <= k. In graph G, $|V_1|$ = $|V_k|$ = 1.

Problem: The problem is to find the minimum cost path from source **s** in V_1 to sink **t** in V_k.

Solution – Forward Approach: In a k- stage graph there are k >= 2 disjoint sets. Each set V_i 1<= i <= k is a 'stage i' in the graph.

Let c(i,j) is the cost of edge <i,j>. Each set V_i is a 'stage i' in the graph.

Let p(i,j) be a minimum cost path from vertex j in V_i (stage i) to **t**.

Let cost(i,j) be the cost of the path p(i,j).

Every path from **s** to **t** is a result of k–2 decisions for a k-stage graph i.e., starting at s (V_1), find and include a vertex in stage 2 (V_2), find and include a vertex in stage 3....., find and include a vertex in stage k–1 (V_{k-1}) then include **t(V_k)**.

We can write that

$$cost(i,j) = min\{c(j,l) + cost(i + 1,l)\}$$

$$l \in V_{i+1}$$

$$<j,l> \in E$$

by using the principle of optimality.

Using the above equation we can work forward and get the solution. This approach is called *forward approach*.

Example:

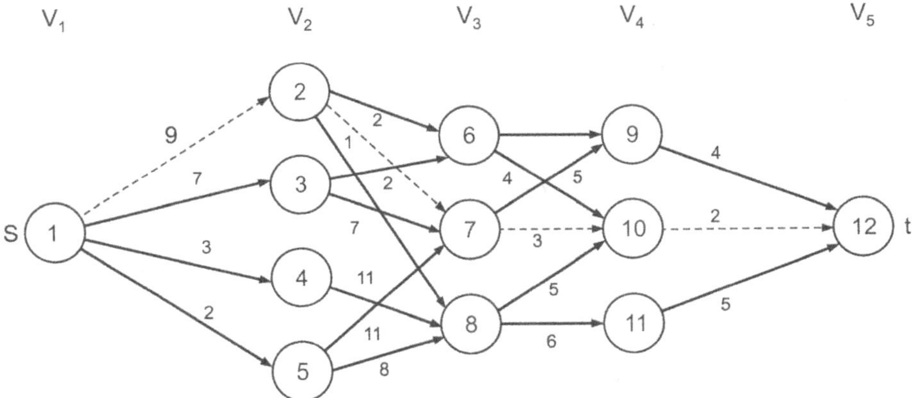

Figure 5.1   A five-stage multi graph

In the above graph: **s is 1 and t is 12**

Cost (i,j) = cost incurred to travel from t to vertex j in stage i

cost(4,9) i.e., cost of the path from vertex 12(t) to vertex 9 in stage 4.

cost(4,9) = 4.

Similarly

cost (4,10) = 2

cost (4,11) = 5

cost (3,6) = min{6 + cost(4,9), 5 + cost(4,10)}

$\qquad$ = min{6 + 4, 5 + 2} = min {10,7} = 7

$$\text{cost }(3,7) = \min\{4 + \text{cost}(4,9), 3 + \text{cost}(4,10)\} = 5$$

$$\text{cost}(3,8) = \min\{5 + \text{cost}(4,10), 6 + \text{cost}(4,11)\}$$
$$= \min\{5 + 2, 6 + 5\} = \min\{7, 11\} = 7$$

$$\text{cost}(2,2) = \min\{4 + \text{cost}(3,6), 2 + \text{cost}(3,7), 1 + \text{cost}(3,8)\}$$
$$= \min\{4 + 7, 2 + 5, 1 + 7\} = \min\{11, 7, 8\} = 7$$

$$\text{cost}(2,3) = \min\{2 + \text{cost}(3,6), 7 + \text{cost }(3,7)\}$$
$$= \min(2 + 7, 7 + 5\} = \min\{9, 12\} = 9$$

$$\text{cost}(2,4) = \min\{11 + \text{cost}(3,8)\} = 11 + 7 = 18$$

$$\text{cost}(2,5) = \min\{11 + \text{cost}(3,7), 8 + \text{cost}(3,8)\}$$
$$= \min\{11+5, 8+7\} = \min\{16, 15\} = 15$$

$$\text{cost}(1,1) = \min\{9 + \text{cost}(2,2), 7 + \text{cost}(2,3), 3$$
$$+ \text{cost}(2,4), 2 + \text{cost}(2,5)\}$$
$$= \min\{9 + 7, 7 + 9, 3 + 18, 2 + 15\}$$
$$= \min\{16, 16, 21, 17\} = 16$$

This path can be determined easily if we record the decision made at each state (vertex).

Let **d(i, j)** be the value of **l** (where l is a node) that minimizes $\{c(j, l) + \text{cost}(i+1, l)\}$.

We can obtain

$$d(3,6) = 10; \ d(3,7) = 10; \ d(3,8) = 10;$$
$$d(2,2) = 7; \ d(2,3) = 6; \ d(2,4) = 8; \ d(2,5) = 8;$$
$$d(1,1) = 2.$$

Let the minimum cost path be s $= 1, v_2, v_3, \ldots\ldots, v_{k-1}, t$. It is easy to see that $v_2 = d(1,1) = 2$, $v_3 = d(2, d(1,1)) = 7$, and $v_4 = d(3, d(2, d(1,1))) = d(3,7) = 10$.

Algorithm

```
1:    Fgraph(G,k,n,p)
2:     // The input is a k-stage graph G with n vertices
       //indexed in order of stages from 1 through n.
3:       //E is the set of edges and c[i,j] is the cost of
       //<i,j>.  p[1:k] is a minimum cost path. cost[i]
       //represents the minimum cost of the path from vertex i
       //to target n.
4:     {
5:             cost[n]:=0.0;
6:             for j:=n-1 to 1 step -1 do
```

```
 7:                    {        // compute cost[j].
 8:                        Let r be a vertex such that <j,r> is an
          edge and  c[j,r]+cost[r]   is min;
 9:                            cost[j]:=c[j,r]+cost[r];
10:                            d[j]:=r;
11:                        }
12:                    // Find a minimum cost path.
13:                    p[1]:=1; p[k]:=n;
14:                    for j:=2 to k-1 do
15:                        p[j]:=d[p[j-1]];
16:    }
```

Note: In the above algorithm instead of writing cost(i,r) where i is the stage, i is skipped for convenience. Similarly for d[i,j], d[j] is written.

5.2.2 Backward Method – Solution

Let bp(i,j) be the min cost path from s to vertex j in V_i.

Let bcost(i,j) be the cost of the path from s to vertex j in V_i.

Using backward approach and principle of optimality

$$\begin{array}{l} \text{bcost}(i, j) = \min\{\text{bcost}(i - 1,l) + c(l, j)\} \\ l \in V_{i-1} \\ \langle l,j \rangle \in E \end{array}$$

Example: For the same graph given in above example.

bcost(2,2) = 9,   bcost(2,3) = 7, bcost(2,4) = 3,   bcost(2,5) = 2

bcost(3,6) = min{bcost(2,2) + c(2,6),

bcost(2,3) + c(3,6)} = min{9 + 4,7 + 2} = 9

bcost(3,7)=11

bcost(3,8) = 10

bcost(4,9) = 15,   bcost(4,10) =14, bcost(4,11) =16

bcost(5,12) = 16

Algorithm

```
1:    Bgraph(G,k,n,p)
2:    {
3:                    bcost[1]:=0.0;
4:                    for j:=2 to n do
5:                    {    // compute bcost[j].
```

```
 6:                          Let  r  be  such  that  <r,j>  is  an
        edge of G and bcost[r]+c[r,j] is minimum;
 7:                          bcost[j]:=bcost[r]+c[r,j];
 8:                          d[j]:=r;
 9:                   }
10:              // Find a minimum cost path.
11:              p[1]:=1; p[k]:=n;
12:              for j:=k-1 to 2 do p[j]:=d[p[j+1]];
13:  }
```

Complexity of both forward and backward approach is $\theta(|V| + |E|)$ or $O(|V| + |E|)$.

5.3   Optimal Binary Search Trees

5.3.1 Binary Search Tree

A Binary Search Tree is a binary tree satisfying the following conditions:

(i)   At every node its left child is smaller and right child is greater.

(ii) All elements in Left Sub-tree of root must be smaller than root and all elements in Right Sub-tree must be greater than root.

Example:

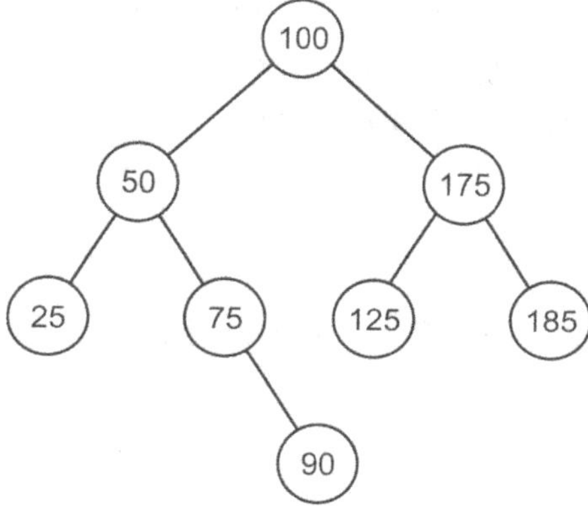

Search Operation: To search for an element X in a binary search tree, initially a pointer (P) is set to the root node then the pointer moves down the tree either to left or to the right depending upon if the element X is less than P or greater.

To search for an element X (=25) the pointer is initially set to the node:

25<100, so P is set to the node:

25<50, so P is set to the node:

Therefore, as the required element is matched with X, the search operation ends by returning the pointer P.

The elements of the above Binary Search Tree in ascending order are:

$\{a_i\}$ →   25   50   75   90   100   125   175   185

The above Binary Search Tree is one of the many possible Binary Search Trees.

The problem of Optimal Binary Search Tree is to construct an Optimal Binary Search Tree given the following data

(i) $a_1, a_2, a_3, \ldots\ldots\ldots\ldots a_n$

(ii) $P_1, P_2, P_3, \ldots\ldots\ldots\ldots P_n$

(iii) $Q_0, Q_1, Q_2, \ldots\ldots\ldots\ldots Q_n$

In the above data P_i is the frequency with which the element a_i is searched for and Q_i is the frequency with which an element belonging to a class E_i is searched for.

The class E_i is explained below:

Let us consider the tree

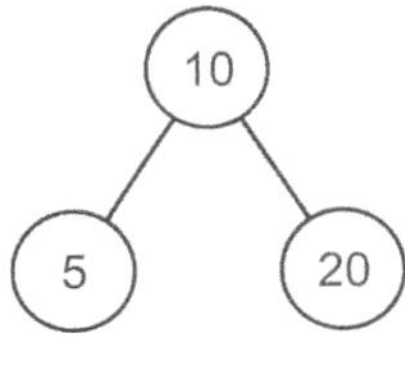

In the above example a_1, a_2, a_3 are 5, 10 and 20 all elements less than a_1 can be represented by an external node as shown below:

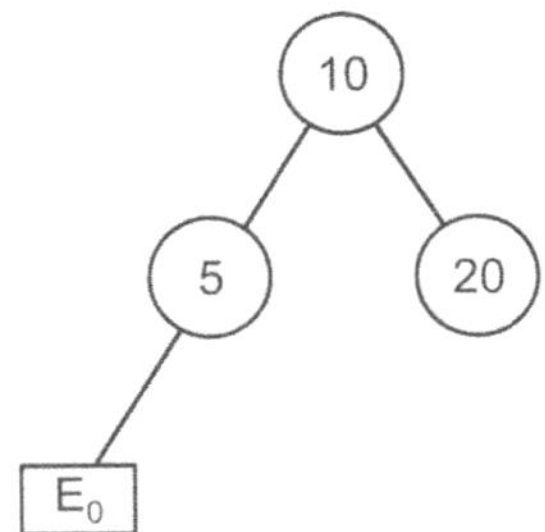

Similarly elements in between a_1 and a_2 ; a_2 and a_3 and the elements greater than a_3 are also shown with external nodes.

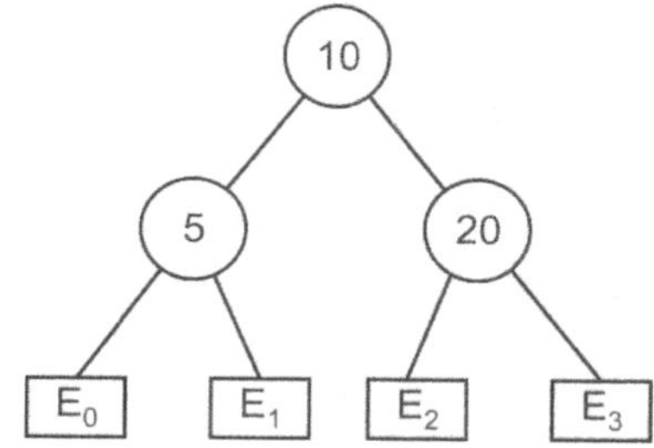

In general all elements corresponding to unsuccessful search operation can be divided into **n+1** classes;

i.e., E_0, E_1, E_2..................E_n

5.3.2 Cost of a Binary Search Tree

Cost of a Binary Search Tree is given the relation:

$$\boxed{\text{Cost} = \sum \text{level}(a_i)*P_i + \sum \text{level}(E_i-1)*Q_i}$$

The problem is to build the binary search tree of identifiers in which the average access cost is minimum. This includes both successful and unsuccessful searches.

Assume that the given set of identifiers is $\{a_1, a_2, ..., a_n\}$ with the ordering $a_1 < a_2 < .... < a_n$.

For 'n' identifiers $2nC_n/(n+1)$ binary search trees can be constructed. For the same set of identifiers different binary search trees gives different performance characteristics. All unsuccessful searches end at external nodes. External nodes are represented using square nodes.

Let $p(i)$ be the probability with which we search for a_i.

Let $q(i)$ be the probability with which we search for x such that $a_i < x < a_{i+1}$.

Assume $a_0 = -\infty$ and $a_{n+1} = +\infty$.

The probability of an unsuccessful search $= \sum_{i=0}^{n} q(i)$

$$\Rightarrow \sum_{i=0}^{n} p(i) + \sum_{i=0}^{n} q(i) = 1.$$

With this data, our target is to construct optimal BST for $\{a_1, a_2, ..., a_n\}$.

Add a fictions node in place of an empty sub tree, which will represent an unsuccessful search. These fictions nodes are called external nodes.

If a binary search tree represents n identifiers, then there will be n internal nodes and n + 1 external nodes.

The expected cost contribution for node $a_i = p(i) * level(a_i)$.

The identifiers not in binary search tree can be partitioned in to n+1 equivalence classes E_i, $0 \le i \le n$.

For all identifiers in the same class E_i, the search terminates at the same external node.

The cost contribution of that node $= q(i) * (level(E_i) - 1)$

The total expected cost of the binary search tree,

$$\sum_{i=0}^{n} p(i) \times level(a_i) + \sum_{i=0}^{n} q(i) \times (level(E_i) - 1)$$

This cost must be minimum for optimal binary search tree.

Example 1: Let n = 3. (a_1, a_2, a_3) = (do, for, while) $p(i) = q(i) = 1/7$ for all i.

P(1:3) = (1/7, 1/7, 1/7) q(0:3) = (1/7, 1/7, 1/7, 1/7)

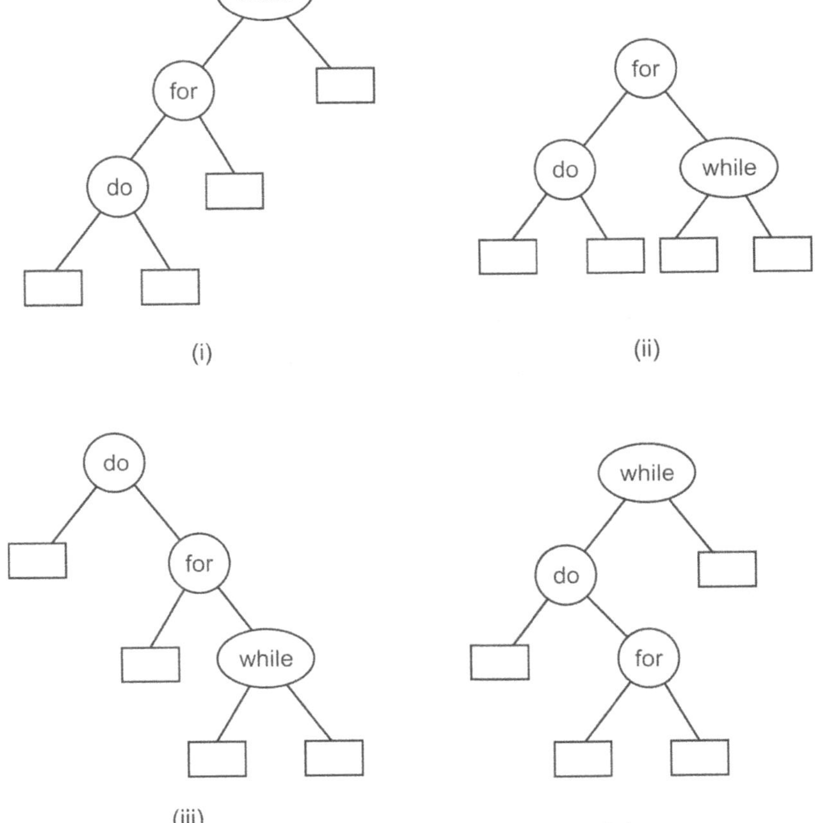

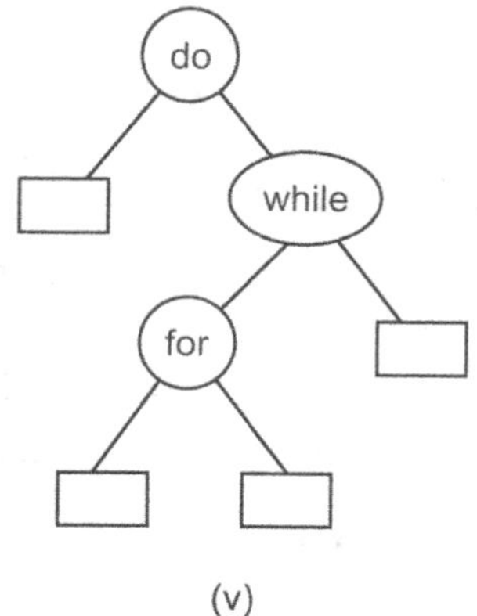

(v)

(i) $(1*1/7) + (2*1/7) + (3*1/7) = 6/7$ => Probability of successful search

$(1*1/7) + (2*1/7) + (3*1/7) + (3*1/7) = 9/7$ => Probability of successful search

$6/7 + 9/7 = 15/7$

(ii) $(1*1/7) + (2*1/7) + (2*1/7) = 5/7$

$(2*1/7) + (2*1/7) + (2*1/7) + (2*1/7) = 8/7$

$5/7 + 8/7 = 13/7$

Tree (ii) is optimal.

Example 2: Let $n = 3$. $(a_1, a_2, a_3) = (do, for, while)$.

$P(1:3) = (0.6, 0.2, 0.1)$ $q(0:3) = (0.045, 0.025, 0.025, 0.01)$

(i) $(1*0.1) + (2*0.2) + (3*0.6) = 2.3$

$(3*0.04) + (3*0.025) + (2*0.025) + (1*0.01) = 0.255$

$2.3 + 0.0255 = 2.555$

(ii) $(1*0.2) + (2*0.6) + (2*0.1) = 1.6$

$(2*0.04) + (2*0.025) + (2*0.025) + (2*0.01) = 0.2$

$1.6 + 0.2 = 1.8$

(iii) $(1*0.6) + (2*0.2) + (3*0.1) = 1.3$

$(1*0.04) + (2*0.025) + (3*0.025) + (3*0.01) = 0.195$

$1.3 + 0.195 = 1.495$

(iv) $(1*0.1) + (2*0.6) + (3*0.2) = 1.9$

$(2*0.04) + (3*0.025) + (3*0.025) + (1*0.01) = 0.24$

$1.9 + 0.24 = 2.14$

(v) $(1*0.6) + (2*0.1) + (3*0.2) = 1.4$

$(1*0.04) + (3*0.025) + (3*0.025) + (2*0.01) = 0.21$

$1.4 + 0.21 = 1.61$

Tree (iii) is optimal.

Cost of a Binary Search Tree in terms of Left Sub-Tree and Right Sub-Tree: Cost of a Left Binary Search Tree (when it is detached from the main tree) is given by cost(l):

$$\text{Cost(l)} = \sum \text{level}(a_i)*P_i + \sum \text{level}(E_i\text{-}1)*Q_i$$

Cost of right Binary Search Tree (detached from main tree) is given by cost(r):

$$\text{Cost(r)} = \sum \text{level}(a_i)*P_i + \sum \text{level}(E_i - 1)*Q_i$$

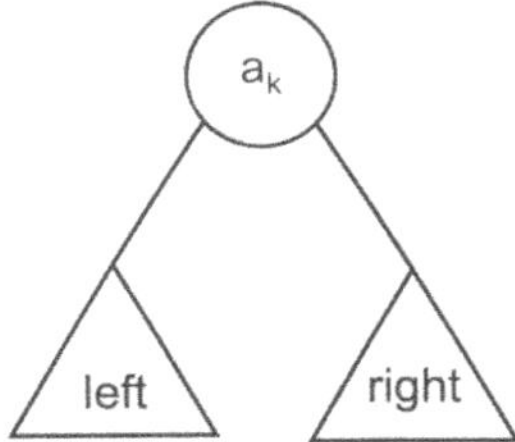

- Left sub-tree consists of a_1,a_2,a_3.........................a_{k-1}
- Right sub-tree consists of a_{k+1},a_{k+2},a_{k+3}...................a_n

$$\text{Cost(t)=Cost(l)+Cost(r)+W(0,n)}$$

where $W(0, n) = \sum P_i + \sum Q_i$

Let t_{ij} be an optimal binary search tree consisting of $a_{i+1},a_{i+2},a_{i+3}.......a_j$

An optimal binary search tree problem is to construct t_{on} (i.e., to construct an optimal binary search tree consisting of $a_1,a_2,a_3.......a_n$).

Let $C(i, j)$ be the cost of t_{ij} then

$$C(0, n) = C(0, k{-}1) + C(k{+}1, n) + W(0, n)$$

Principle of Optimality: The Principle of Optimality states that in an optimal sequence of decisions, all the subsequence must also be optimal.

$$C(0, n) = \min_{1 \le k \le n} \{C(0, k{-}1) + C(k{+}1, n)\} + W(0, n)$$

Generalizing the above expression:

$$C(i, j) = \min_{i+1 \leq k \leq j} \{C(i, k-1) + C(k+1, j)\} + W(i, j)$$

Solution-Using Dynamic Programming Technique:

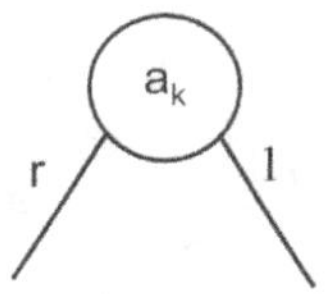

1. Let the tree contains the identifiers $a_1, a_2, \ldots, a_n$.

2. Let the binary search tree (BST) contains a_k at root as shown,

$$\Rightarrow \text{total cost} = p(k) + cost(l) + cost(r) + w(0, k-1) + w(k.n)$$

where $cost(l) = \sum_{1 \leq i < k} p(i) * level(a_i) + \sum_{0 \leq i < k} q(i) * (level(E_i)-1)$

$$cost(r) = \sum_{k < i \leq n} p(i) * level(a_i) + \sum_{k < i \leq n} q(i) * (level(E_i)-1)$$

$w(i,j) = q(i) + \sum_{l=i+1 \text{ to } j} (q(l) + p(l))$ for tree to be optimal, $cost(l)$ and $cost(r)$ should be minimum.

$\Rightarrow$ Let $c(i,j)$ represents the cost of optimal BST containing $a_{i+1}, a_{i+2} \ldots \ldots, a_j$ and E_i to E_j

$\Rightarrow cost(l)$ should be $c(0, k-1)$ and $cost(r)$ should be $c(k,n)$ and

cost of BST $= p(k) + c(0, k-1) + c(k,n) + w(0, k-1) + w(k,n)$

$$\Rightarrow c(0,n) = \min_{1 \leq k \leq n} \{p(k) + c(0, k-1) + c(k,n) + w(0, k-1) + w(k,n)\}$$

we can generalize to

$$c(i,j) = \min_{1 < k \leq j} \{p(k) + c(i, k-1) + c(k,j) + w(i, k-1) + w(k,j)\}$$

$$= \min_{1 < k \leq j} \{c(i, k-1) + c(k,j)\} + w(i,j)$$

using this equation beginning with $c(i,i)=0$ and $w(i,i)=q(i)$ we can solve for $c(0,n)$.

In this process we will recover root $r(i,j)$ for t_{ij}.

Example: Let $n = 4$ and $(a_1, a_2, a_3, a_4) = $ **(do, if, int, while)**.

Let $p(1:4) = (3,3,1,1)$ and $q(0:4) = (2,3,1,1,1)$.

Solution: Initially, we have $w(i,i) = q(i)$, $c(i,i) = 0$ and $r(i,i) = 0$, $0 \leq i \leq 4$.

We have $w(i,j) = p(j) + q(j) + w(i, j-1)$, we get

Optimal Binary Search Tree consisting of one node each:

t_{01}

cost $= 0 + 0 + 8 = 8$

C (0, 1) = 8

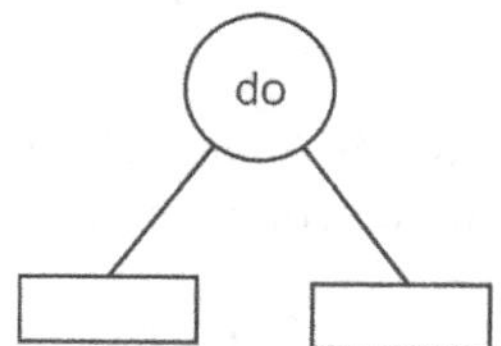

t_{12}

cost $= 0 + 0 + 7 = 7$

C (1, 2) = 7

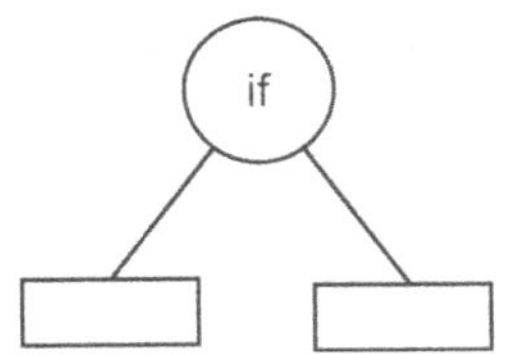

t_{23}

cost $= 0 + 0 + 3 = 3$

C (2, 3) = 3

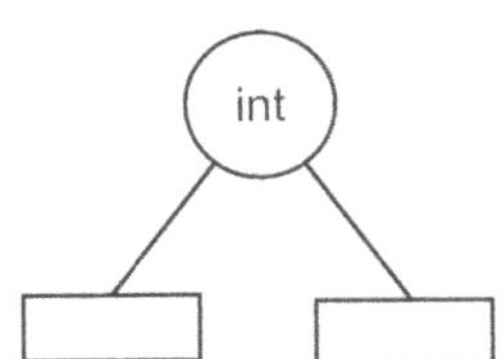

t_{34}

cost $= 0 + 0 + 3 = 3$

C (3, 4) = 3

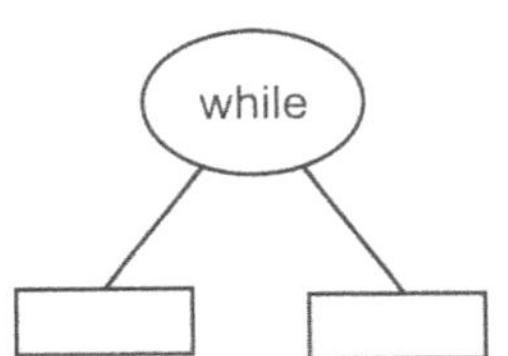

Optimal Binary Search Tree consisting of two nodes each:

t_{02}

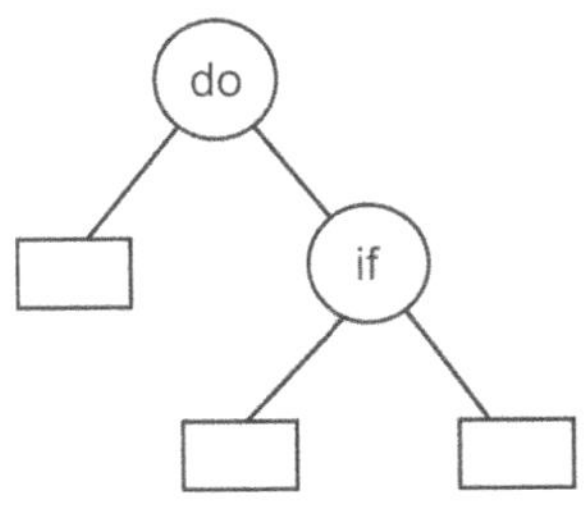
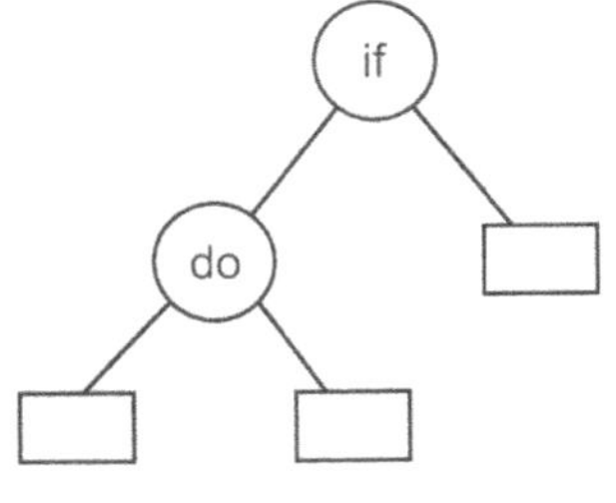

cost $= 0 + 7 + 12 = 19$ cost $= 8 + 0 + 12 = 20$

C (0, 2) = 19; r (0, 2) = 1

t_{13}

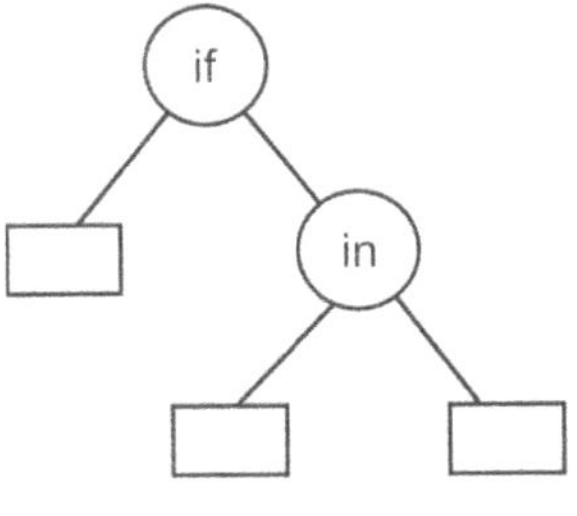
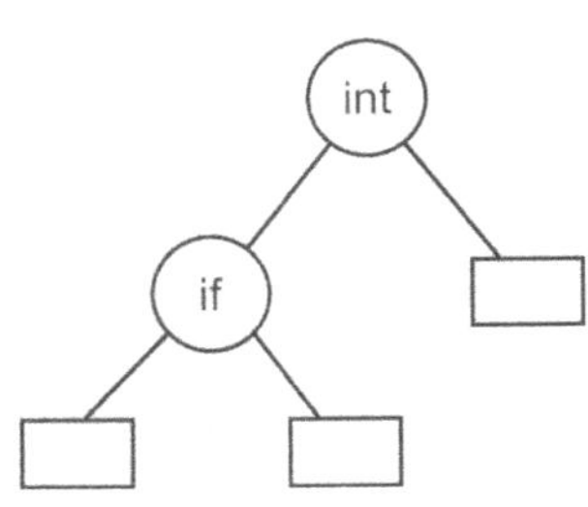

cost $= 0 + 3 + 9 = 12$ cost $= 7 + 0 + 9 = 16$

C (1, 3) = 12; r (1, 3) = 2

t_{24}

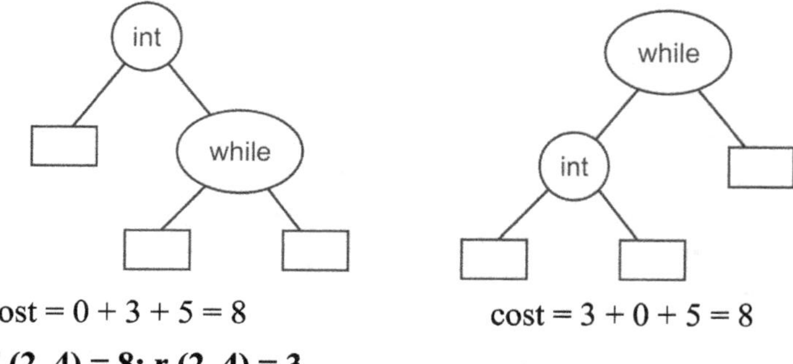

$$\text{cost} = 0 + 3 + 5 = 8 \qquad\qquad \text{cost} = 3 + 0 + 5 = 8$$

C (2, 4) = 8; r (2, 4) = 3

Optimal Binary Search Tree consisting of three nodes each:

t_{03}

(i)

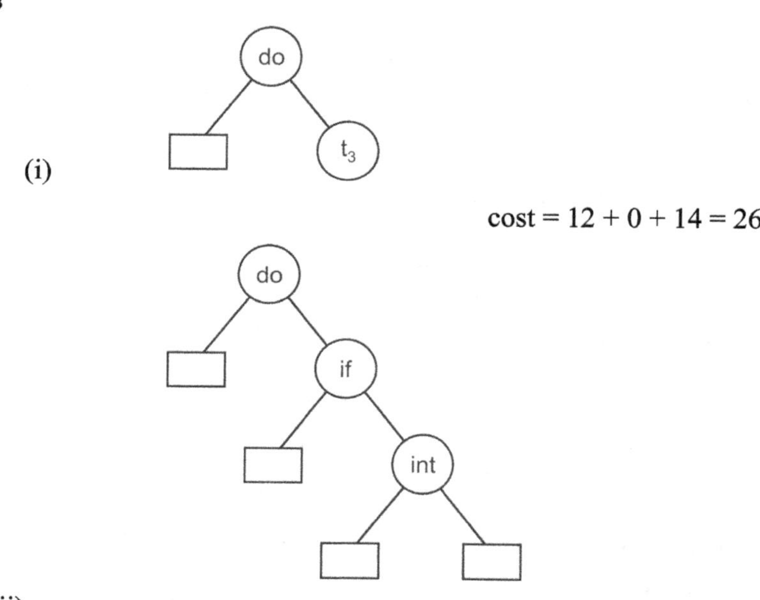

$$\text{cost} = 12 + 0 + 14 = 26$$

(ii)

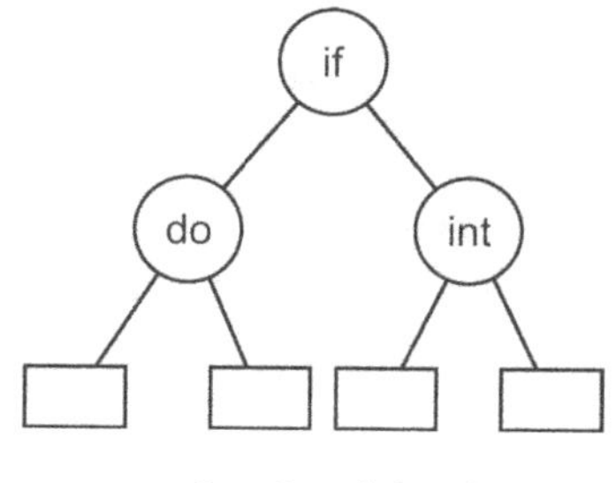

$$\text{cost} = 8 + 3 + 14 = 25$$

(iii)

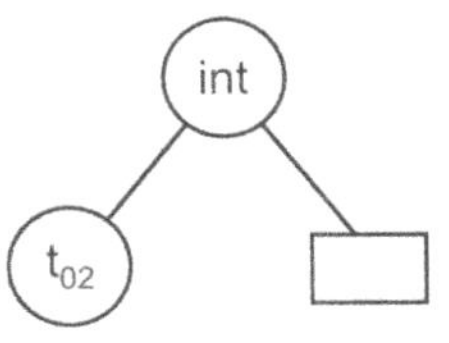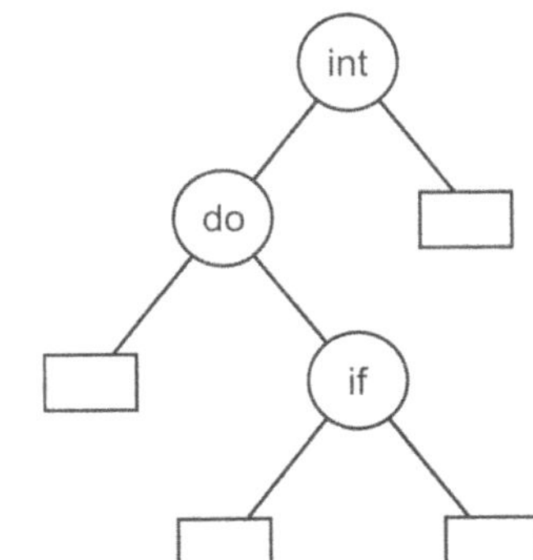

cost = 19 + 14 + 0 = 33
C (0, 3) = 25; r (0, 3) = 2

t_{14}

(i)

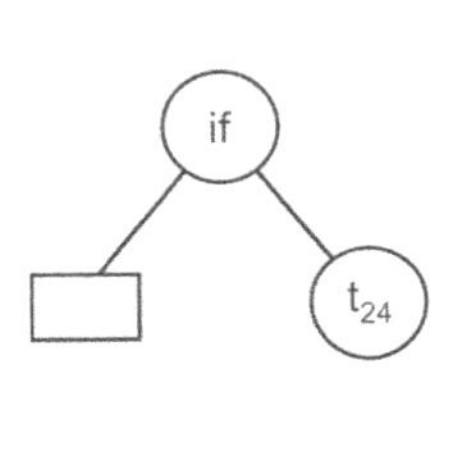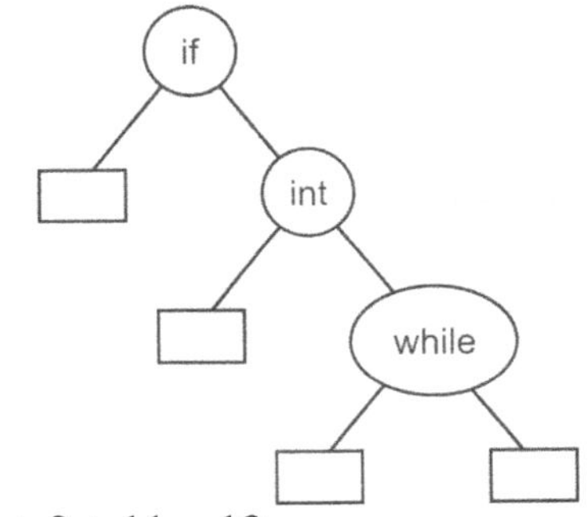

cost = 0 + 8 + 11 = 19

(ii)

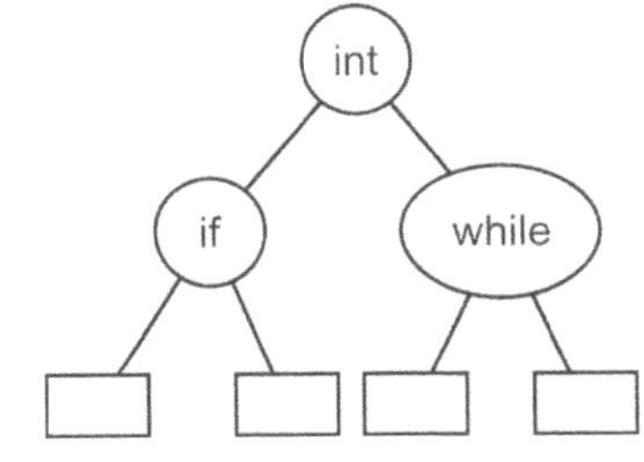

cost = 7 + 3 + 11 = 21

(iii)

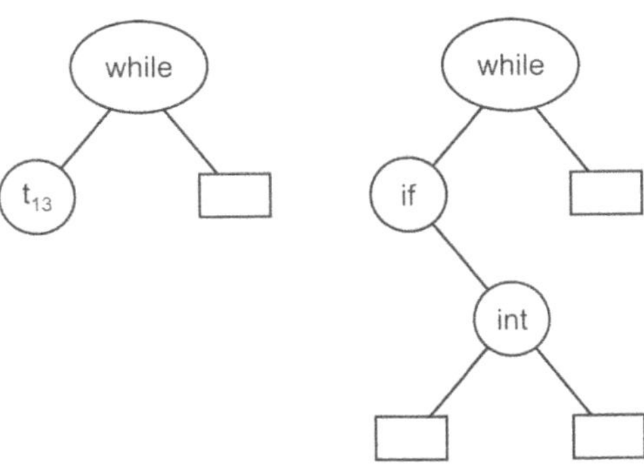

cost = 12 + 0 + 11 = 23; **C (1, 4) = 19; r (0, 3) = 2**

Optimal binary search tree consisting of all four nodes

t_{04}

As per the previous iterations we can find the costs of four possible binary trees and then choose the minimum cost tree as an optimal binary search tree.

There is a shortcut to this. The given keywords are grouped such that each group contains **n–1** consecutive keywords.

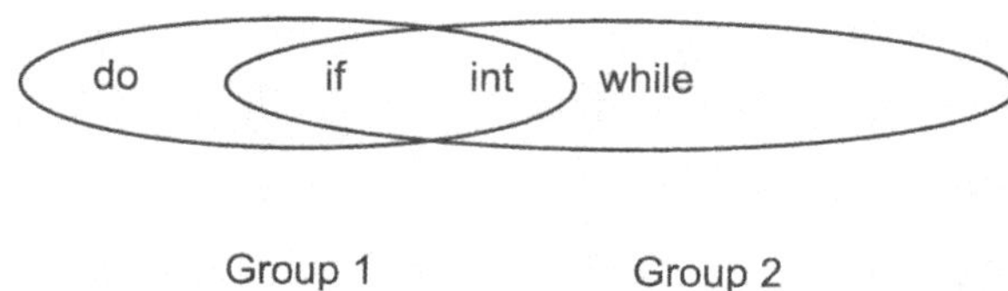

Let the root of group-1 is r_1 and the root of group-2 is r_2, then we need to find the costs of the trees with root as r_1 and the one with root as r_2. In our example $r_1 = 2(a_2)$ and $r_2 = 2(a_2)$.

Therefore, we construct only one binary search tree consisting of four nodes and that is the Optimal Binary Search Tree.

Therefore, the optimal binary search tree for the given data is:

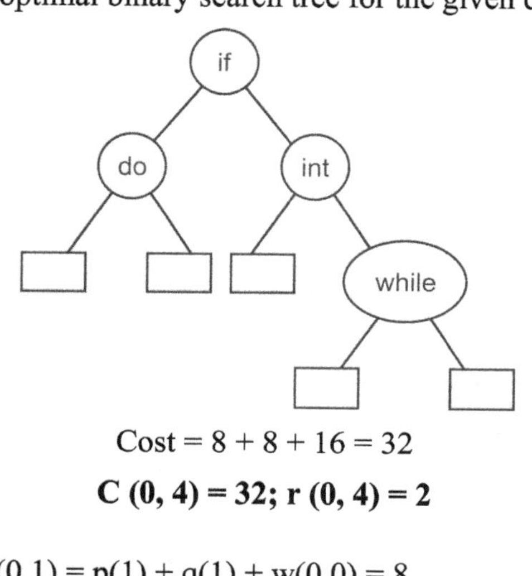

$$\text{Cost} = 8 + 8 + 16 = 32$$

$$C\,(0, 4) = 32;\ r\,(0, 4) = 2$$

$$w(0,1) = p(1) + q(1) + w(0,0) = 8$$

$$c(0,1) = w(0,1) + \min\{c(0,0) + c(1,1)\} = 8$$

$$r(0,1) = 1$$

$$w(1,2) = p(2) + q(2) + w(1,1) = 7$$

$$c(1,2) = w(1,2) + \min\{c(1,1) + c(2,2)\} = 7$$

$$r(1,2) = 2$$

$$w(2,3) = p(3) + q(3) + w(2,2) = 3$$

$$c(2,3) = w(2,3) + \min\{c(2,2) + c(3,3)\} = 3$$

$$r(2,3) = 3$$

$$w(3,4) = p(4) + q(4) + w(3,3) = 3$$

$$c(3,4) = w(3,4) + \min\{c(3,3) + c(4,4)\} = 3$$

$$r(3,4) = 4$$

This process can be repeated until $w(0,4)$, $c(0,4)$, and $r(0,4)$ are obtained. The results are,

	0	1	2	3	4
0	$w_{00} = 2$ $c_{00} = 0$ $r_{00} = 0$	$w_{11} = 3$ $c_{11} = 0$ $r_{11} = 0$	$w_{22} = 1$ $c_{22} = 0$ $r_{22} = 0$	$w_{33} = 1$ $c_{33} = 0$ $r_{33} = 0$	$w_{44} = 1$ $c_{44} = 0$ $r_{44} = 0$
1	$w_{01} = 8$ $c_{01} = 8$ $r_{01} = 1$	$w_{12} = 7$ $c_{12} = 7$ $r_{12} = 2$	$w_{23} = 3$ $c_{23} = 3$ $r_{23} = 3$	$w_{34} = 3$ $c_{34} = 3$ $r_{34} = 4$	
2	$w_{02} = 12$ $c_{02} = 19$ $r_{02} = 1$	$w_{13} = 9$ $c_{13} = 12$ $r_{13} = 2$	$w_{24} = 5$ $c_{24} = 8$ $r_{24} = 3$		
3	$w_{03} = 14$ $c_{03} = 25$ $r_{03} = 2$	$w_{14} = 11$ $c_{14} = 19$ $r_{14} = 2$			
4	$w_{04} = 16$ $c_{04} = 32$ $r_{04} = 2$				

From the table we see that $c(0,4) = 32$ is the minimum cost of binary search tree for (a_1, a_2, a_3, a_4). The root of tree t_{04} is a_2. Hence, the left subtree is t_{01} and the right subtree is t_{24}. Tree t_{01} has root a_1 and subtrees t_{00} and t_{11}. Tree t_{24} has root a_3; its left subtree is t_{22} and its right subtree is t_{34}. Thus, with the data in the table it is possible to reconstruct t_{04}. Following Fig shows optimal search tree t_{04}.

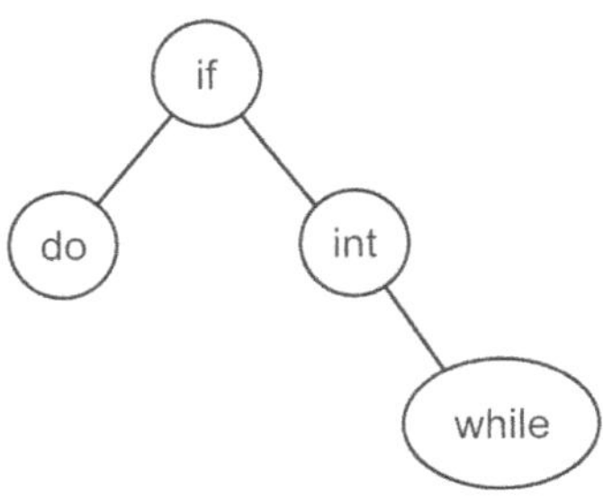

Algorithm:

Algorithm OBST(p, q, n)

```
 1:    /* Given n distinct identifiers a₁ < a₂ <....< aₙ and
            probabilities //p[i],1<=i<=n,and
            q[i],0<=i<=n,this algorithm computes the cost
            c[i,j] of  OBST tᵢⱼ  for identifiers
            aᵢ₊₁,....,aⱼ.It also computes r[i,j],the root of
            tᵢⱼ.  w[i,j] is the weight of tᵢⱼ.*/
 2:    {
 3:            for i:=0 to n-1 do
 4:            {    // Initialise.
 5:                    w[i, j]:=q[i];     r[i, i]:=0;
        c[i, i]:= 0.0;
 6:                    //Optimal trees with one node
 7:            w[i, i+1]:=q[i]+q[i+1]+p[i+1];
 8:        r[i, i+1]:=i+1;
 9:                    c[i, i+1]:= q[i]+q[i+1]+p[i+1];
10:        }
11:            w[n, n]:=q[n];    r[n, n]:=0; c[n, n]:=0.0;
12:            for m:=2 to n do // find optimal trees with
        //m nodes
13:            {      for i:=0 to n-m do
14:        {  j:=i+m;      w[i, j]:=w[i, j-1]+p[j]+q[j];
15:          k:=Find(c, r, i, j);
16:          // The value of l in the range r[i,j-1] <=
        l<=r[i+1,j] that minimizes c[i, l-1]+c[l, j].
17:            c[i, j]:=w[i, j]+c[i, k-1]+c[k, j];
18:            r[i, j]:=k;
19:        }
20:            }
21:            Write (c[0, n],w[0, n],r[0, n]);
22: }
```

Algorithm Find(c, r ,i ,j)

```
 1:    {
 2:       min:= ∞;
 3:       for m:=r[i, j-1] to r[i+1, j] do
 4:       if (c[i, n-1]+c[m, j]) < min then
 5:       {     min:=c[i, m-1]+c[n, j]; l:=m;
 6:       }
 7:       return l;
 8: }
```

5.4 0/1 KNAPSACK PROBLEM

In 0/1 knapsack problem we have a knapsack of capacity "**C**". This knapsack is to be filled with the given objects such that we get a maximum profit. Associated with the "n" objects profits $\{P_1, P_2, P_3.......P_n\}$ and weights $\{W_1, W_2, W_3.......W_n\}$ are given. The selection of the objects should meet the following constraints:

(i) $x_i \in \{0, 1\}$, where x_i is "i^{th}" selected object

(ii) $\sum x_i w_i \leq C$

Knapsack problem and 0/1 Knapsack problem are different. For solving knapsack problem we use **"GREEDY METHOD"**. For solving 0/1 knapsack problem, **"DYNAMIC PROGRAMMING"** method is used because greedy method for this problem doesn't give correct solution.

It is the same knapsack problem with additional constraint that $x_i \in \{0,1\}$ i.e., part of an object can't be put in the knapsack. Let $f_j(y)$ is the profit on including the objects between 1 and j subject to the weight y i.e., **KNAP (1, j, y).**

By using principle of optimality we can write that

$$f_n(m) = max\{ f_{n-1}(m),\ f_{n-1}(m-w_n)+p_n\}$$

In general for i>0

$$f_i(y) = max\{ f_{i-1}(y),\ f_{i-1}(y-w_i)+p_i\}$$

where $f_0(y) = 0$ for any weight y.

We need to calculate $f_n(m)$ by beginning with the knowledge $f_0(y)=0$ for all y   and $f_i(y)=-\infty$, y<0. We need to calculate this for 0<y<m. if w_i's are integers, the complexity is $\theta(nm)$. If w_i's are real numbers then f_i's can't be computed for all y values.

The solution set is represented by a tuple called (P,W). where 'P' is profit and 'W' is weight.

In the case where w_i's can be real numbers $s^i = \{(p.w)/p=f_i(y_i)$ and $w=y_i\}$.

Let s^i be the solution set by including only the objects from 1 to i. $s^0=\{0,0\}$.

When generating the S^i's, we can also purge all pairs (P,W) with W>m, as these pairs determine the value of $f_n(x)$ only for x>m. since the knapsack capacity is m, we are not interested in the behavior of f_n for x>m. When all pairs (P_j,W_j) with W_j>m are purged from the S^i's, $f_n(m)$ is given by the P values of the last pair in S^n. Note also that by computing S^n, we can find the solutions to all the knapsack problems KNAP(1,n,x), $0 \leq x \leq m$, and not just KNAP(1,n,m). Since, we want only a solution to KNAP(1,n,m), we can dispense with the computation of S^n. The last pair in S^n is either the last one in S^{n-1} or it is (P_j+p_n, W_j+w_n), where $(P_j, W_j) \in S^{n-1}$ such that $W_j+w_n \leq m$ and W_j is maximum.

If (P_1, W_1) is the last tuple in S^n, a set of 0/1 values for the x_i's such that $\sum p_i x_i = P_1$ and $\sum w_i x_i = W_1$ can be determined by carrying out a search through the S^i's. We can set $x_n = 0$ if $(P_1, W_1) \in S^{n-1}$. If $(P_1, W_1) \notin S^{n-1}$, then $(P_1-p_n, W_1-w_n) \in S^{n-1}$ and we can set $x_n=1$. This leaves us to determine how either (P_1, W_1) or (P_1-p_n, W_1-w_n) was obtained in S^{n-1}. This can be done recursively.

5.4.1 Dominance Rule

S^{i+1} contains two pairs (P_1, W_1) and (P_2, W_2) with the property that $P_1 \leq P_2$ and $W_1 \geq W_2$ then the pair (P_1, W_1) can be discarded because containing with (P_1, W_1) will not lead to optimal solution.

S^i represents the possible states resulting from the 2^i decision sequence for $x_1, x_2 \ldots \ldots x_i$.

A state refers to a pair (P_j, W_j), W_j the total weight of objects included in the knapsack and P_j is the corresponding profit.

$$S^0 = \{(0, 0)\}; \text{ Empty knapsack profit pair is}$$

Empty knapsack is represented by $S^0 = \{(0, 0)\}$

By adding the first tuple to the solution set S_0, the solution set becomes

$$S^0_1 = \{(P_1, W_1)\}$$
$$S^{i+1} = S^i \cup S^i_1$$
$$S^1 = S^0 \cup S^0_1 = \{(0, 0), (P_1, W_1)\}$$

S^i is a solution set by including --- the objects from 1 to i. S^1 is solution set by including one object.

For one object we have two alternatives:

1. Object is not included in knapsack then profit = 0, weight = 0. (P, W) pair = (0, 0).

2. Object is included in knapsack then profit = P_1, weight = W_1. (P, W) pair = (P_1, W_1).

    Hence $S^1 = \{(0, 0), (P_1, W_1)\}$.

Now on S^1 we place second object (P_2, W_2). It is represented by S^1_1.

$$S^1_1 = \{(0 + P_2, 0 + w_2), (P_1 + P_2, W_1 + W_2)\}$$
$$S^1_1 = \{(P_2, W_2), (P_1 + P_2, W_1 + W_2)\}$$
$$S^2 = S^1 + S^1_1 = \{(0, 0), (P_1, W_1) (P_2, W_2) (P_1 + P_2, W_1 + W_2)\}$$

For two objects we have four alternatives:

1. Two objects are not selected P=0, W=0, (P, W)=(0, 0).

2. First object is selected and second object is not selected.

    $P = P_1, W = W_1, (P, W) = (P_1, W_1)$

3. First object is not selected and second object is selected.

    $P = P_2, W = W_2, (P, W) = (P_2, W_2)$

4. Both objects are selected.

    $P = P_1 + P_2, W = W_1 + W_2, (P, W) = (P_1 + P_2, W_1 + W_2)$

Example 1: Let $s_1^i =\{ (p,w)/(p-p_i,w-w_i) \in s^i\}$ is a set of solutions by including $(i+1)^{th}$ object in s^i. Then $s^{i+1} = s^i \cup s_1^i$

Here we will apply 'discarding' or 'purging' rule i.e., if s^{i+1} contains two pairs (p_j,w_j) and (p_k,w_k) with the property that $p_j < p_k$ and $w_j > w_k$ then the pair (p_j,w_j) can be discarded.

Example 2: Consider the knapsack instance n = 3, $(w_1,w_2,w_3) = (2,3,4)$, $(p_1,p_2,p_3) = (1,2,5)$, and m = 6. For these data we have

$(P_1, W_1) = (1, 2) (P_2, W_2) = (2, 3) (P_3, W_3) = (5, 4)$

S0 = {(0, 0)}   empty knapsack

S_1^0

$S^0 = \{(0,0)\}; S_1^0 = \{(1,2)\}$

$S^1 = \{(0,0),(1,2)\}; S_1^1 = \{(2,3),(3,5)\}$

$S^2 = \{(0,0),(1,2),((2,3),(3,5)\}; S_1^2 = \{(5,4),(6,6),(7,7),(8,9)\}$

$S^3 = \{(0,0),(1,2),((2,3),(5,4),(6,6),(7,7),(8,9)\}$

On empty knapsack we place object one

Hence $S_1^0=\{(1, 2)\}$

$S^1 = S^0 + S_1^0 = \{(0, 0) (1, 2)\}$

With one object we have two alternatives i.e., object is selected and object is not selected.

$S_1^1 \rightarrow$ on S^1 object 2 is placed.

$S_1^1 = \{S^1 + (2, 3)\}$

$= \{(0, 0) (1, 2)\} + (2, 3)$

$S_1^1 = \{(2, 3), (3, 5)\}$

$S^2 = S^1 \cup S_1^1$

$= \{(0, 0), (1, 2)\} \cup \{(2, 3)(3, 5)\}$

$= \{(0, 0)(1, 2)(2, 3)(3, 5)\}$

$S^2_1 \rightarrow$ on S^2 object 3 is placed.

$S^2_1 = \{S^2 + (5, 4)\}$

$\quad = \{(0, 0)\,(1, 2)(2, 3)(3, 5)\} + (5, 4)$

$S^2_1 = \{(5, 4)\,(6, 6)(7, 7)(8, 9)\}$

$S^3 = S^2 \text{ U } S^2_1$

$\quad = \{(0, 0)\,(1, 2)(2, 3)(3, 5)(5, 4)\,(6, 6)(7, 7)(8, 9)\}$

From this solution set some pairs are removed. Pairs (7, 7), (8, 9) are removed as the weight of the above pair is more than knapsack capacity. By using dominance rule/purging rule pair (3, 5) is compared with (5, 4). In this pair (3, 5) is dominated by pair (5, 4) because profit of (3, 5) is less than (5, 4) and weight is more. So that the pair (3,5) has been eliminated from S^3 as a result of the purging rule. Now solution set S^3 consider of :

$\quad S^3 = \{(0, 0)(1, 2)(2, 3)(5, 4)(6, 6)\}$

From the above solution maximum profit is (6, 6).

Hence the maximum profit that can be obtained $= 6$

Pair (6, 6) is available in S^3 but not available in S^2.

Hence object 3 is selected.

$\quad (6, 6) - (5, 4) = (1, 2)$

Pair (1, 2) is present in S^2 and in S^1. Hence object 2 is not selected. Pair (1, 2) is present in S^1 and not present in S^0.

Hence object 1 is selected.

$\quad$ object 1 is selected (P, W) $= (1, 2)$

$\quad$ object 3 is selected(P, W) $= (5, 4)$

Solution is (1, 0, 1).

Algorithm:

```
 1:   DKP(p,w,n,m)
 2:   {
 3:         S⁰ := { (0,0) };
 4:         for i := 1 to n-1 do
 5:             {
 6:                 S₁ⁱ⁻¹ := { (P,W) | (P-pᵢ,W-wᵢ) ∈ Sⁱ⁻¹ and W ≤ m};
 7:                 Sⁱ := MergePurge(Sⁱ⁻¹ , S₁ⁱ⁻¹);
 8:             }
 9:         (PX,WX) := last pair in Sⁿ⁻¹;
10:      (PY,WY) := (P' + pₙ , W' +wₙ) where W' is the largest
         W         in        any        pair         in         Sⁿ⁻¹
         such that W+wₙ ≤ m;
```

```
11:        // Trace back for xₙ,xₙ₋₁,....,x₁.
12:        if (PX>PY) then xₙ :=0;
13:        else   xₙ := 1;
14:        TraceBackFor(xₙ₋₁,...,x₁);
15:   }
```

5.5 ALL PAIRS SHORTEST PATH PROBLEM

All Pairs Shortest Path problem is to find the shortest distances between every pair of nodes of the given graph. Let $G = (V,E)$ be a directed graph where 'V' is a set of vertices or nodes and 'E' is the set of edges. Each edge has an associated non-negative length. The problem is to calculate the length of the shortest path between each pair of nodes.

Suppose the nodes of G are numbered from 1 to n, so $V = \{1,2,...n\}$. Let cost be an adjacency matrix which stores weight of edges of graph G. Graph G has n vertices, cost $(i,i)=0$, $1<=i<=n$. Vertices that are not adjacent i.e., vertices which are not connected with an edge, if the edge (i,j) does not exist for them cost$(i,j) = \infty$.

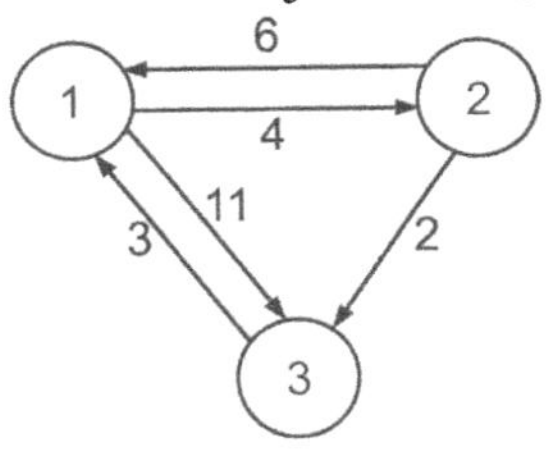

The principle of optimality applies: if k is the node on the shortest path from i to j then the part of the path from i to k and the part from k to j must also be optimal, that is shorter. First, create a cost adjacency matrix for the given graph.

Consider the above example graph, its adjacency matrix is given below:

$$A = \begin{bmatrix} 0 & 4 & 11 \\ 6 & 0 & 2 \\ 3 & \infty & 0 \end{bmatrix}$$

To solve this problem we introduce vertex-1 as an intermediate vertex to find shorter distances between every pair of rows.

$$(V_i ,V_j) \text{ where } 1\leq i \leq n ; 1\leq j \leq n$$

By following this method the shorter distances between every pair of vertices are given in the following matrix

$$A_1 = \begin{bmatrix} 0 & 4 & 11 \\ 6 & 0 & 2 \\ 3 & 7 & 0 \end{bmatrix}$$

In the above matrix: $A_1(3,2) = \min (A(3,2), A(3,1) + A(1,2))$

$$= \min (\infty, 3+4) = 7$$

In the second step the intermediate vertex is 2, the shorter distances matrix A_2 is given below:

$$A_2 = \begin{bmatrix} 0 & 4 & 6 \\ 6 & 0 & 2 \\ 3 & 7 & 0 \end{bmatrix}$$

In the above matrix: $A_2(2,3) = \min (A_1(3,1), A_1(3,2) + A_1(2,1))$
$$= \min (3, 7 + 6)$$
$$= 3$$

In the third step the intermediate vertex is 3, the shorter distance matrix A_3 is given below:

$$A_3 = \begin{bmatrix} 0 & 4 & 6 \\ 5 & 0 & 2 \\ 3 & 7 & 0 \end{bmatrix}$$

In the above matrix: $A_3(2,1) = \min (A_2(2,1), A_2(2,3) + A_2(3,1))$
$$= \min (6, 2 + 3)$$
$$= 5$$
$$A_3(1,2) = \min (A_2(1,2), A_2(1,3) + A_2(3,2))$$
$$= \min (4, 6 + 7)$$
$$= 4$$

The above matrix gives the shortest distances between every pair of vertices.

Algorithm All paths(cost, X, n)

```
for i=1 to n do
{
  for j= 1 to n do
  {
  X[i, j]= cost[i, j];
  }
}
for i=1 to n do
{
  for j= 1 to n do
  {
  for k= 1 to n do
  {
  X[i, j] = min (X[i, j] , X[i, k] +
  X[k, j]);
  }
                 }
                 }
        }
```

Parameters: Cost $\rightarrow$ Adjacency matrix of the graph, this is the input parameter.

X $\rightarrow$ It is an output parameter at the termination of the algorithm, this matrix holds the shortest distances (mxn) matrix.

n $\rightarrow$ Number of vertices in the graph.

The first nested loop is to initialize matrix "A" to cost matrix.

The second nested loop is to find the shorter distances between every pair of vertices using vertex 1, 2, 3.........n as intermediate vertices.

The time complexity of above algorithm is equals to $O(n^3)$, because the statement **X[i, j] = min (X[i, j] , X[i, k] + X[k, j]);** gets executed n^3 times, as the other nested loop statements has the less complexity of the order of n^2.

Therefore, the time complexity of the algorithm is $O(n^3)$.

5.6 THE TRAVELLING SALESPERSON PROBLEM

Let $G = (V,E)$ be a directed graph with n vertices. Let c_{ij} is the cost of the edge between i and j. $c_{ij} > 0$ and $c_{ij} = \infty$ if $<i,j> \notin E$. Let $V = n$ and assume $n>1$. A tour of G is a directed simple cycle that includes every vertex in V. The problem is to find a tour of minimum cost. The cost of the tour is the sum of cost of the edges on the tour. The tour is the shortest path that starts and ends at the same vertex (i.e.,) vertex 1. Travelling salesman problem is a permutation problem, these problems are harder to solve.

Applications: water pipelines, mail delivery, transport etc.

Suppose we have to route a postal van to pick up mail from the mail boxes located at 'n' different sites. An n+1 vertex graph can be used to represent the situation. One vertex represent the post office from which the postal van starts and return. Edge $<i,j>$ is assigned a cost equal to the distance from site 'i' to site 'j'. the route taken by the postal van is a tour and we are finding a tour of minimum length. every tour consists of an edge $<1,k>$ for some $k \in V-\{\}$ and a path from vertex k to vertex 1. The path from vertex k to vertex 1 goes through each vertex in $V-\{1,k\}$ exactly once.

The function which is used to find the path is $g(1,V-\{1\}) = min\{ c_{ij} + g(j,s-\{j\})\}$ g(i,s) be the length of a shortest path starting at vertex i, going through all vertices in S, and terminating at vertex 1. The function $g(1,v-\{1\})$ is the length of an optimal tour.

Solution: Let **g(i,s)** be the length of a shortest path starting at vertex i, going through all vertices in s and terminating at vertex 1. Then **g(1,V-{1})** is the length of the optimal sales person tour.

Using principle of Optimality:

$$g(1,V-\{1\}) = \min \ \{ \ c_{1k}+g(k,V-\{1,k\})\}$$
$$2 \leq k \leq n$$
$$\text{In general, } g(i,s) = \min \ \{ \ c_{ij}+g(j,s-\{j\})\}$$
$$j \in s$$

We know that $g(i,\phi) = c_{i1}$, $1 \leq i \leq n$. From this we can compute for $g(i,s)$ for $|s| = 1,2,\ldots,n-1$

When $|s| < n-1$, the values of i, j are $i \neq 1$, $1 \notin s$ and $I \notin s$.

Example:

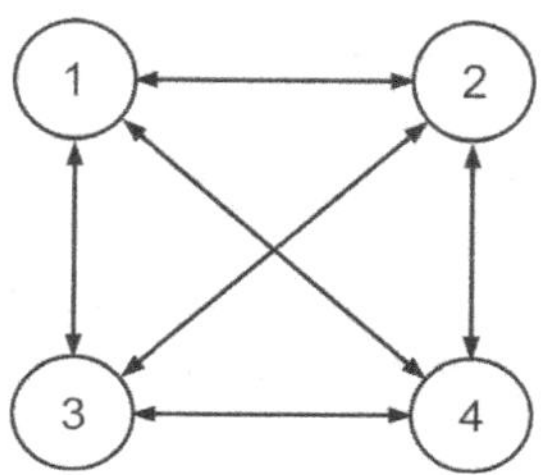

$$\begin{bmatrix} 0 & 10 & 15 & 20 \\ 5 & 0 & 9 & 10 \\ 6 & 13 & 0 & 12 \\ 8 & 8 & 9 & 0 \end{bmatrix}$$

Let $g(i, s)$ be the length of the shortest path in which we start at vertex i, visit all vertices in s and reach the vertex 1.

Therefore, the required solution is $g(1, v - \{1\})$

Let us find the optimal solutions for $|s| = 0, 1, 2,\ldots\ldots\ldots,(n-1)$.

When $|s| = 0$,

The optimal solution: $g(2, \emptyset) = C_{21} = 5$

$$g(3, \emptyset) = C_{31} = 6$$
$$g(4, \emptyset) = C_{41} = 8$$

When $|s| = 1$,

The optimal solution: $g(2, \{3\}) = C_{23} + C_{31} = 9+6 = 15$

$$g(2, \{4\}) = C_{24} + C_{41} = 10+8 = 18$$
$$g(3, \{4\}) = C_{34} + C_{41} = 12 + 8 = 20$$
$$g(3, \{2\}) = C_{32} + C_{21} = 13 + 5 = 18$$
$$g(4, \{2\}) = C_{42} + C_{21} = 8 + 5 = 13$$
$$g(4, \{3\}) = C_{43} + C_{31} = 9 + 6 = 15$$

When $|s| = 2$,

The optimal solution:

$$g(2, \{3,4\}) = \min\{ C_{23} + g(3, \{4\}), C_{24} + g(4, \{3\}) \}$$
$$= \min\{29, 25\}$$
$$= 25$$

$$g(3, \{2,4\}) = \min\{ C_{32} + g(2, \{4\}), C_{34} + g(4, \{2\}) \}$$
$$= \min\{31, 25\}$$
$$= 25$$

$$g(4, \{2,3\}) = \min\{ C_{42} + g(2, \{3\}), C_{43} + g(3, \{2\}) \}$$
$$= \min\{23, 27 \}$$
$$= 23$$

When $|s| = 3$,

The optimal solution is given by:

$$g(1, \{2, 3, 4\}) = \min\{C_{12} + g(2, \{3, 4\}), C_{13} + g(3, \{2, 4\}), C_{14} + g(4, \{2, 3\})\}$$
$$= \min\{(10+25, 15+25, 20+23)\}$$
$$= \min\{35, 40, 43\} = 35$$

Having calculated all possible g terms, we are at a position to take decisions on solving the given problem. The shortest distance of travelling sales person problem, in this example is $g(1, \{2, 3, 4\})$.

Therefore, at this stage we can take a decision to reach vertex 2 because reaching vertex 2 (from vertex 1) gives the minimum distance i.e.,

$$= \min\{C_{12} + g(2, \{3, 4\}), C_{13} + g(3, \{2, 4\}), C_{14} + g(4, \{2, 3\})\}$$
$$= \min\{(10 + 25, 15 + 25, 20 + 23)\}$$
$$= \min\{35, 40, 43\}$$
$$= 35$$

Having taken this decision to reach vertex 2, we are in a position to take the next decision. The next decision is on visiting the next vertex after v2.

As, $\{ C_{12} + g(2, \{3, 4\}) \}$ is minimum, we need to follow $g(2, \{3, 4\})$ [not $C_{13} + g(3, \{2, 4\})$ and $C_{14} + g(4, \{2, 3\})$].

By following $g(2, \{3, 4\})$ we need to visit vertex 4 after vertex 2.

As $g(2, \{3, 4\}) = \min\{ C_{23} + g(3, \{4\}), C_{24} + g(4, \{3\}) \}$
$$= \min\{29, 25\}$$
$$= 25$$

And the next decision is to visit vertex 3 because that is the only possibility and the last decision is to reach 1.

An optimal tour of the graph has a length of 35. This tour can be retained by retaining with each g(i, S) the value of j that minimizes the right hand side of the equation. Let J(i, S) be this value.

Then, J(1,{2,3,4}) = 2. Thus the tour starts from 1 and goes to 2.

J(2,{3,4}) = 4, and J(4, {3}) = 3. Hence the optimal tour is 1,2,4,3,1.

Analysis of the problem: Let N be the number of $g(i, S)$'s that have to be computed before computing $g(1,V-\{1\})$. For each value of $|s|$ there are $n-1$ choices for i. The number of distinct sets S of size k not including 1 and i is $\binom{n-2}{k}$.

$$\Rightarrow \quad N = \sum_{k=0}^{n-2} (n-1) \binom{n-2}{k} = (n-1)2^{n-2}$$

but $g(i,S)$ with $|s| = k$ requires $k-1$ comparisons

$\Rightarrow$ time complexity $= \theta(n^2,2^n)$ and space complexity $= \theta(n2^n)$.

The drawback of this algorithm is its space complexity.

5.7   RELIABILITY PROBLEM

In this problem a system is to be designed using multiplicative optimization function. System consist of several devices. Let r_i be the reliability of device D_i. Let us suppose there are three devices D_1, D_2, & D_3 having reliability 0.9 each, then the reliability of the entire system is 0.9*0.9*0.9=0.729 i.e., system will work when all three devices are working and system will fail even one device fails. Though each device reliability is high the reliability of entire system is less. Our problem is to increase the reliability of the system by duplicating devices. Multiple copies of the same device are connected in parallel by the switching circuits, they determine which devices in a group are functioning properly. At each stage they make use of one such device.

Let us suppose store i has m_i copies of device D_i, the probability that all m_i copies fail is $(1 - r_i)^{m_i}$. The reliability of store i is $1 - (1 - r_i)^{m_i}$.

Hence the reliability improve with m_i. if r_i=0.9 and m_i=2 the stage reliability becomes

$$1 - (1 - 0.9)^2 = 0.99.$$

Let us assume that the reliability of stage i is given by a function $\phi_i(m_i)$.

The reliability of the entire system is $\pi_{1\leq i\leq n}\phi_i(m_i)$.

Our problem is to maximize reliability using device duplication. As the devices are duplicated the cost of the system is also increased. The reliability maximization is to be carried out under a cost constraint.

Let C_i be the cost of each unit of device i and let C be the maximum allowable cost of the system being designed. The maximization problem is

$$\text{maximize } \pi_{1\leq i\leq n}\phi_i(m_i)$$

$$\text{subject to} \sum_{1\leq i\leq n}c_i(m_i)\leq c$$

$$m_i \geq 1 \text{ and integer, } 1\leq i\leq n$$

We use S^i to represent the set of all undominated tuples (r, c) where 'r' is reliability and 'c' is cost.

Problem: The problem is to construct a system of n types of devices D_i, $1\leq i\leq n$ with some multiplicity for each device $m_i \geq 1$, $1\leq i\leq n$ such that to maximize the reliability subject to total cost of the system $\leq c$.

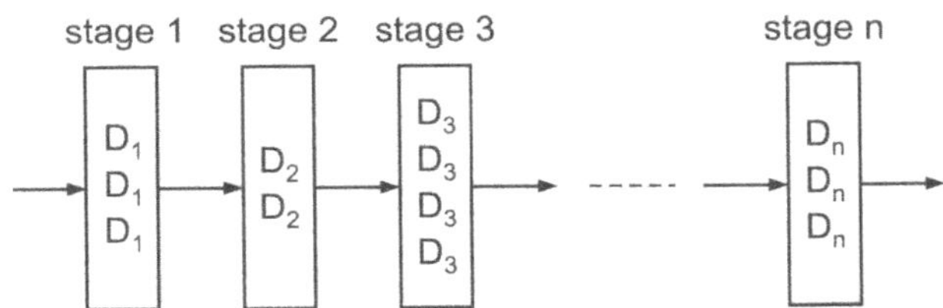

Figure 5.2 Multiple devices connected in parallel in each stage

Let r_i be the reliability of device D_i. If the multiplicity of D_i is m_i then the reliability of stage $i = 1-(1-r_i)^{m_i}$. Here reliability will improve rapidly with m_i.

Let the reliability of stage $i = \phi_i(m_i)$, $1\leq i\leq n$.

$\Rightarrow$ **Reliability of total system =** $\pi_{1\leq i\leq n}\phi_i(m_i)$

Formally the **problem is to maximize** $\pi_{1\leq i\leq n}\phi_i(m_i)$

subject to $\sum_{1\leq i\leq n}c_i(m_i)\leq c$ $m_i \geq 1$ and integer, $1\leq i\leq n$

where c_i is the cost of D_i.

Solution: This can be solved using dynamic programming technique similar to the knapsack problem. Here each $c_i > 0$. We have to find each m_i ,

$$1\leq m_i\leq u_i.$$

where u_i(upper limit to m_i) $= \lfloor (c + c_i - \sum_1^n c_j)/c_i \rfloor$

An optimal solution m_1, m_2, m_3,.....m_n is the result of a sequence of decisions, one decision for each m_i.

Let $f_i(x)$ represent the maximum value of $\Pi_{1 \leq j \leq i} \phi_j(m_j)$ subject to $\Sigma_{1 \leq j \leq i}$ $c_j m_j \leq x$ and $1 \leq m_j \leq u_j$, $1 \leq j \leq i \Rightarrow$ the value of an optimal solution is $f_n(c)$.

Using the principal of optimality:

$$f_n(c) = \max \quad \{ \phi_n(m_n) \, f_{n-1}(c - c_n m_n)\}$$

$$1 \leq m_n \leq u_n$$

for any $f_i(x)$, $i \geq 1$ this generalizes to

$$f_i(x) = \max \quad \{ \phi_i(m_i) \, f_{i-1}(x - c_i m_i)\}$$

$$1 \leq m_i \leq u_i$$

Clearly $f_0(x) = 1$ for all x, $0 \leq x \leq c$.

Let s^i consist of tuples of the form (f,x), where $f = f_i(x)$.

Let s_j^i is the set of all tuples obtainable from s^{i-1} by choosing $m_i = j$

$$\Rightarrow \quad s^i = \cup_{1 \leq j \leq uj} \, s_j^i$$

Dominance Rule: (f_1, x_1) dominates (f_2, x_2) if $f_1 \geq f_2$, $x_1 \leq x_2$.

Example: Devices $D_1, D_2, D_3 \Rightarrow n = 3$ $c_1 = 30$, $c_2 = 15$, $c_3 = 20$, $c = 105$; $r_1 = 0.9$, $r_2 = 0.8$, $r_3 = 0.5$

$$\Rightarrow \quad u_1 = \lfloor (c + c_1 - \Sigma_1^3 \, c_j)/c_1 \rfloor = \lfloor (105 + 30 - (30 + 15 + 20)/30 \rfloor = \lfloor (135 - 65)/30 \rfloor = \lfloor 75/30 \rfloor = 2$$

Similarly $u_2 = 3$, $u_3 = 3$

$s^0 = \{(1,0)\}$

$s^1 = s_1^1 \cup s_2^1 = \{(0.9,30)\} \cup \{(0.9,30),(0.99,60)\} = \{(0.9,30), (0.99,60)\}$

$s^2 = s_1^2 \cup s_2^2 \cup s_3^2 = \{(0.72,45),(0.792,75)\} \cup \{(0.864,60)\} \cup \{(0.892,75)\}$

$$= \{(0.72,45),(0.864,60),(0.892,75)\}$$

Note: As the tuple $(0.792, 75)$ has been dominated by $(0.864,60)$, $(0.792, 75)$ has been eliminated.

$s^3 = s_1^3 \cup s_2^3 \cup s_3^3 = \{(0.36,65),(0.432,80),(0.4464,95)\} \cup \{(0.54,85),(0.648,100)\}$

$$\cup \{(0.63,105)\}$$

$$= \{(0.36,65),(0.432,80),(0.54,85),(0.648,100)\}$$

back track for $m_1 = 1$, $m_2 = 2$, $m_3 = 2$.

Algorithm:

```
REL_DESIGN(C, n, c, r)
{  s⁰ = { (1,0) }
        for i=1 to n do { find uᵢ }
        for i=1 to n do
        {
                sⁱ = ∪₁≤ⱼ≤uⱼ sⱼⁱ
                sⁱ=mergepurge(sⁱ)
        }
        for i=n; i ≥1;i--)
        {       trace back mᵢ   }
}
```

Objective Question Bank

1. ______ is used for solving 0/1 knapsack problem.   [   ]

   A. $S^i = S^{i-1} + S_1^i$ B. $S^i = S^{i-1} - S_1^i$

   C. $S^i = S^{i+1} + S_1^i$ D. $S^i = S^{i+1} - S_1^i$

2. Time complexity of travelling salesperson problem is____   [   ]

   A. $O(n)$ B. $O(n^2)$

   C. $O(1)$ D. $O(2^n)$

3. If there are n nodes, the possible binary search trees are   [   ]

   A. n   B. n + 1

   C. $\dfrac{1}{n+1}2nC_n$ D. n_{c2}

4. If there are 4 nodes, the possible binary search tress are   [   ]

   A. 10   B. 5

   C. 14   D. 16

5. What is the time complexity of optimal binary search tree?   [   ]

   A. $O(n)$ B. $O(1)$

   C. $O(n^2)$ D. $O(2^n)$

6. What is the time complexity of Travelling sales person problem   [   ]

   A. $O(n^2\, 2^n)$ B. $O(1)$

   C. $O(n^2)$ D. $O(2^n)$

7. Which one of the following algorithm design techniques is used in finding all pairs of shortest distances in a graph?   [   ]

   A. Dynamic programming   B. Backtracking

   C. Greedy   D. Divide and Conquer

8. Dynamic programming is applicable when   [   ]
    A. sub problems are independent
    B. sub problems are not independent
    C. sub problems are not dependent
    D. sub problems are dependent

9. Let (a_1, a_2, a_3) = (do,if,while), $p(i) = q(i) = 1/7$ for all i. The number of possible binary search trees are____   [   ]
    A. 5   B. 4
    C. 6   D. 7

10. Cost of searching a successful identifier can be calculated in OBST is___   [   ]
    A. frequency * level   B. frequency * (level -1)
    C. frequency * (level $+1$)   D. frequency * (level $+1$) -1

11. Cost of searching an unsuccessful identifier can be calculated in OBST is____   [   ]
    A. frequency * (level -1)   B. frequency * (level $+1$)
    C. frequency * level   D. frequency * (level $+2$)

12. Mission of Travelling Sales person Problem (TSP) is ___   [   ]
    A. To determine the shortest tour.
    B. Minimize the total distance traveled.
    C. Providing *distances* between the cities.
    D. Both a & b.

13. Time Complexity of Floyd-Warshall Algorithm is_____   [   ]
    A. $O(n^3)$ B. $O(n)$
    C. $O(1)$ D. $O(\log n)$

14. Let r_i be the reliability of device D_i (that is, r_i is the probability that device i will function properly). Then, the reliability of entire system is ________   [   ]
    A. $\pi\, r_i$ B. r_i
    C. π D. None

15. Let Φ_i (m_i) be the reliability of stage i, $i \le n$ then, the reliability of system of n stages is _____.   [   ]
    A. $\pi\ \Phi_i(m_i)$ B. $\Phi_i(m_i)$
    C. $\pi\ m_i$ D. None

16. Dynamic programming follows ____ technique.   [   ]
    A. Bottom-up   B. Top-bottom
    C. Divide & conquer   D. both a & b

17. Suppose the nodes of G are numbered from 1 to n, so N = {1,2,...N},and
    suppose G matrix L gives the length of each edge, with $L(i,j) = 0$ for
    $i = 1,2...n$, $L(i,j) > =$ for all i & j, if the edge (i,j) does not exist then
    $L(i,j) = ?$.   [   ]
    A. 0   B. 1
    C. infinity   D. Null

18. MULISTAGE GRAPH problem can be solved in ____ways.   [   ]
    A. Forward Method.   B. Backward Method.
    C. Both a & b   D. None

19. The cost of a path from source (s) to destination (t) is the sum of the
    costs of the edger on the path. The *MULTISTAGE GRAPH* problem is
    to find a minimum cost path from ____.
    A. 's' to 't'   B. 't' to 's'
    C. Both a &b   D. None

20. In ________ approach, finds out the cost of each and every node
    starting from the 'k' th stage to the 1st stage.   [   ]
    A. forward   B. backward
    C. a & b   D. None

21. Travelling Sales Person problem is used to find a ________   [   ]
    A. Tour of minimum cost   B. Tour of maximum cost
    C. Cost   D. None

Fill in the Blanks

1. __________ states that in an optimal sequence of decisions, all the
   subsequences must also be optimal.

2. If there are three nodes, the possible binary search trees are ________ .

3. Let 'R' be the reliability of the device 'D'.   If we provide two 'D' in
   the system then the reliability of the device is given by the formulae
   ____

Review Questions

1. (a) What is Dynamic Programming? Explain with suitable
        illustration.

(b) You are given a list of words, W_1, W_2, W_3,..., W_n and their corresponding probabilities of occurrence $p_1, p_2, p_3, ..., p_n$. The problem is to arrange these words in a binary search tree in a way that minimizes the expected total access time. Suggest a good algorithm to implement it. Also prove the complexity of the algorithm derived by you.

R09 Set 2 December 2011

2. Devise a "binary" search algorithm that splits the set not into two sets of almost equal sizes but into two sets, one of which is twice the size of the other. How does this algorithm compare with binary search?

R09 Set 4 December 2011

3. Construct an optimal binary search tree for the following data: n=4, (a_1, a_2, a_3, a_4) = (do, if, int, while), p(1:4) = (3,3,1,1) and q(0:4) = (2,3,1,1,1).

R09 Set 4 December 2011

4. (a) Explain forward and backward approach of problem solving in Dynamic programming?

   (b) Find an optimal solution to the 0/1 knapsack instance, given n=3, weights and profits as (w_1, w_2, w_3) = (2,3,4), (p_1, p_2, p_3) = (1,2,5) and knapsack capacity = 6 generate the sets Si using dynamic programming.

R09 Set 1 December 2011

5. (a) Discuss the general method for the dynamic programming.

   (b) How the reliability of the system can be increased?

R09 Set 3 December 2011

6. (a) Define OBST. How will you construct an optimal binary search tree?

   (b) Use function OBST to compute w(i, j), r(i, j) and c(i, j), 0 < = i < j < = 4, for the identifier set (a_1, a_2, a_3, a_4) = (count, float, if, while) with p(1) = 1/20, p(2) = 1/5, p(3) = 1/10, p(4)=1/20, q(0) = 1/5, q(1) = 1/10, q(2) = 1/5, q(3) = 1/20, and q(4) = 1/20. Using the r(i, j)'s, construct the Optimal Binary Search Tree.

R09 November / December-2013

7. (a) How reliability design problem can be solved with dynamic programming? Give example.

   (b) Discuss about all pairs shortest path problem with suitable example.

R09 June-2014

8. (a) Solve the following 0/1 Knapsack problem using dynamic programming $P = (11, 21, 31, 33)$, $W = (2, 11, 22, 15)$, $C = 40$, $n = 4$.

    (b) Consider three stages of a system with $r_1 = 0.3$, $r_2 = 0.5$, $r_3 = 0.2$ and $c_1 = 30$, $c_2 = 20$, $c_3 = 30$. Where the total cost of the system is $C = 80$ and $u_1 = 2$, $u_2 = 3$, $u_3 = 2$ find the reliability design.

R09 May-2013

9. Derive the recurrence equation used in Optimal Binary Search Tree Problem. With an example explain how to compute all $c(i,j)$, $w(i,j)$ and $r(i,j)$.

R09 December-January, 2011-2012

10. Write the pseudocode of a simpler version of Dijkstra's algorithm that finds only the distances (i.e., the lengths of shortest paths but not shortest paths themselves) from a given vertex to all other vertices of a graph represented by its weight matrix.

R09 December-January, 2011-2012

11. How would you construct an optimal binary search tree for a set of n keys if all the keys are equally likely to be search for? What will be the average number of comparisons in the tree if $n = 2k$.

R09 December-January, 2011-2012

12. Discuss the dynamic programming solutions for the problems of
     (a) Reliability design
     (b) Traveling salesperson problem.

$$6$$

BACKTRACKING

6.1 THE GENERAL METHODS

Backtracking is one of the most general algorithm design techniques. The backtracking algorithms are used for obtaining an optimal solution satisfying some constraints. The desired solution must be expressible as an n-tuple $(x_1 \ldots x_n)$ where x_i is chosen from some finite set S_i. It is used to find a vector which maximizes or minimizes a criterion function $P(x_1 \ldots x_n)$. The advantage of the backtracking algorithm is once we know that a partial vector $(x_1, \ldots x_i)$ will not lead to an optimal solution that $(m_{i+1} \ldots \ldots \ldots m_n)$ possible test vectors may be ignored entirely. Backtracking is an application of recursion. While solving a problem, a guess made can go wrong, so to make next move we may backup and try again. Implementation of backtracking becomes easy by using recursion, because stack is maintained by recursion.

The solution for a backtracking problem can be represented by a tree on which a modified depth first search is performed to provide one or all possible solutions to the given problem. The solutions to the problems that are to be solved by the backtracking technique may require to satisfy a complex set of constraints. The constraints are classified into two types of categories, they are:

(i) Explicit constraints

(ii) Implicit constraints

(i) Explicit constraints: The rules that restrict each X_i to take values only from a given set are called as explicit constraints.

Examples:

$X_i \geq 0$ or $S_i = \{\text{all non-negative real nos.}\}$

$X_i = 0$ or 1 or $S_i = \{0, 1\}$

$L_i \leq X_i \leq U_i$ or $S_i = \{a: L_i \leq a \leq U_i\}$

(ii) Implicit constraints: The rules that determine which of the tuples in the solution space I can actually satisfy the criterion functions are called as implicit constraints.

Algorithm Backtrack(k)

```
// A recursive backtracking procedure is described. On
//entering, the first k-1 values
 // x[1], x[2],…., x[k-1] of the solution vector x[1:n]
//have been assigned. X[] and n //are global.
{
    for (each x[k] ∈ T(x[1],…..,x[k-1]) do
    {
       if(B_k(x[1], x[2],….,x[k]≠ 0) then
       {
          if(x[1],x[2],…,x[k] is a path to an answer node)
             then write(x[1:k]);
          if(k<n) then Backtrack(k+1);
       }
    }
}
```

Algorithm IBacktracking(n)

```
// A backtracking procedure is described. All solutions
//are generated in X[1:n]
//and printed as soon as they are determined.
 {
    k=1;
    While (k≠0) do
    {
if (there remains all untried
      X[k]∈T(X[1],[2],…..X[k-1])and   B_k   (X[1],…..X[k])
is true ) then
      {
if(X[1],……X[k] )is the path to the answer node)
       Then write(X[1:k]);
       k=k+1;              //consider the next step.
    }
else k=k-1; //consider backtracking to the previous set.
 }
}
```

T(X[1]…..X[k–1]) is all possible values of X[k] gives that X[1],……..X[k–1] have already been chosen. All solutions are generated in X[1:n] and printed as soon as they are determined. B_k(X[1]………X[k]) is a boundary function which determines the elements of X[k] which satisfies the implicit constraint.

The efficiency of the above backtracking algorithms depends on the following four factors: (i) the time to generate the next x_k, (ii) the number of x_k satisfying the explicit constraints, (iii) the time for the bounding functions B_k, and (iv) the number of x_k satisfying the B_k.

The problems which are solved using backtracking method are:

(a) N-Queens problem

(b) Sum of subsets

(c) Graph coloring

(d) Hamiltonian cycle

6.2 N-QUEENS PROBLEM

The n-queens problem is to place n-queens on an nXn chessboard in such a way that no two queens attack each other i.e., no 2 queens to be placed on same row, same column and same diagonal. For writing an algorithm to solve n-queens problem the input is 'n' & output is n-tuple.

Solution: The solution vector X ($X_1...X_n$) represents a solution in which X_i is the column of the ith row where ith queen is placed. First, check if any two queens are in same row next check that no two queens are in same column. The function, which is used to check these two conditions, is [i, X (j)], which gives position of the ith queen, where i represents the row and X (j) represents the column position. We have to check no two queens are in it diagonal. If two queens are in positions (i, j) and (k, 1) then two queens lie on the same diagonal, if and only if $|j–1|=|i–k|$.

For example when n = 4, then the problem becomes 4-Queen problem and for n = 8 then the problem becomes 8-Queen problem.

6.2.1 4-Queens Problem

The 4-queens problem is to place 4-queens on an 4 × 4 chessboard in such a way that no two queens attack each other. The solution to 4- queen problem is shown in the Figure 6.1.

The output is x = (2, 4, 1, 3) and this vector x indicates the positions of 4-queens as shown in Figure 6.1. To solve n-queens problem using brute force approach requires the testing of n!, n-tuples. For 4-queen problem where n = 4, 24, 4-tuples are to be tested. Therefore this approach has a time complexity of O(n!) and this time complexity is not practically acceptable. We solve this problem by systematically searching for a solution in a solution space.

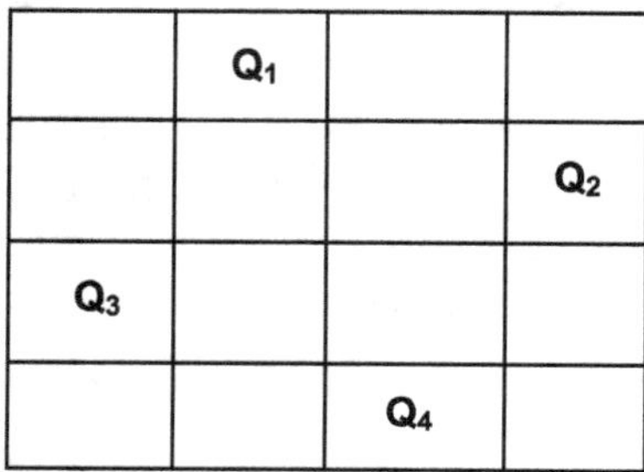

Figure 6.1

Solution space for the n-queens problem when n = 4 is give below

(1,2,3,4)}

(1,2,4,3)} 4!(4-tuples)

.

.

.

.

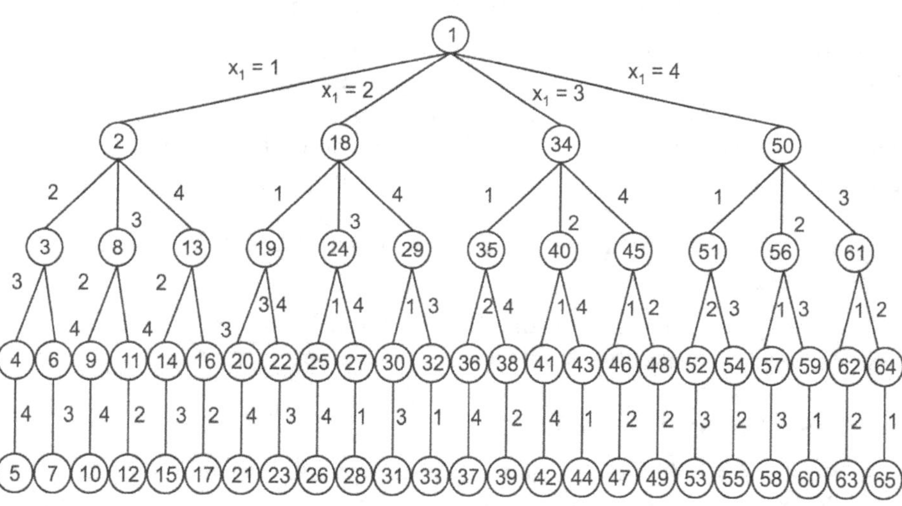

Figure 6.2

Backtracking approach: The above tree has two types of nodes they are (i) Promising nodes (ii) Non promising nodes. Promising node is a node that indicates there is a chance of finding an answer by proceeding further. Whereas non promising node is a node from which when we proceed there is no chance of reaching an answer node.

For example node 3 in the Figure 6.2 is a non-promising node, we reach node 3 from root via node 2. Reaching from node 1 to node 2 is represented in partial solution vector as X=(1,-,-,-), then move to node 3 updates the partial vector as X=(1,2,-,-). This partial vector indicates that first queen at cell (1,1) & second queen at cell (2,2) as shown in figure 6.3.

<table>
<tr><td>Q_1</td><td></td><td></td><td></td></tr>
<tr><td></td><td>Q_2</td><td></td><td></td></tr>
<tr><td></td><td></td><td></td><td></td></tr>
<tr><td></td><td></td><td></td><td></td></tr>
</table>

Figure 6.3

Irrespective of the elements x_3, x_4 the partial vector can't lead to an answer. Therefore once we reach a non promising node instead of proceeding, we back track (because if we proceed there are no chances of reaching a solution). Therefore we back track from node 3. Backtracking from node 3 has an advantage of skipping the two permutations efficiently. For backtracking the bounding function is used. The tree in Figure 6.2 gives the solution space for the given problem for a 4 queen problem we have 24, 4-tuples vectors. The first vector is given by a path from root node or node-1 to node-5 (node 5 is a leaf node). The second vector is given by the path from root node or node-1 to node 7 and so on. By searching this tree (figure 6.2) using DFS we construct vector 'x' element by element. When one element is added to vector x, we test whether proceeding in this direction has a chance of leading to the solution. If we find that there is no chance of leading to this solution we back track from that node.

Steps to generate the solution:

1. Initialize x array to zero.

2. Place first queen in k = 1 in the first row.

3. To find the column position start from value 1 to n.

4. If k = 1 then x (k) = 1. So (k, x(k)) will give the position of the kth queen. Here we have to check whether there is any queen in the same column or diagonal.

   X (i) = X(k) for column

   $|X(i) - X(k)| = (i-k)$ for the same diagonal.

5. If any one of the conditions is true then return false indicating that k^{th} queen can't be placed in position X (k).

6.   If the condition fails, increment X (k) value by one and proceed until the position is found.

7.   If the position X (k) $\leq$ n and k = n then the solution is generated completely.

8.   If k < n, then increment the 'k' value and find position of the next queen.

9.   If the position X (k) > n then k^{th} queen cannot be placed as the size of the matrix is 'N*N'.

10.   So decrement the 'k' value by one i.e., we have to backtrack and after the position of the previous queen.

Example:

4 queens: Two possible solutions are

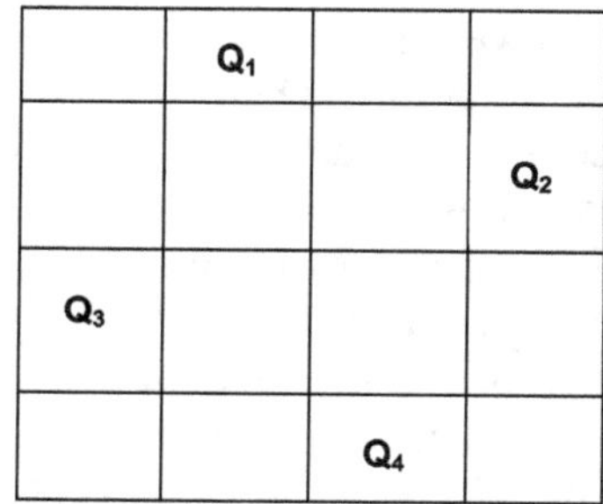

Figure 6.4

Algorithm place (k, i)

```
//return true if a queen can be placed in kth row and ith
//column otherwise it returns false. X[ ] is a global
//array whose first k-1 values have been set. Abs(n)
//returns the //absolute value of n.
{
   for j=1 to k-1 do
      If ((X [j]=i) //two queens in same column.
      Or (abs (X [j]-i)=abs (j-k)))
then return false;
return true;
}
Algorithm Nqueen (k, n)
```

```
//using backtracking it prints all possible positions of
//n queens in 'n*n' chessboard. So that they are non-
//tracking.
{
     for i=1 to n do
         {
             if place (k, i) then
                {
                    X[k]=i;
                     if (k=n) then write (X[1:n]);
                      else nqueens(k+1,n)     ;
                }
         }
}
```

6.2.2 Tracing of Solution to 4-queen Problem

The problem is to place 4 queens in a non attacking mode on a 4 × 4 chess board. So we have to place 4 queens in four different rows. Each row should accommodate one queen, therefore we place queen1 (Q_1) in first row, Q_2 in second row, Q_3 in third row and Q_4 in fourth row. First we place Q_1 in first column as shown in Figure 6.5 (a) and the same is shown in Figure 6.6 as move from node 1 to node 2. Now we start placing Q_2 in second row, fist we try to place Q_2 in first column it is not possible as Q_1 is in first column then

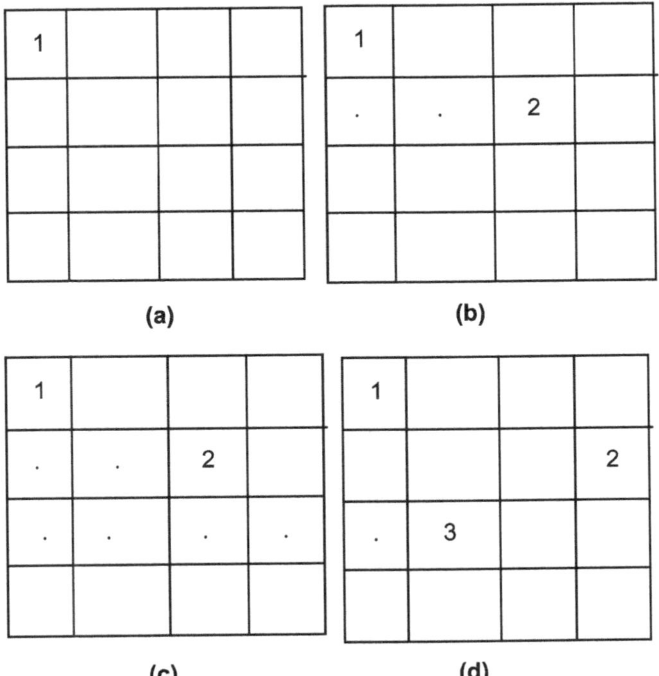

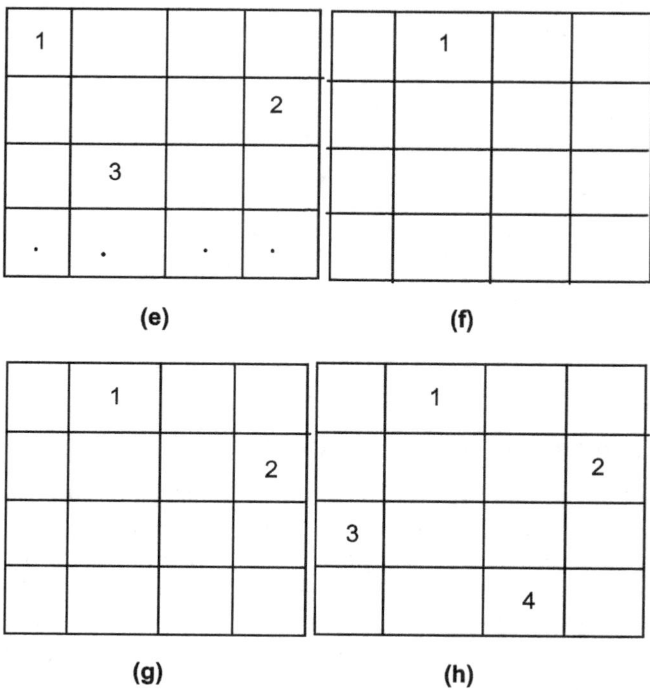

Figure 6.5(a, b, c, d, e, f, g, h)

we try to place Q_2 in second column this is also not possible because Q_1 and Q_2 are on the same diagonal, therefore Q_2 is placed in third column as shown in Figure 6.5 (b) and the same is shown in Figure 6.6 as move from node 2 to node 8. Now we start placing Q_3 in third row and it is not possible as shown in Figure 6.5 (c). So proceeding further is waist i.e., no need to try to place queens in fourth row because we cannot place 4- queens on the board. Now we backtrack and try to place Q_2 in next column i.e., fourth column as shown in Figure 6.5 (d).

Now we try to place Q_3 in third row, first we look at first column it fails then we try to place it in second column. Q_3 is placed in second column successfully as shown in Figure 6.5(d) same thing is shown by an edge from node 13 to node 14 in Figure 6.6.

Now we try to place Q_4 in fourth row and it is not successful. So we cannot place Q_4 in fourth row as shown in figure 6.5(e). Same thing is shown by an edge from node 14 to node 15 in figure 6.6. We go back and try to explore another possibility for Q_3 i.e., we try to place Q_3 in 3rd column and it is failed due to the bounding function i.e., Q_2 and Q_3 are on the same diagonal as shown try an edge from node 13 to node 16 in Figure 6.6. Now we go to back and try to explore another possibility for Q_3 and there is no other possibility. Now we further go back and explore another possibility for

Q_2. This process of going back and exploring all possibilities is called Back Tracking. After back tracking there are no other possibilities for Q_2, again we backtrack and try other possibility for Q_1. Q_1 is placed in 2nd column as shown in Figure 6.5(f) and the same is represented by an edge from node 1 to node 18. Q_2 is tried in first 3 columns and it is failed, finally Q_2 is placed in 4th column as shown in figure 6.5(g). Q_3 is placed in first column and Q_4 is placed in 3rd column as shown in figure 6.5(h) and same thing is shown by an edge from node 18 to node 29 and node 30 to node 31 in figure 6.6. A part of figure 6.2 that is generated is shown in figure 6.6. The numbering of nodes in figure 6.6 are taken from figure 6.2. A node that is killed by a bounding function has B under it. If two Queens are on the same diagonal are eliminated by bounding function.

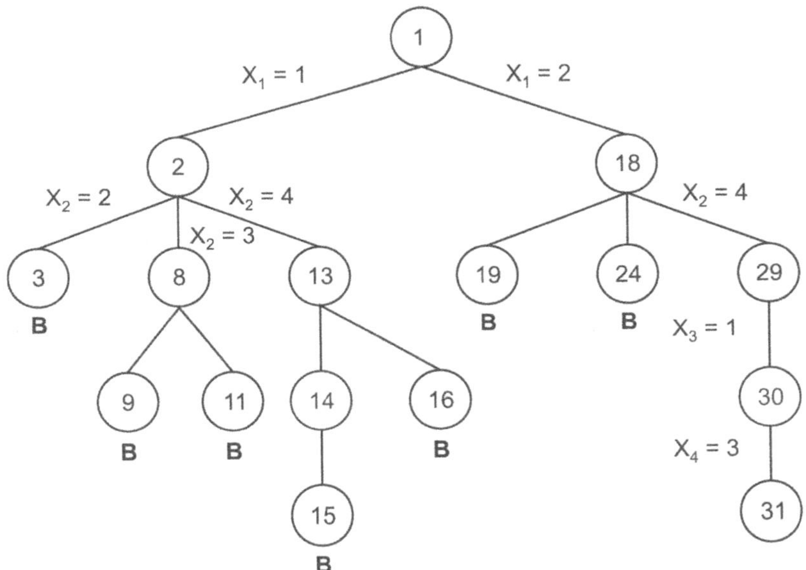

Figure 6.6

The solution to back tracking algorithm are found by systematically searching the solution space for the given problem instance for a solution space. This systematic search is done with the help of tree organization.

Terminology of tree organization: A problem state is defined by each node of the tree organization. The state space of the problem is defined by all paths from the root to other nodes. Any node S for which the path from the root to S defines a tuple in the solution space is called solution state. If this solution state satisfies implicit constraint of the problem then they are called answer states. State space tree is the tree organization of the solution space. Tree organization that are independent of problem instances are called static trees, if they are dependent of problem instances they are called dynamic trees. A generated node, whose children are not yet generated is called live node. The live node whose children are currently generated is called E–Node. A generated node, all of whose children are already generated is called dead node.

There are two ways of generating nodes i.e., problem states. They are (i) back tracking (ii) branch and bound. In back tracking method a new child X of the current E-node Y is generated, this child node X becomes E-node after it is fully explored again node Y becomes E-node. In branch and bound technique an E-node remain as E-node until it becomes dead node. Bounding functions are used in both methods to kill live nodes without generating all children nodes. In back tracking method nodes are generated using depth first search with bounding functions.

6.2.3 8-Queen Problem

The 8-queens problem is to place 8-queens on an 8×8 chessboard in such a way that no two queens attack each other.

Monte carlo method is used to estimate the number of nodes that are going to be generated by a back tracking algorithm. In this process of estimation, a random path Y is generated in the state space tree. The number of children n_i that do not get bounded are determined by the bounding function. One of these n_i children is randomly selected and is identical as the next node of the path. Once we reach terminal node or there is no child node that do not get bounded i.e., n_i becomes zero at that node the path generation terminates. Using these n_i one can estimate the total number of nodes m in the state space tree that will not get bounded. When we are searching all answer nodes. This number M is very useful. In the solution of a given problem instance 'i' the estimated number of nodes is m and is given by

$$M = 1 + n_1 + n_1 * n_2 + n_1 * n_2 * n_3 + \text{------}$$

	1						
		2					
3							
		4					
			5				

$(8,5,4,3,2) = 1649$

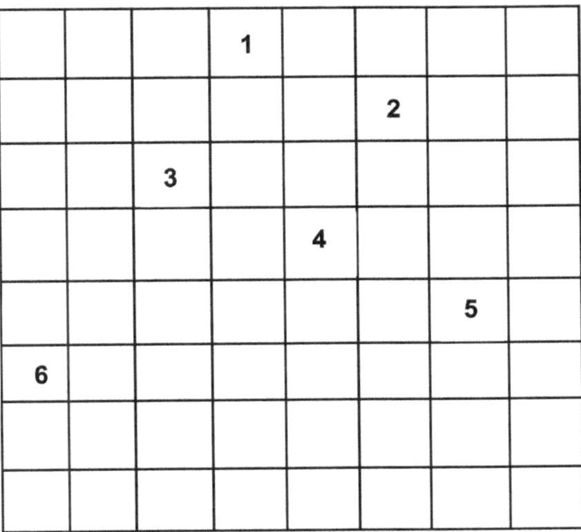

(8,5,3,1,2,1) = 769

Figure 6.7(a)& (b)

The above function estimate can be used to estimate the number of nodes generated by the 8-queen problem. Using the function estimate function 8×8 chess boards are created as shown in Figure 6.7. The placement of each queen on the chess board was chosen randomly. The first queen can be placed in 8 different ways in the first row. Let us assume 6, is placed in 2nd column. Now Q_2 can be placed in any of the 5 positions (4, 5, 6, 7, 8) in second row. Among these randomly we have selected 4th column as shown in Figure 6.7(a).

Q_3 can be placed in any of the four positions i.e., (1, 6, 7, 8) among these randomly we have chosen column 1 and Q_3 is placed in column 1. Q_4 can be placed in three positions i.e., (3, 7, 8) among these randomly we have chosen column 3 and Q_4 is placed in column 3. Q_5 can be placed in two positions i.e., (5, 8) among the two positions randomly we have chosen column 5 and Q_5 is placed in column 5. There is no place for Q_6. So algorithm estimate terminates, so the number of nodes generated are:

$$1 + 8 * 5 + 8 * 4 * 5 + 8 * 5 * 4 * 3 + 8 * 5 * 4 * 3 * 2$$

$$=1 + 40 + 160 + 480 + 960$$

$$=1649 \text{ as shown in Figure 6.7(a).}$$

Similarly for Figure 6.7(b) number of nodes generated is 769, for figure 6.7(c) number of nodes generated are 1401 and for figure 6.7(d) number of nodes generated are 2329.

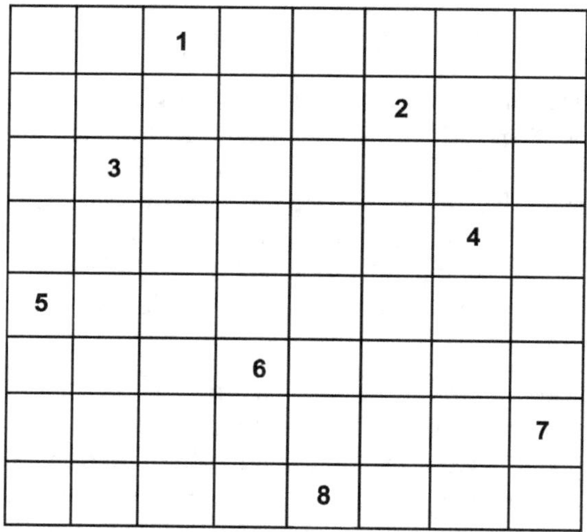

(8,6,4,2,1,1,1) = 1401

(8,5,3,2,2,1,1,1) = 2329

Figure 6.7(c)&(d)

6.3 SUM OF SUBSETS

In sum of subsets problem, n positive numbers called weights are given and we need to find all combinations of these numbers whose sum is M. The explicit constraint requires $x_i \in \{ j \mid j$ is an integer and $1 \leq j \leq n\}$. The implicit constraints require that no two solutions be the same and the sum of the corresponding weights must be equal to m. The solution of sum of subset problem can be expressed in two ways. They are fixed tuple size solution and variable tuple size solution.

Example: If n = 4, (w_1, w_2, w_3, w_4) = (11, 13, 24, 7) and m = 31

The derived solution is (11, 13, 7) and (24, 7).

Using variable tuple size solution the two solutions are given as (1, 2, 4) and (3, 4) indicating in the first solution 1st, 2nd and 4th objects are selected and in the second solution 3rd and 4th objects are selected.

Using fixed tuple size solution the two solutions are given as (1, 1, 0, 1) and (0, 0, 1, 1). Objects selected are represented by 1 and not selected are represented by 0. The solution for a given problem instance are determined by the back tracking algorithm by systematically searching the solution space. This search is done by using a tree organization for the solution space. The variable tuple size formulation for n = 4 is shown in figure 6.8 and nodes are numbered as Depth first Search. There are 16 possible solution i.e., 2^4. One among them is ( ), this corresponds to empty path the root itself. The possible solutions are: ( ), (1), (1, 2), (1, 2, 3), (1, 2, 3, 4), (1, 2, 4), (1, 3), (1, 3, 4), (1, 4), (2), (2, 3), (2, 3, 4), (2, 4), (3),(3, 4), (4). The number of nodes generated by the tree equal to number of possible solutions i.e., 16 as shown in Figure 6.8.

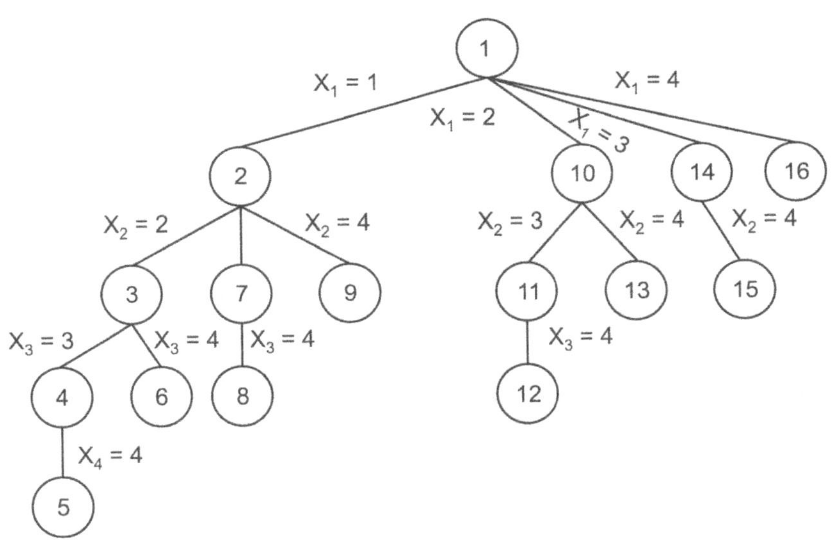

Figure 6.8

The fixed tuple size formulation for n = 4 is shown in Figure 6.9. The nodes at depth 1 are for item 1, nodes at depth 2 are for item 2 and so on. The tree in Figure 6.9 is a full binary tree each node has two children. The left child of the node includes corresponding item and the right child of the root excludes the item. All paths from the root to a terminal node define the solution space. There are 16 possible solutions i.e. 2^4 leaf nodes. Total number of nodes are 31.

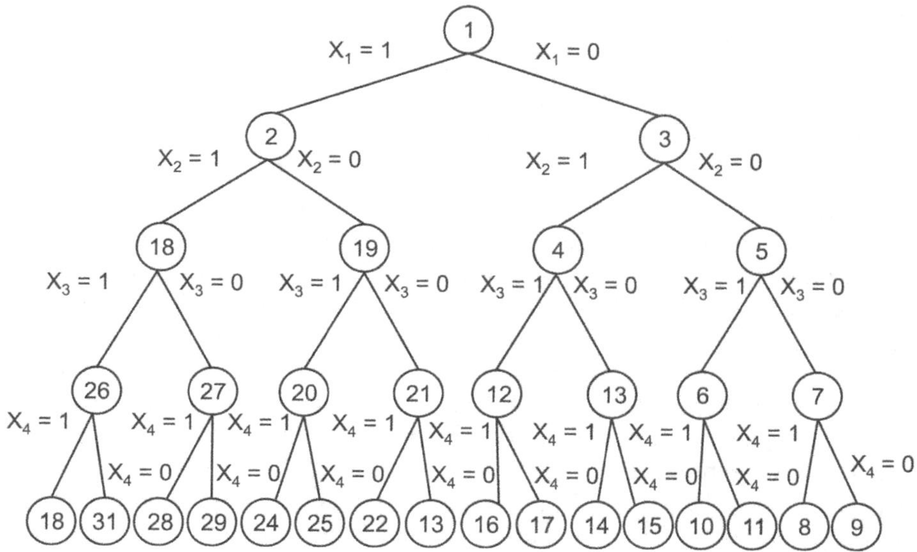

Figure 6.9

A backtracking solution for sum of subset problem using fixed tuple size strategy is given below. In the solution vector element x_i is one if weight w_i is included otherwise x_i is zero. Initially all w_i's are arranged in non decreasing order.

The bounding function is:

$$B_k(x_1,...,x_k) = \Sigma_{i=1}^{k} W_i X_i + \Sigma_{i=k+1}^{n} W_i \geq m$$

and $\Sigma_{i=1}^{k} W_i X_i + W_{k+1} \leq m$

In fixed tuple strategy, the elements x(i) of the solution vector is either 1 or 0 depending on if the weight W(i) is included or not.

Note: In the state space tree of the solution, for a node at level i, the left child corresponds to X(i)=1 and right to X(i) = 0.

Example: Given n = 6, M = 30 and W(1...6) = (5,10,12,13,15,18).

We have to generate all possible combinations of subsets whose sum is equal to the given value M = 30. In state space tree of the solution the rectangular node lists the values of s, k, r; where s is the sum of subsets, 'k' is the iteration and 'r' is the sum of elements after 'k' in the original set.

The state space tree for the above problem is shown in Figure 6.10.

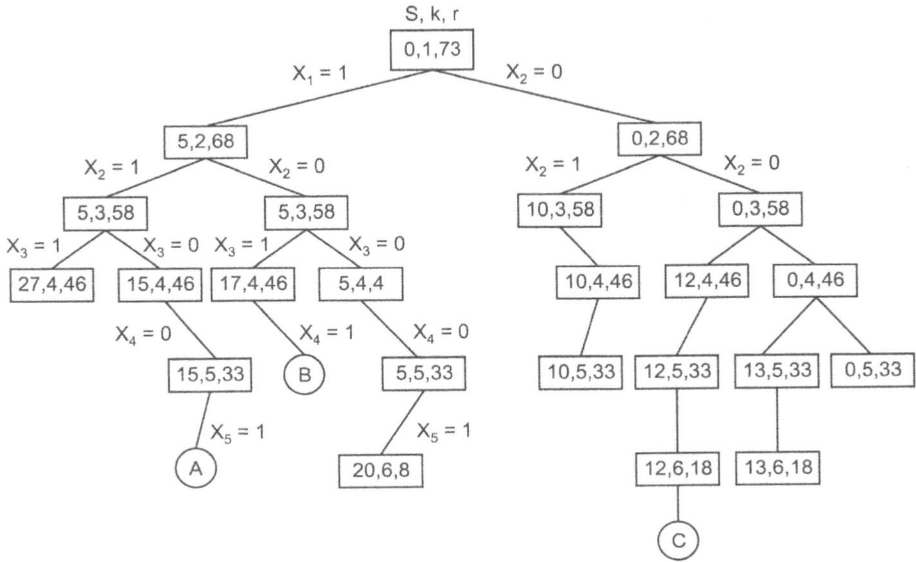

Figure 6.10

There are three solutions for the above problem:

1st solution is A → 1 1 0 0 1 0

2nd solution is B → 1 0 1 1 0 0

3rd solution is C → 0 0 1 0 0 1

In the tree, Edges from level 'i' nodes to 'i+1' nodes are labeled with the values of X_i, which is either 0 or 1. The left sub tree of the root defines all subsets containing W_i. The right subtree of the root defines all subsets, which does not include W_i.

Algorithm sum of sub set has 3 parameters s, k, r, where s is the sum of selected items, k is the iteration number and r is the sum of remaining items. In each iteration an item is considered sequentially it may be selected or not if it is selected its weight is added to sum otherwise not after the iteration the weight is deducted from parameter r. Initially of root s, k, r value are (0, 1, 73) where 73 is the sum of all items. At level 2 first item is selected or not selected then the tuple is (5, 2, 68) and (0, 2, 68) respectively. At third level the tuples are (15, 3, 68), (5, 3, 68), (10, 3, 68) and (0, 3, 68). Similarly at level four the tuples are (27, 4, 46), (15, 4, 46), (17, 4, 46), (5, 4, 46), (10, 4, 46), (12, 4, 46), (0, 4, 46). For the tuple (10, 3, 58) only one child is generated i.e., (10, 4, 46), other child is not generated due to the bounding function. If that item is selected then 'S' will be become 22 and the weight of next item will be greater than 12 then 'S' value will be greater than 34 which is greater than 30 i.e., ' M' value. So this is a non-promising node that's why they are not generated by the bounding function. Therefore the tuple (10, 3, 58) has only one child. Similarly the tuple (15, 4, 46), (5, 4, 46), (10, 4, 46), (12, 4, 46) has one child and other childs are killed by bounding function. In the figure 6.10 the circular nodes represents the subsets with sum 'M'. The circular nodes are A, B and C. The output is (11001), (1011), (001001). Number of nodes generated in the above tree using bounding function are 23 as shown in the Figure 6.10 where as the full state space tree without bounding function contains 63 nodes.

Generation of state space tree:

1. An array X is maintained.

2. The value of X_i indicates whether the weight W_i is included or not.

3. Initialize sum to zero i.e., s = 0.

4. Check each node starting from the first node.

5. Assign X(k) ← 1.

6. If S + X(k) = M then we print the subset because the sum is the required output.

7. If the above condition is not satisfied then check S + X(k) + W(k + 1) <= M. If so, we have to generate the left sub tree. It means W(t) can be included so the sum will be incremented and we have to check for the next k.

8. Now right sub tree is to be generated. For this the condition is S + W(k + 1)<= M. Because W(k) is omitted and W(k + 1) has to be selected.

9. Repeat the process and find all the possible combinations of the subset.

Algorithm sumofsubset(s, k, r)

```
{
//generate the left child. Note s+w(k)<=M since Bk-1 is
//true.
X[k]=1;
If   (S+W[k]=m)   then   write(X[1:k]);   //   there   is   no
//recursive call here as W[j]>0,1<=j<=n.
Else   if   (S+W[k]+W[k+1]<=m)   then   sum   of   sub   (S+W[k],
k+1,r- W[k]);
//generate right child and evaluate Bk.
If ((S+ r- W[k]>=m)and(S+ W[k+1]<=m)) then
{
X{k]=0;
sum of sub (S, k+1, r- W[k]);
}
}
```

6.4 GRAPH COLORING

If all vertices of graph G can be colored using *m* colors in such a way that no two adjacent vertices will have the same color, then the graph G is said to be *m-colorable*. The problem of assigning colors to every vertex is termed as *'m-colorability decision problem'*. A graph G containing *n* vertices can always be colored using n colors, But, yet there may be a smaller $m(m<n)$ such that using *m*, G can be colored. The smallest possible integer m is called as the *chromatic number* of G. The problem of finding the chromatic number of a graph is termed as *'m-colorability optimization problem'*.

Example: The following graph shown in Figure 6.11 can be colored using the colors 1, 2 and 3. One can also observe that it can not be colored using less than 3 colors. Hence chromatic number of that graph is 3.

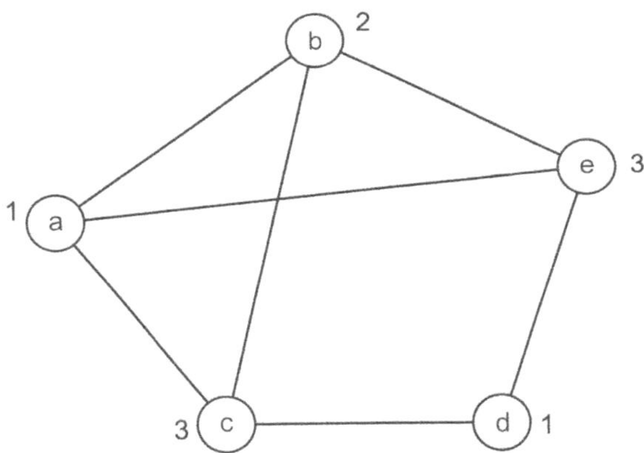

Figure 6.11 An example of a graph and it's coloring

Problem: The problem is to determine all the different ways in which a given graph can be colored using at most *m* colors.

Solution: Let G[1:n, 1:n] be the adjacency matrix of the graph G where G[i,j] = 1 if (i,j) is an edge of G, and G[i,j] = 0 otherwise. The colors are represented by the integers 1, 2, 3, 4,....,m and the solutions are given by the n-tuple $(x_1, x_2, ... x_n)$, where x_i is the color of node i. Using the recursive formulation of the backtracking, the algorithm for this problem is given below.

Algorithm for finding all *m-colorings* of a graph with *n* vertices: The following recursive backtracking algorithm uses boolean adjacency matrix G[1:n, 1:n] to represent a Graph, the vertices of the graph are numbered such that adjacent vertices are assigned distinct integers are printed.

Algorithm mColoring(k)

```
{
    repeat
    { // Generate all legal assignments for x[k].
       NextValue(k); // Assign to x[k] a legal color.
    if(x[k]=0) then return;   // No new color possible.
    if(k=n) then  // At most m colors have been used to
color the n vertices.
       write(x[1:n]);
          else mColoring(k+1);
          } until(false);
}
```

In the following algorithm $x[1],....,x[k-1]$ have been assigned integer values in the range $[1,m]$ such that adjacent vertices have distinct integers. A value for $x[k]$ is determined in the range $[0,m]$. $x[k]$ is assigned the next highest numbered color while maintaining distinctness from the adjacent vertices of vertex k. If no such color exists, then $x[k]$ is 0.

Algorithm NextValue(k)

```
{
    repeat
      {
        x[k]:=(x[k] + 1) mod (m+1); // Next highest color.
        if(x[k]=0)then return;//All colors have been used.
          for j:=1 to n do
            {
                // Check if this color is distinct from
                //the adjacent colors
              if((G[k,j] != 0) and (x[k]=x[j])) then
                  break;
              // If (k,j) is an edge and if adjacent
              //vertices have the same color.
            }
          if(j=n+1) then return; // New color found.
          } until (false);
}
```

Function m-coloring is begun by first assigning the graph to its adjacency matrix, *setting the array x[] to zero,* and then invoking the statement *m-coloring(1).* The time complexity of graph coloring is $O(nm^n)$.

Consider a map with five regions and its graph shown in Figure 6.12.

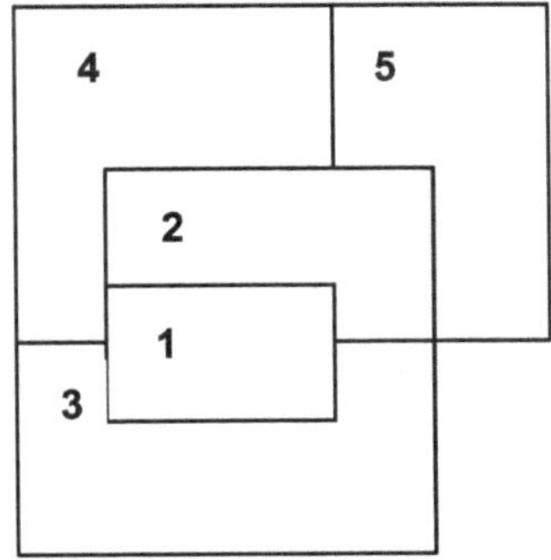

Figure 6.12

1 is adjacent to 2, 3, 4

2 is adjacent to 1, 3, 4, 5

3 is adjacent to 1, 2, 4

4 is adjacent to 1, 2, 3, 5

5 is adjacent to 2, 4

Graph of Figure 6.12 is redrawn in Figure 6.13

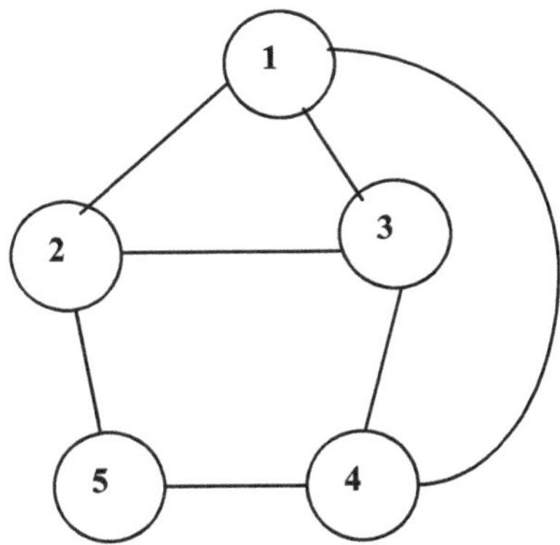

Figure 6.13

Steps to color:

1. Create the adjacency matrix graph(1:m,1:n) for a graph.

2. If there is an edge between i, j then $C(i, j) = 1$ otherwise $C(i, j) = 0$.

3. The Colors will be represented by the integers 1,2,…..m and the solutions will be stored in the array $X(1)$, $X(2)$,…………, $X(n)$, X(index) is the color, index is the node.

4. The formula used to set the color is $X(k) = (X(k) + 1) \% (m + 1)$

5. First one chromatic number is assigned, after assigning a number for 'k' node, we have to check whether the adjacent nodes has got the same values if so then we have to assign the next value.

6. Repeat the procedure until all possible combinations of colors are found.

7. The function which is used to check the adjacent nodes and same color is,   if((Graph (k,j) == 1) and X(k) = X(j))

Example:

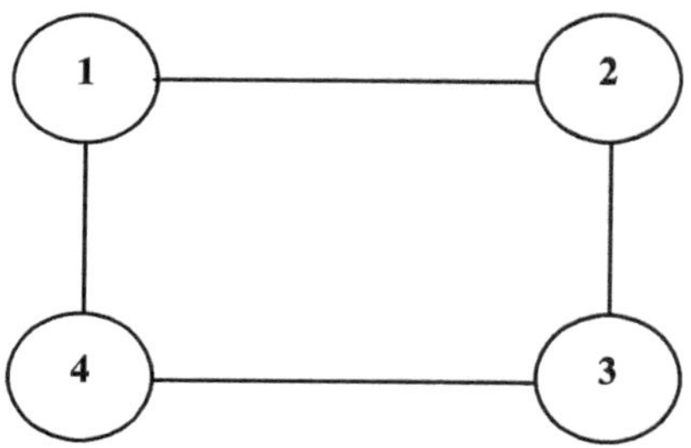

N = 4

M = 3

$$\text{Adjacency Matrix:} \begin{bmatrix} 0 & 1 & 0 & 1 \\ 1 & 0 & 1 & 0 \\ 0 & 1 & 0 & 1 \\ 1 & 0 & 1 & 0 \end{bmatrix}$$

Problem is to color the given graph of 4 nodes using 3 colors. The above graph can be colored using two colors also.

State Space Tree: In the state space tree the numbers in the nodes are the vertices of the graph where as the weights of the edges are the colors. In the tree we have three different weights they are 1, 2, and 3. Node 1 can be colored with any of the three colors 1, 2 and 3 as shown in the tree (Figure 6.14). If node 1 is colored with color 1 then node 2 can be colored with either color 2 or color 3. Similarly if node 1 is colored with color 2 then node 2 can be colored with either color 1 or color 3. In the state space tree at level 1 different possibilities for node1 are shown, at level 2 different possibilities for node 2 are shown, at level 3 different possibilities for node 3 are shown, at level 4 different possibilities for node 4 are shown.

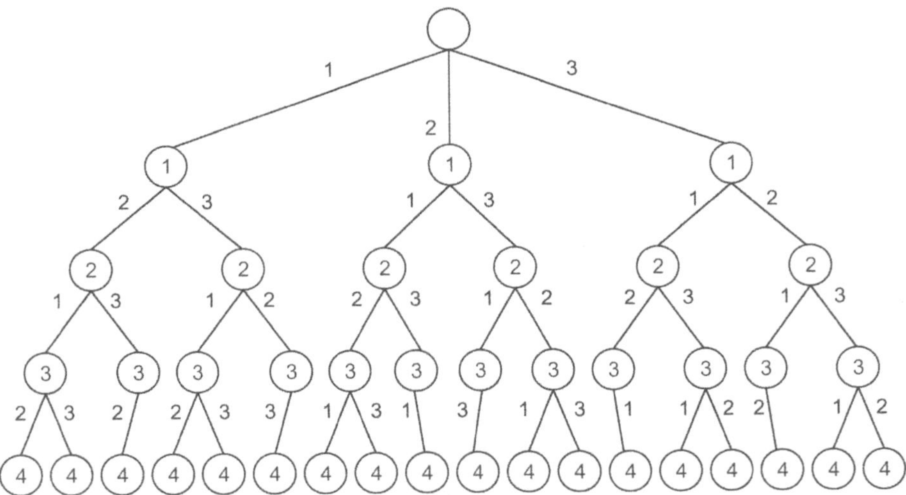

Figure 6.14

6.5 HAMILTONIAN CYCLES

A Hamiltonian cycle is a closed path that includes every vertex exactly once. Let $G = (V,E)$ be a connected graph with 'n' vertices.

Consider an example graph G1.

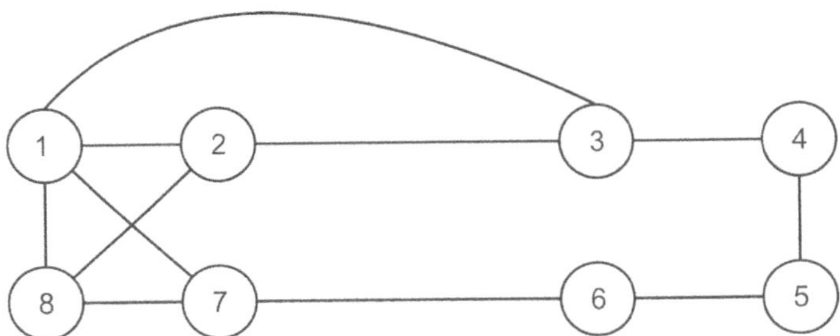

The above graph has two Hamilton cycles:

1, 3, 4,5,6,7,8,2,1 and

1,2,8,7,6,5,4,3,1.

The backtracking algorithm can be used to find the Hamilton cycle of any graph.

Procedure:

1. Define a solution vector $X(X_i........X_n)$ where X_i represents the ith visited vertex of the proposed cycle.

2. Create a cost adjacency matrix for the given graph.

3. The solution array should be initialized to all zeros except $X(1) = 1$, because the cycle should start at vertex '1'.

4. Now the second vertex to be visited in the cycle should be found.

5. The vertex from 1 to n are included in the cycle one by one by checking the following two conditions

6. There should be a path from previous visited vertex to current vertex.

7. The current vertex must be distinct and should not have been visited earlier.

8. When the above two conditions are satisfied the current vertex is included in the cycle, else the next vertex is tried.

9. When the nth vertex is visited we have to check, is there any path from nth vertex to first 8 vertices. If no path, then go back one step and after the previous visited node, repeat the above steps to generate possible Hamiltonian cycle.

The below algorithm is used to find all Hamiltonian cycle.

Algorithm Hamiltonian (k)

```
{
Loop
   Next value (k)
if (x (k)=0) then return;
{
   if k=n then
       Print (x)
else
Hamiltonian (k+1);
end if
}
repeat
}
Algorithm Nextvalue (k)
{
 repeat
{
   X [k]=(X [k]+1) mod (n+1); //next vertex
   if (X [k]=0) then return;
   if (G [X [k-1], X [k]] ≠0) then
```

```
{
   for j=1 to k-1 do if (X [j]=X [k]) then break;
   // Check for distinction.
   if (j=k) then   //if true then the vertex is distinct.
     if ((k<n) or ((k=n) and G [X [n], X [1]] ≠ 0)) then
return;
}
} Until (false);
}
```

Objective Question Bank

1. Which statement is not true in case of backtracking Method?   [   ]

   A. For a given solution space and unique tree organization is possible.

   B. Backtracking is a variation of the basic dynamic programming idea.

   C. Many problems which deal with searching for a set of solutions can be solved using the backtracking method.

   D. Using backtracking method, we can solve problems in an efficient way, when compared to greedy method.

2. What is the problem statement of N-Queens problem?   [   ]

   A. N Queens are to be placed on a N × N chessboards so that no two Queens are on the same row, column or diagonal.

   B. N Queens are to be placed on a N × N chessboard.

   C. N Queens are to be placed on a 8 × 8 chessboard.

   D. N Queens are to be placed on a large chessboard.

3. Painting all the vertices of a graph with colors such that no two adjacent vertices have the same color is called of the graph.   [   ]

   A. Coloring   B. N - chromatic

   C. Hi - color   D. bi chromatic

4. In backtracking, are the rules that determine which of the tuples in the solution space of satisfy the criterion function.   [   ]

   A. Implicit constraints   B. Explicit constraints

   C. Bounding function   D. Permutation tree

5. Number of leaf nodes are available in tree organization of the 4-Queens solution space.   [   ]
   A.   16   B.   4
   C.   24   D.   8

6. A sufficient condition for a simple graph G with n vertices have a Hamiltonian cycle is that the degree of every vertex in G is at least [   ]
   A.   n   B.   n / 3
   C.   n / 4   D.   n / 2

7. In state space tree of the 4-queens problem, initially, Node 1 is the only one live node. This represents   [   ]
   A.   All the 4-queens are placed randomly on the chess board.
   B.   All the 4-queens a replaced at four corners of the chess board.
   C.   Sixteen queens have been placed on the chess board.
   D.   No queen has been placed on the chess board.

8. In many applications of the backtrack method, the desired solution is expressible as   [   ]
   A.   An algebraic equation
   B.   A matrix
   C.   An n-tuple $(x_1, x_2 \ldots \ldots x_n)$
   D.   A set of binary trees

9. In 8 Queens problem, after applying the conditions, the size of solution space is   [   ]
   A.   8 tuples   B.   16 tuples
   C.   Factorial 8 tuples   D.   32 tuples

10. Which statement is not true in case of Hamiltonian cycle?   [   ]
    A.   A Hamiltonian cycle in a graph of n vertices consists of exactly n edges.
    B.   A graph may contain more than one Hamiltonian cycle.
    C.   Every connected graph has at least one Hamiltonian cycle.
    D.   A Hamiltonian cycle is a round-trip path along n edges of G that visit several vertexes once and returns to t_s starting position.

11. In state space tree of the 4- queen's problem, initially, Node 1 is the only one live node. This represents   [   ]
    A.   All the 4-queens are placed at four corners of the chess board.
    B.   All the 4-queens are placed randomly on the chess board.
    C.   No queen has been placed on the chess board.
    D.   Sixteen queens have been placed on the chess board.

12. For N Queens problem, the time complexity is   [   ]

   A. O (n)   B. O (log n)

   C. O (n*n)   D. O (n!)

13. If d is the degree of the given graph, then it can be colored with colors

                                                                                                                       [   ]

   A. d   B. 2*d

   C. d + 1   D. d − 1

14. A sufficient condition for a simple graph G with n vertices have a Hamiltonian cycle is that the degree of every vertex in G is at least

                                                                                                                      [   ]

   A. n / 2   B. n / 4

   C. n   D. n / 3

15. Which statement is not true in case of backtracking Method?   [   ]

   A. Explicit constraints are rules that restrict each x_i to take on values only from a given set.

   B. Backtracking cannot be used for N queen's problem.

   C. Implicit constraints describe the way in which the x_i must relate to each other.

   D. Often the problem to be solved using backtrack method, calls for finding one vector that maximizes or minimizes or satisfies a criterion function.

16. The solution space tree of 8 queens contain   [   ]

   A. 8*8*8 tuples   B. 8 tuples

   C. 8 to the power of 8 tuples   D. 8 * 8 tuples

17. In sum of subsets problem, if n weights are considered then the solution space consists of   [   ]

   A. n*n tuples   B. n! tuples

   C. 2 to the power of n distinct tuples   D. n tuples

18. To check whether the nodes of G can be colored in such a way that no two adjacent nodes have the same color yet only m colors are used. This is termed as   [   ]

   A. Planar color problem

   B. m - coloring problem

   C. Coloring problem

   D. m - colorability decision problem

19. In backtracking Method, modified criterion function is also known as
    [   ]

    A. Bounding function   B. Implicit constraints

    C. Solution space   D. Explicit constraints

20. If two queens are placed at position (i, j) and (k, l), then they are on the
    same diagonal if and only if   [   ]

    A. $i / j = k/l$ B. $i + j = k + l$

    C. $i * j = k * l$ D. $i \% j = k \% l$

21. What is the time complexity of graph coloring problem?   [   ]

    A. $O(m\,n)$

    B. $O(m - n)$

    C. $O(m + n)$

    D. $O(n * m$ to the power of $n)$

22. The total number of different Hamiltonian cycles in a complete graph of
    n vertices is   [   ]

    A. $1\,2 * (n + 2)!$ B. $1\,2 * n!$

    C. $1\,2 * (n - 1)!$ D. $1\,2 * (n + 1)!$

Fill in the Blanks

1. n-queens problem solved by the _____________________method.

2. Backtracking is a _____________________search with some
   bounding function.

3. Graph coloring can be solved by _____________________method.

4. The name backtrack was first coined by _____________________in
   the 1950s.

5. _____________________constraints are rules that restrict each x_i
   to take on values only from a given set.

6. The implicit constraints are rules that determine which of the tuples in
   the solution space I satisfy the _____________________ function.

7. In the Sum of Subsets problem all paths from the root to other nodes
   define the _____________________ of the
   problem.

Review Questions

1. (a) Let w = (6; 15; 20; 10; 11; 18; 29) and m = 35. Find all possible subsets of w that sum to m. Draw the portion of the state space tree that is generated.

   (b) Differentiate between Live node and E-node.

   December 2011

2. Draw the state space tree for m-coloring problem for n = 3 and m = 3.

   December 2011

3. (a) Briefly explain 8-queen problem using backtracking. Explain its application.

   (b) Draw the state space tree for m coloring when n = 3 and m = 3.

   November / December-2013

4. (a) What is Hamiltonian cycle? Discuss a backtracking algorithm that finds all the Hamiltonian cycles in a graph.

   (b) Write a recursive backtracking algorithm for sum of subsets problem.

   June-2014

5. (a) Explain the Back Tracking Strategy with an example.

   (b) State and explain the n-Queen problem using backtracking

   May-2013

6. Compare and contrast between fixed and variable tuple size formulation and illustrate it for the following sum of subset problem given below.

   Let w = {7; 4; 10; 23; 35; 20; 32} and m = 55. Find all possible subsets of w that sum to m. Draw the portion of the state space tree that is generated.

   April-May, 2012

7. Differentiate between Backtracking and Branch & Bound technique by considering 4-queen problem. Explain how nodes are generated and numbered in state space tree in the above two techniques.

   April-May, 2012

8. Explain Sum of subsets Problem. Design its algorithm using Backtracking.

   December 2011

9. (a) Modify General Backtracking algorithm to find only a single solution rather than all solutions.

   (b) How do you decide whether any two queens can not threaten each other by mapping n-Queens problem onto a chess board?

   December 2011

10. Write a Backtracking algorithm for the sum of subsets problem using the state space tree corresponding to the variable tuple size formulation.

December-January, 2011-2012

11. Define the following terms:

    State space, explicit constraints, implicit constraints, problem state, solution states, answer states, live node, E-node, dead node, bounding functions.

December-January, 2011-2012

7

BRANCH AND BOUND

7.1 INTRODUCTION

The branch and bound is a systematic method for handling optimization problems. This method is applied where greedy method and dynamic programming fails. Its worst case complexity is of exponential order which if handled carefully, runs reasonably fast on average. Its rudimentary functionality is like BFS for searching optimal solution and it uses Bounding functions (which kill the live nodes), rather it determines which node & when to expand and thereby provides the optimal solution. Collection of every possible path from root to each node is called as state space.

The problem states for which the tuple is defined in the solution space are called solution states. **Answer states** are those solution states 's' for which the path from the root to *'s'* defines a tuple that is a member of the set of solutions (i.e., It satisfies the implicit constraints) of the problem. State space tree is a tree organization of solution space.

A live node is one which is generated and all children of 'n' are not completely generated. A dead node is one which cannot be expanded further or all the children of 'n' are generated. The **live node** whose children are currently being generated is called the *E*-node (node being expanded).

Breadth first node generation with bounding function is called branch and bound. Depth first node generation with bounding function is called backtracking. Branch-and-bound includes all state space search methods in which all children of the E-node are generated before any other live node can become the E-node. In branch and bound E-node remains as E-node until it becomes dead node. The backtracking algorithm is effective for decision problems, but it is not designed for optimizing problems. This drawback is rectified in case of branch and bound technique. In this also we use bounding function i.e., similar to backtracking. The essential difference between backtracking and branch and bound is, if we get a solution then we will terminate the search procedure in backtracking, whereas in branch and bound, we will continue the process (search) until we get an optimal solution. Branch and bound technique is applicable for optimization problems only.

There are three common search strategies of branch and bound technique. They are

1.   FIFO branch and bound

2.   LIFO branch and bound

3.   Least Cost branch and bound

A branch and bound method searches a state space tree using any search mechanism in which all the children of the E – node are generated before another node becomes the E – node.

In branch-and-bound terminology, Breadth first search (BFS) will be called FIFO (First In First Output) search or FIFO branch and bound and **D-search** (depth search) state space search will be called LIFO (Last In First Out) or LIFO branch and bound. Bounding functions are used to avoid the generation of sub trees that do not contain an answer node. Usually, the goal here is to find a configuration for which the cost function is minimized.

7.2   FIFO BRANCH AND BOUND

FIFO Branch and Bound uses queue data structure for its implementation. All live nodes are stored in queue. The Figure 7.1 shows how nodes are generated in FIFO branch and bound. Assume the node 12 is an answer node. To begin with node 1 is E-node, next the children of node 1 are generated (node 2, 3, 4) and these live nodes are placed in the queue as shown in Figure 7.2 (a).

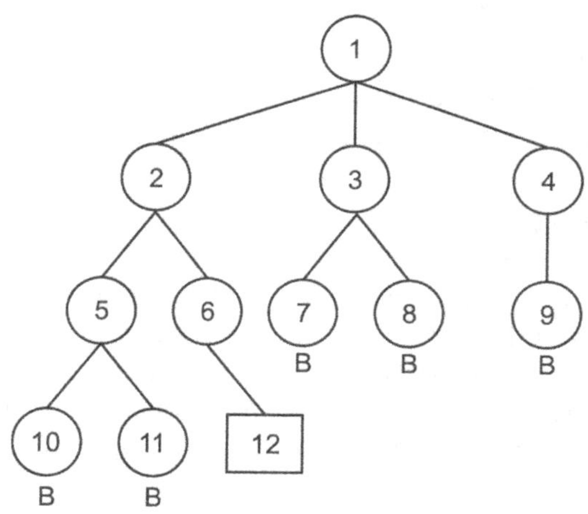

Figure 7.1 State space tree

Now we will delete an element from queue i.e., node 2, now node 2 becomes E-node, its children are generated (node 5 and 6) and placed in the queue as shown in figure 7.2 (b).

Node 3 is deleted from queue and it becomes E – node. Children of node 3 are generated (node 7 and 8) and these live nodes are killed by bounding functions. So we will not include these nodes in the queue as shown in Figure 7.2 (c). Node 4 is deleted from queue and it becomes E – node. Child of node 4 is generated (node 9) and this live node is killed by bounding function. So we will not include node 9 in the queue as shown in Figure 7.2 (d).

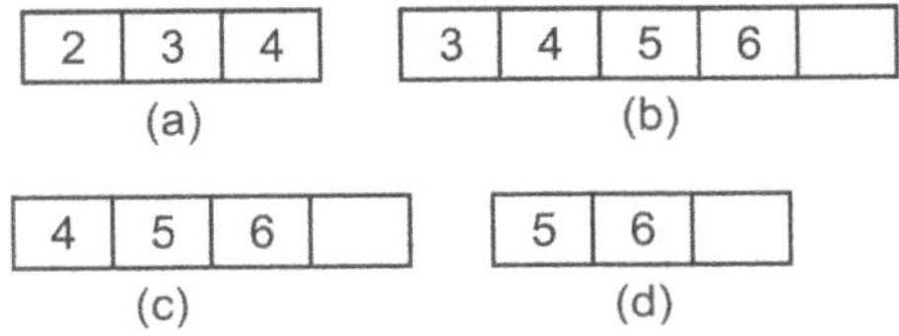

Figure 7.2 (a), (b), (c), (d) Queue storing live nodes

Next delete an element from queue, generate children of node 5 i.e., nodes 10 and 11 are generated and they are killed by bounding function. Last node in queue is 6. The child of node 6 is 12, it satisfies the conditions of the problem which is the answer node, so search terminates.

7.3 LIFO BRANCH AND BOUND

LIFO Branch and Bound uses stack data structure for its implementation. All live nodes are stored in stack. The figure 7.3 shows how nodes are generated in LIFO branch and bound.

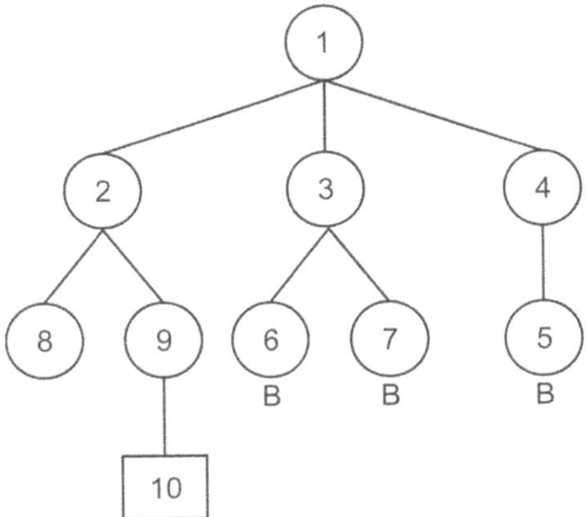

Figure 7.3 State space tree

Initially stack is empty. Assume the node 10 is an answer node. To begin with node1 is E-node, next the children of node1 are generated (node 2, 3, 4) and these live nodes are placed in the stack as shown in Figure 7.4 (a). After generation of nodes 2,3 and 4 node1 becomes dead node.

Remove top most element from stack i.e., node 4, it becomes E-node, its child i.e., node 5 is generated and it is killed by the bounding function, so it is not placed on the stack as shown in Figure 7.4 (b). Now node 3 is on the top of the stack it is deleted from the stack and it becomes E-node. Children of node 3 i.e., node 6 and node 7 are generated and they are killed by the bounding function. So node 6 and node 7 are not placed on the stack as shown in Figure 7.4 (c). Node 2 is on the top of the stack, it is deleted from the stack and it becomes E-node. Children of node 2 i.e., node 8 and node 9 are generated and these live nodes are placed on the stack as shown in Figure 7.4 (d). Delete an element from stack i.e., node 9. Generate child of node 9 i.e., node 10 which is the answer node, so search process terminates.

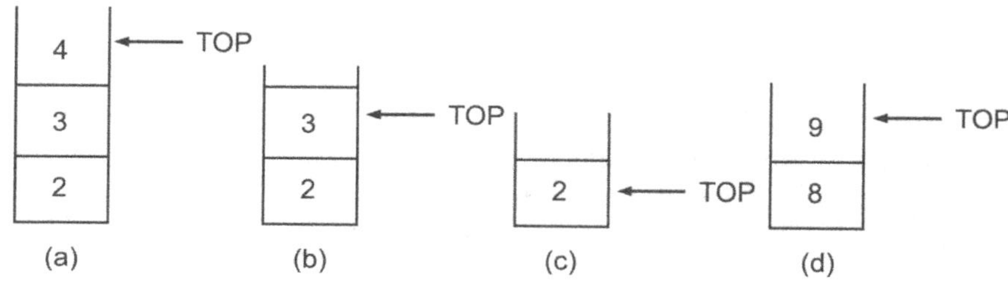

Figure 7.4 (a), (b), (c), (d) Stack storing live nodes

7.4 LEAST COST BRANCH AND BOUND

In LIFO and FIFO branch and bound, selection rule for the next E-node does not give any preference to a node that has a very good chance of getting the search to an answer node quickly. Least Cost branch and bound uses intelligent ranking function or cost function which is denoted by $\hat{c}$ (x) and it is always depends on the problem. After generation of all live nodes cost function generates cost of all nodes, the node which has minimum cost becomes E – node among all live nodes.

Initially node1 is taken as E – node and its children are generated i.e., node 2, 3 and 4 are generated. By using ranking function cost is calculated and the cost of node 2, 3 and 4 are $\hat{c} = 5$, $\hat{c} = 3$ and $\hat{c} = 4$ respectively. The node with minimum cost becomes E-node, i.e., node 3 becomes E-node. The children of node 3 are generated and they are node 5 and 6 where as node 2 and node 4 are not expanded as shown in Figure 7.5. By using ranking function cost of node 5 and 6 are calculated. Among these node 5 is selected due to its minimum cost and node 5 becomes E-node. Generate children of node 5 i.e., node 7 and node 8. Among these node 7 is selected since its cost ($\hat{c}$ = 1) is minimum. Node 7 is the answer node, so we terminate search process.

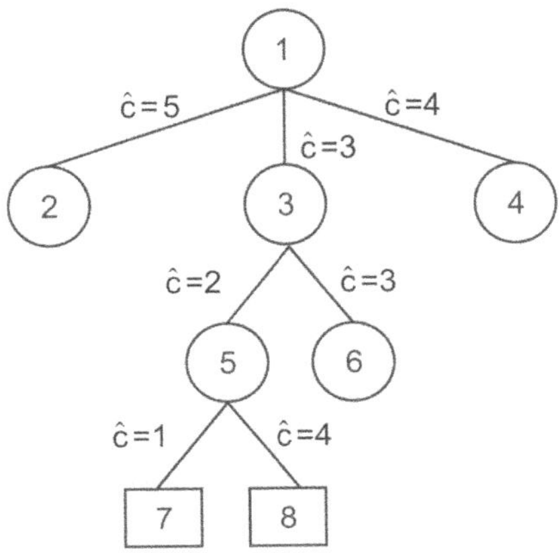

Figure 7.5 State space tree generated during LC search

7.5 4-QUEENS PROBLEM

In 4-queens problem, the four queens are to be arranged in a non attacking mode on the 4X4 chessboard. Let us see how a FIFO branch-and-bound algorithm would search the state space tree for the 4-queens problem. The state space tree is given in Figure 7.1, the nodes are numbered according to depth first search and the weight of the edge shows the column number in which queen is placed.

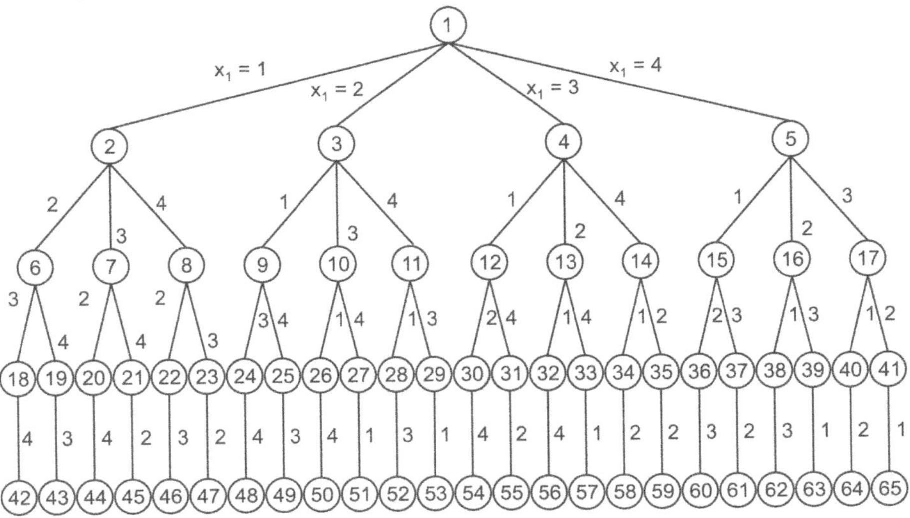

Figure 7.6 State space tree for 4-queen problem

Node 1 is the initial node which represents that none of the queens is placed on the chess board and now there are 4 places in the first row (i.e., column 1, 2, 3, 4) on which the first queen can be placed. It is represented by the nodes 2, 3,4 and 5.

The nodes 2, 3, 4 and 5 are live nodes and the node 2 becomes the next E-node which will be further expanded to nodes 6, 7 and 8 which represents that if queen 1 is placed in row 1 and column 1 then the queen 2 can be placed in one of the three places in row 2 i.e., column 2, 3, 4 (shown in graph by nodes 6, 7, 8 respectively) and similarly it continues to all the nodes as shown in Figure 7.6.

Nodes 2, 3, 4 and 5 are live nodes and initially node 2 is an E-node and is extended and nodes 6, 7, 8 are generated. Node 6 is killed by the bound function and nodes 7 and 8 are added to the queue of live nodes as shown in Figure 7.7. If two queens are placed in the same diagonal then they are killed by bound function.

Next E-node to be expanded is node 3 and nodes 9, 10, 11 are generated. Nodes 9 and 10 are killed by the bound function and node 11 is added to the queue of live nodes.

Node 4 is the next E-node and the process is continued.

The graph after applying the FIFO branch and bound search is shown in the Figure 7.7, 'B' is written under the nodes which are killed by the bound function. Numbers inside the nodes correspond to the numbers in Figure 7.6, and numbers outside the nodes give the order in which the nodes are generated by adding bounding function. At the time the answer node, node 52, is reached, the only live nodes remaining are nodes 31 and 37.

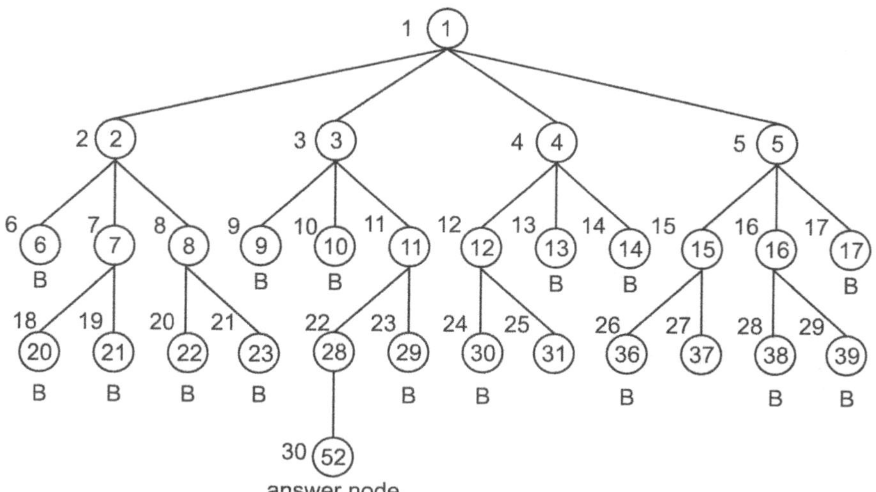

Figure 7.7 Portion of 4-queens state space tree generated by
FIFO branch and bound

7.6 FORMULATION OF LEAST COST SEARCH

In this method a cost estimation function decides among all live nodes which node should become E-node. Whereas in LIFO and FIFO branch and bound, selection rule is based on the data structure used. In this method preference to a node will be given which has a very good chance of getting the answer node quickly.

In the above 4-queen problem the rigid FIFO rule first requires the expansion of all live nodes generated before node 28 was expanded. But node 28 leads to answer node in one more move which is not taken care by the rigid FIFO rule.

A ranking function $\hat{C}$ (.) can be used to speed up the searching process in which the ranks are given to the nodes and the E-nodes are selected on the basis of these ranks. If the ranking function is used in 4-queens example as shown in Figure 7.7, then it assigns node 28 a better rank than all other live nodes, then node 28 will become *E*-node, following node 11. The remaining live nodes will never become *E*-nodes as the expansion of node 28 results in the generation of an answer node (node 52). The ranks are assigned to the nodes based on additional computational effort (or cost) needed to reach an answer node from the live node. For the node 'x', the cost would be:

1. The number of nodes on the sub-tree x that need to be generated before any answer node is generated or, more simply,

2. The number of levels the nearest answer node (in the sub-tree x) is from x.

If the second cost method is used on above 4-queen problem the cost of the root of the tree is 4(since node 52 is four levels from node 1). The costs of nodes 3 & 4, 11 & 12 and 28 & 31 are respectively 3, 2, and 1 and the costs of all remaining nodes on levels 2, 3, and 4 are respectively greater than 3, 2, and 1. If this cost is used as a basis for selecting the next E-node, then the order of E-nodes are 1, 3, 11 & 28 and the other nodes that get generated are nodes 2, 4, 5, 9, 10, 29, and 52. The first method generates minimum number of nodes.

The difficulty in using the ideal cost function is computing the cost of a node which involves a search of the sub-tree x for an answer node. By the time the cost of a node is determined, the sub-tree will be searched and there is no need to explore x again.

Hence search algorithms usually rank nodes only based on an estimate $\hat{g}$ (.) of their cost. Let $\hat{g}$ (x) be an estimate of the additional effort needed to reach an answer node from x. Node x is assigned a rank using a function (.) such that $\hat{C}$ (x) =f (h(x)) + $\hat{g}$ (x),

Where h(x) is the cost of reaching x from the root and f (.) is any non-decreasing function.

LC-search (least cost search) is a search strategy that uses a cost function $\hat{C}(x) = f(h(x)) + \hat{g}(x)$, to select the next e-node and chooses a live node with least (.) as its next e-node.

The following lines define Cost function c (.). The c(x) is the cost (level, computational difficulty, etc.) of reaching x from the root of the state space tree, if x is an answer node. If x is not an answer node, then c(x) = infinity, providing the sub-tree x contains no answer node; Otherwise c(x) is equal to the cost of a minimum cost answer node in the sub-tree x. From now on c(x) is referred to as the cost of x.

7.6.1 Control Abstractions for LC-Search

Let 't' be a state space tree and c( ) a cost function for the nodes in 't'. if 'x' is a node in 't', then c(x) is the minimum cost of any answer node in the sub tree with root 'x'. A Least Cost Branch and Bound search of tree uses two functions Least( ) and Add( ). The output of Least Cost search is tracing the path from the answer node to the root node of the tree. The algorithm of the Least Cost Search is given bellow as shown in algorithm 7.1.

Algorithm LCSearch(*t*)

```
 1:   //Search t for an answer node.
 2:   {
 3:   if (t is an answer node) then
 4:   {
 5:   output(t);
 6:   return;
 7:   }
 8:   E ← t;
 9:   repeat
10:   {
11:   for each child x of E do
12:   {
13:   if(x is an answer node) then
14:   {
15:   Output is the path from x to t;
16:   return;
17:   }
18:   Add(x);              //x is a new live node
19:   (x→parent) :=E;  //pointing the path from x to root
20:   }
21:   if   (there are no more live nodes) then
22:   {
```

```
23:    Write(" No answer node"); return;
24:    }
25:    E :=Least( );
26:    }until(false);
27:    }
28:    Algorithm 7.1 LC-Search
```

7.7 BOUNDING

A state space tree is searched using any of the search mechanism and all the children of the E-node are generated before any another node becomes the E-node. Let us consider that the node x has a cost c(x) associated with it. The objective is to find the minimum cost answer node. Three common search strategies that are used are FIFO, LIFO, and LC.

The condition $\hat{C}$ (x) <= c(x) is used to provide lower bounds on solutions obtainable from any node x. where $\hat{C}$ (x) is a cost function. If upper is an upper bound on the cost of a minimum-cost solution, then all live nodes x with $\hat{C}$ (x) > upper may be killed as all answer nodes reachable from x have cost c(x)> = $\hat{C}$ (x) >upper. The starting value for upper can be set to infinity. Each time a new answer is found, the value of upper can be updated.

Example: Consider the problem of job scheduling with deadlines. We generalize this problem to allow jobs with different processing times.

There are n jobs and one processor. Each job i has associated with it a three tuple (p_i, d_i, t_i), job i requires t_i units of processing time, if its processing is not completed by the deadline di, and then a penalty pi is incurred. A subset of jobs j among all jobs should be found such that the penalty incurred is minimum among all possible subsets, such as j is optimal.

The objective is to select a subset j of the n jobs such that all jobs in j can be completed by their deadlines. Hence, a penalty can be incurred only on those jobs not in j.

Consider the following instances: n = 4, $(p_1, d_1, t_1) = (5, 1, 1)$, $(p_2, d_2, t_2) = (10, 3, 2)$, $(p_3, d_3, t_3) = (6, 2, 1)$, and $(p_4, d_4, t_4) = (3, 1, 1)$. The solution space for this instances consists of all possible subsets of the job index set {1,2,3,4}. The solution space can be organized into a tree by means of either of the two formulations used for the sum of subsets problem.

The costs of the answer nodes of Figure 7.9 are given below the nodes. Figure 7.8 corresponds to the variable tuple size formulations while Figure 7.9 corresponds to the fixed tuple size formulation. All non-square nodes are answer nodes.

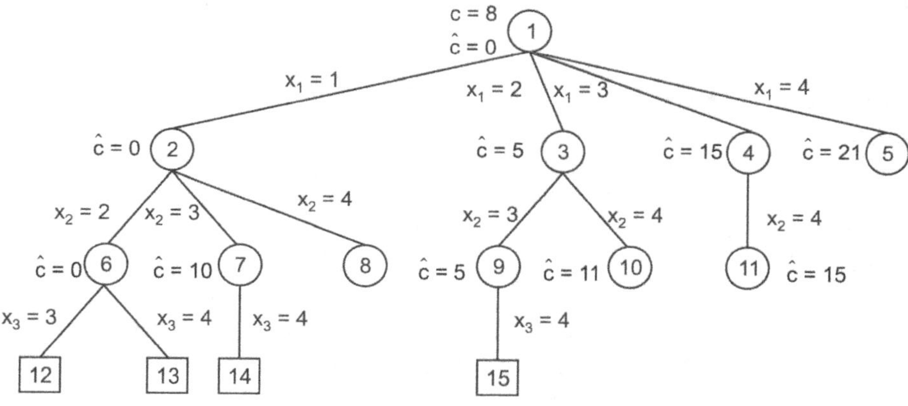

Figure 7.8 State space tree corresponding to variable tuple size formulation

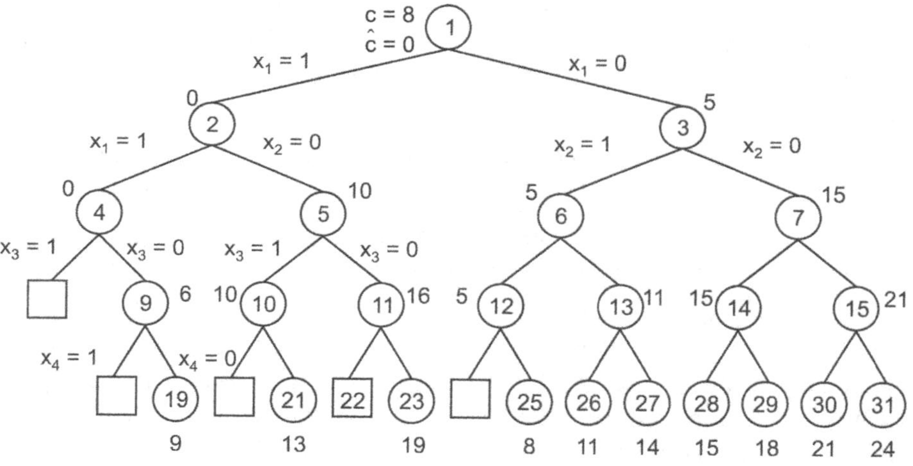

Figure 7.9 State space tree corresponding to fixed tuple size formulation

In both figures square nodes represent infeasible subsets. In Figure 7.8, Node 9 represents an optimal solution and is the only minimum-cost answer node. For this node j = {2, 3} and the penalty (cost) is 8. In Figure 7.9, Node 25 represents the optimal solution and is also a minimum-cost answer node. This node corresponds to j = {2, 3} and a penalty of 8.

7.8 TRAVELLING SALES PERSON PROBLEM

If there are 'n' cities and cost of travelling from one city to other city is given. A salesman has to start from any one of the city and has to visit all the cities exactly once and has to return to the starting place with shortest distance or minimum cost.

Let G = (V, E) be a directed graph defining an instance of the travelling salesperson problem. Let C_{ij} be the cost of the edge (i, j) and $C_{ij} = \infty$ if (i, j) !∈ E(G) and let $|v| = n$. Solution to Travelling Salesman Problem using dynamic programming having time complexity $O(n^2 2^n)$ has been discussed in chapter 6. Let us see how a branch and bound algorithm would search the state space tree for the Travelling salesman problem. Worst case time complexity of this algorithm is same as dynamic programming algorithm and it is $O(n^2 2^n)$. The running time of the branch and bound algorithm may be much less than $O(n^2 2^n)$ by the use of good bounding functions. Assume that every tour starts and ends at vertex 1. To use least cost branch and bound to search the travelling salesperson state space tree, we must define a cost function c(x) and two other functions ĉ (x) and û (x) such that ĉ (x) ≤ c (x) ≤ û (x).

The following Figure 7.10 shows the state space tree organization for the case of a complete graph with n = 4. Each leaf node L is a solution node. The tour is defined by the path from the root to the leaf node L.

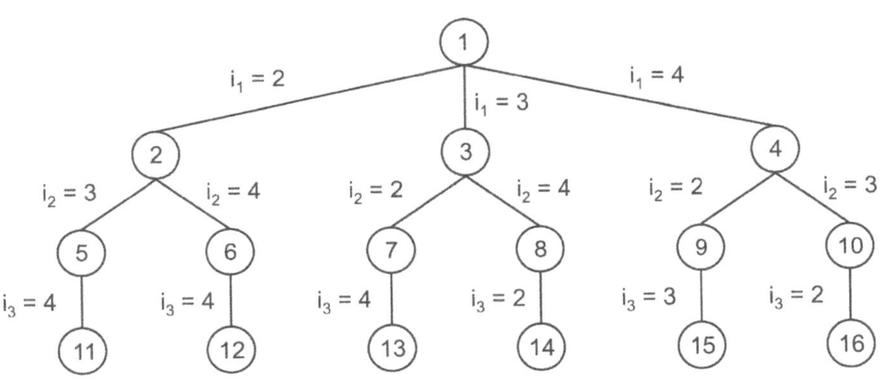

Figure 7.10 State space tree for the travelling salesperson problem with n = 4 and $i_0 = i_4 = 1$

7.8.1 Reduced Cost Matrix

A row or column is said to be reduced if it contains at least one zero and all remaining entries are non-negative. A matrix is reduced if every row and column is reduced. If a constant 't' is chosen to be minimum entry in row 'i' or column 'j' then subtracting it from all entries in row 'i' (column j) will introduce a zero into a row 'i'(column j). The total amount subtracted from the columns and rows is lower bound on the length of a minimum cost tour and can be used as the ĉ (x) value for the root of state space tree. With every node in state space tree, we associate a reduced cost matrix.

Let 'A' be the reduced cost matrix for node R. Let 'S' be the child of 'R' such that the edge (R, S) corresponds to including edge (i, j) in the tour. If 'S' is not a leaf node then the reduced cost matrix for node 'S' can be obtained as follows.

1. Change all entries in row i column j of 'A' to ∞.

2. Set A(j, 1) to ∞.

3. Apply row reduction and column reduction except for rows and columns containing ∞.

4. The total cost for node 'S' can be calculated as

$\hat{c}$ (S) = $\hat{c}$ (R) + A(i, j) + r where 'r' is the total amount subtracted in step 3.

Example: Solve the following instance of travelling sales person cost matrix as shown in Figure 7.11 using LCBB.

$$\begin{bmatrix} \infty & 20 & 30 & 10 & 11 \\ 15 & \infty & 16 & 4 & 2 \\ 3 & 5 & \infty & 2 & 4 \\ 19 & 6 & 18 & \infty & 3 \\ 16 & 4 & 7 & 16 & \infty \end{bmatrix}$$

Figure 7.11 Cost matrix

Reduce the first row of cost matrix by 10, then the cost matrix becomes

$$R_1 - 10 \rightarrow \begin{bmatrix} \infty & 10 & 20 & 0 & 1 \\ 15 & \infty & 16 & 4 & 2 \\ 3 & 5 & \infty & 2 & 4 \\ 19 & 6 & 18 & \infty & 3 \\ 16 & 4 & 7 & 16 & \infty \end{bmatrix}$$

Reduce the Second row of cost matrix by 2, then the cost matrix becomes

$$R_2 - 2 \rightarrow \begin{bmatrix} \infty & 10 & 20 & 0 & 1 \\ 13 & \infty & 14 & 2 & 0 \\ 3 & 5 & \infty & 2 & 4 \\ 19 & 6 & 18 & \infty & 3 \\ 16 & 4 & 7 & 16 & \infty \end{bmatrix}$$

Reduce the 3rd row of cost matrix by 2, then the cost matrix becomes

$$R_3 - 2 \rightarrow \begin{bmatrix} \infty & 10 & 20 & 0 & 1 \\ 13 & \infty & 14 & 2 & 0 \\ 1 & 3 & \infty & 0 & 2 \\ 19 & 6 & 18 & \infty & 3 \\ 16 & 4 & 7 & 16 & \infty \end{bmatrix}$$

Reduce the 4th row of cost matrix by 3, then the cost matrix becomes

$$R_4 - 3 \rightarrow \begin{bmatrix} \infty & 10 & 20 & 0 & 1 \\ 13 & \infty & 14 & 2 & 0 \\ 1 & 3 & \infty & 0 & 2 \\ 16 & 3 & 15 & \infty & 0 \\ 16 & 4 & 7 & 16 & \infty \end{bmatrix}$$

Reduce the 5th row of cost matrix by 4, then the cost matrix becomes

$$R_5 - 4 \rightarrow \begin{bmatrix} \infty & 10 & 20 & 0 & 1 \\ 13 & \infty & 14 & 2 & 0 \\ 1 & 3 & \infty & 0 & 2 \\ 16 & 3 & 15 & \infty & 0 \\ 12 & 0 & 3 & 12 & \infty \end{bmatrix}$$

Reduce the First column of cost matrix by 1, then the cost matrix becomes

$$C_1 - 1 \rightarrow \begin{bmatrix} \infty & 10 & 20 & 0 & 1 \\ 12 & \infty & 14 & 2 & 0 \\ 0 & 3 & \infty & 0 & 2 \\ 15 & 3 & 15 & \infty & 0 \\ 11 & 0 & 3 & 12 & \infty \end{bmatrix}$$

Reduce the 3rd column of cost matrix by 3, then the cost matrix becomes

$$C_3 - 3 \rightarrow \begin{bmatrix} \infty & 10 & 17 & 0 & 1 \\ 12 & \infty & 11 & 2 & 0 \\ 0 & 3 & \infty & 0 & 2 \\ 15 & 3 & 12 & \infty & 0 \\ 11 & 0 & 0 & 12 & \infty \end{bmatrix}$$

Finally, the reduced cost matrix is shown in Figure 7.12.

$$\begin{bmatrix} \infty & 10 & 17 & 0 & 1 \\ 12 & \infty & 11 & 2 & 0 \\ 0 & 3 & \infty & 0 & 2 \\ 15 & 3 & 12 & \infty & 0 \\ 11 & 0 & 0 & 12 & \infty \end{bmatrix}$$

Figure 7.12 Reduced cost matrix L = 25

Consider the path (1, 2): The first row and Second column of reduced matrix are made infinity (∞) and element (2, 1) is also made ∞ as shown in Figure 7.13.

$$\begin{bmatrix} \infty & \infty & \infty & \infty & \infty \\ \infty & \infty & 11 & 2 & 0 \\ 0 & \infty & \infty & 0 & 2 \\ 15 & \infty & 12 & \infty & 0 \\ 11 & \infty & 0 & 12 & \infty \end{bmatrix}$$

Figure 7.13 Path 1, 2; node 2

Apply row and column reduction r = 0.

$$\hat{c}\,(2) = \hat{c}\,(1) + A(1, 2) + r = 25 + 10 + 0 = 35$$

Consider the path (1, 3): The first row and Third column of reduced matrix are made infinity (∞) and element (3, 1) is also made ∞ as shown in Figure 7.14.

$$\begin{bmatrix} \infty & \infty & \infty & \infty & \infty \\ 12 & \infty & \infty & 2 & 0 \\ \infty & 3 & \infty & 0 & 2 \\ 15 & 3 & \infty & \infty & 0 \\ 11 & 0 & \infty & 12 & \infty \end{bmatrix}$$

Figure 7.14 Path 1, 3; node 3

Above matrix is not reduced. Subtract 11 from 1st column then the matrix is reduced and given in Figure 7.15 bellow.

$$\begin{bmatrix} \infty & \infty & \infty & \infty & \infty \\ 1 & \infty & \infty & 2 & 0 \\ \infty & 3 & \infty & 0 & 2 \\ 4 & 3 & \infty & \infty & 0 \\ 0 & 0 & \infty & 12 & \infty \end{bmatrix}$$

Figure 7.15 Path 1, 3; node 3

Apply row and column reduction r = 11.

$$\hat{c}\,(3) = \hat{c}\,(1) + A(1, 3) + r = 25 + 17 + 11 = 53$$

Consider the path (1, 4): The first row and Fourth column of reduced matrix are made infinity (∞) and element (4, 1) is also made ∞ as shown in Figure 7.16.

$$\begin{bmatrix} \infty & \infty & \infty & \infty & \infty \\ 12 & \infty & 11 & \infty & 0 \\ 0 & 3 & \infty & \infty & 2 \\ \infty & 3 & 12 & \infty & 0 \\ 11 & 0 & 0 & \infty & \infty \end{bmatrix}$$

Figure 7.16 Path 1, 4; node 4

Apply row and column reduction r=0.

$$\hat{c}\,(4) = \hat{c}\,(1) + A(1, 4) + r = 25 + 0 + 0 = 25$$

Consider the path (1, 5): The first row and Fifth column of reduced matrix are made infinity (∞) and element (5, 1) is also made ∞ as shown in Figure 7.17.

$$\begin{bmatrix} \infty & \infty & \infty & \infty & \infty \\ 12 & \infty & 11 & 2 & 0 \\ 0 & 3 & \infty & 0 & \infty \\ 15 & 3 & 12 & \infty & \infty \\ \infty & 0 & 0 & 12 & \infty \end{bmatrix}$$

Figure 7.17 Path 1, 5

Above matrix is not reduced. Subtract 2 from 2nd row and 3 from 4th row then the matrix is reduced and given in Figure 7.18.

$$\begin{bmatrix} \infty & \infty & \infty & \infty & \infty \\ 10 & \infty & 9 & 0 & \infty \\ 0 & 3 & \infty & 0 & \infty \\ 12 & 0 & 9 & \infty & \infty \\ \infty & 0 & 0 & 12 & \infty \end{bmatrix}$$

Figure 7.18 Path 1, 5; node 5

Apply row and column reduction $r = 5 + 0 = 5$.

$$\hat{c}\,(4) = \hat{c}\,(1) + A(1, 5) + r = 25 + 1 + 5 = 31.$$

Since the minimum cost is 25, so select node 4. The matrix obtained for path (1, 4) is considered as reduced cost matrix as shown in Figure 7.19 and a part of space tree generated by procedure LCBB is shown in Figure 7.20.

$$\begin{bmatrix} \infty & \infty & \infty & \infty & \infty \\ 12 & \infty & 11 & \infty & 0 \\ 0 & 3 & \infty & \infty & 2 \\ \infty & 3 & 12 & \infty & 0 \\ 11 & 0 & 0 & \infty & \infty \end{bmatrix}$$

Figure 7.19 Reduced Cost Matrix

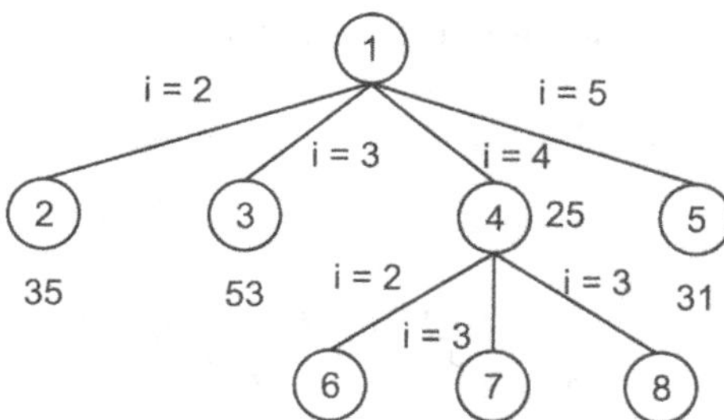

Figure 7.20 Part of space tree generated by procedure LCBB

Consider the path (1, 4, 2): The fourth row and second column of reduced matrix are made infinity (∞) and element (2, 1) is also made ∞ as shown in Figure 7.21.

$$\begin{bmatrix} \infty & \infty & \infty & \infty & \infty \\ \infty & \infty & 10 & \infty & 0 \\ 0 & \infty & \infty & \infty & 2 \\ \infty & \infty & \infty & \infty & \infty \\ 11 & \infty & 0 & \infty & \infty \end{bmatrix}$$

Figure 7.21 Path 1, 4, 2; node 6

Apply row and column reduction r = 0.

$$\hat{c}\,(2) = \hat{c}\,(4) + A(4, 2) + r = 25 + 3 + 0 = 28$$

Consider the path (1, 4, 3): The fourth row and third column of reduced matrix are made infinity (∞) and element (3, 1) is also made ∞ as shown in figure 7.22.

$$\begin{bmatrix} \infty & \infty & \infty & \infty & \infty \\ 12 & \infty & \infty & \infty & 0 \\ \infty & 3 & \infty & \infty & 2 \\ \infty & \infty & \infty & \infty & \infty \\ 11 & 0 & \infty & \infty & \infty \end{bmatrix}$$

Figure 7.22 Path 1, 4, 3

Above matrix is not reduced. Subtract 11 from 1st column and 2 from 3rd row then the above matrix is reduced and is given in Figure 7.23 below.

$$\begin{bmatrix} \infty & \infty & \infty & \infty & \infty \\ 1 & \infty & \infty & \infty & 0 \\ \infty & 1 & \infty & \infty & 0 \\ \infty & \infty & \infty & \infty & \infty \\ 0 & 0 & \infty & \infty & \infty \end{bmatrix}$$

Figure 7.23 Path 1, 4, 3; node 7

Apply row and column reduction r = 2 + 11 = 13.

$$\hat{c}\,(3) = \hat{c}\,(4) + A(4, 3) + r = 25 + 12 + 013 = 50$$

Consider the path (1, 4, 5): The fourth row and fifth column of reduced matrix are made infinity (∞) and element (5, 1) is also made ∞ as shown in Figure 7.24.

$$\begin{bmatrix} \infty & \infty & \infty & \infty & \infty \\ 12 & \infty & 11 & \infty & 0 \\ 0 & 3 & \infty & \infty & \infty \\ \infty & \infty & \infty & \infty & \infty \\ \infty & 0 & 0 & \infty & \infty \end{bmatrix}$$

Figure 7.24 Path 1,4, 5

Above matrix is not reduced. Subtract 11 from 2nd row then the above matrix is reduced and is given in Figure 7.25 below.

$$\begin{bmatrix} \infty & \infty & \infty & \infty & \infty \\ 1 & \infty & 0 & \infty & \infty \\ 0 & 3 & \infty & \infty & \infty \\ \infty & \infty & \infty & \infty & \infty \\ \infty & 0 & 0 & \infty & \infty \end{bmatrix}$$

Figure 7.25 Path 1,4, 5; node 8

Apply row and column reduction $r = 11 + 0 = 11$.

$$\hat{c}\,(5) = \hat{c}\,(4) + A(4, 5) + r = 25 + 0 + 11 = 36$$

Since the minimum cost is 28, so select node 2. The matrix obtained for path (1, 4, 2) is considered as reduced cost matrix as shown in Figure 7.26 and a part of space tree generated by procedure LCBB is shown in Figure 7.27.

$$\begin{bmatrix} \infty & \infty & \infty & \infty & \infty \\ \infty & \infty & 11 & \infty & 0 \\ 0 & \infty & \infty & \infty & 2 \\ \infty & \infty & \infty & \infty & \infty \\ 11 & \infty & 0 & \infty & \infty \end{bmatrix}$$

Figure 7.26 Reduced cost matrix

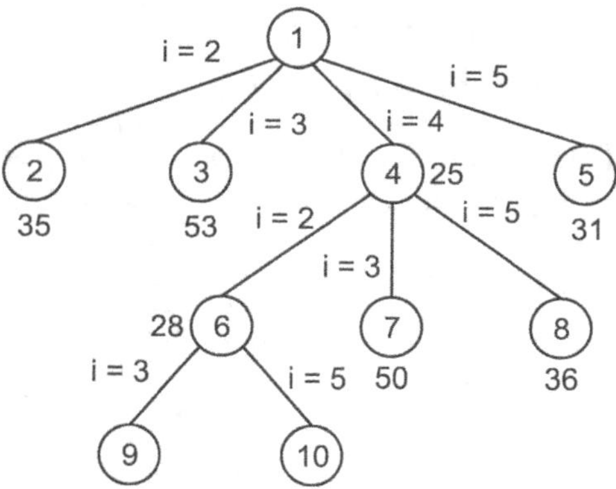

Figure 7.27 Part of space tree generated by procedure LCBB

Consider the path (1, 4, 2, 3): The 2nd row and 3rd column of reduced matrix are made infinity (∞) and element (3, 1) is also made ∞ as shown in Figure 7.28.

$$\begin{bmatrix} \infty & \infty & \infty & \infty & \infty \\ \infty & \infty & \infty & \infty & \infty \\ \infty & \infty & \infty & \infty & 2 \\ \infty & \infty & \infty & \infty & \infty \\ 11 & \infty & \infty & \infty & \infty \end{bmatrix}$$

Figure 7.28 Path 1, 4, 2, 3

Above matrix is not reduced. Subtract 11 from 1st column and 2 from last column then the above matrix is reduced and is given in Figure 7.29 bellow.

$$\begin{bmatrix} \infty & \infty & \infty & \infty & \infty \\ \infty & \infty & \infty & \infty & \infty \\ \infty & \infty & \infty & \infty & 0 \\ \infty & \infty & \infty & \infty & \infty \\ 0 & \infty & \infty & \infty & \infty \end{bmatrix}$$

Figure 7.29 Path 1, 4, 2, 3; node 9

Apply row and column reduction $r = 2 + 11 = 13$.

$$\hat{c}\,(9) = \hat{c}\,(6) + A(2, 3) + r = 28 + 11 + 13 = 52$$

Consider the path (1, 4, 2, 5): The 2nd row and 5th column of reduced matrix are made infinity (∞) and element $(5, 1)$ is also made ∞ as shown in Figure 7.30.

$$\begin{bmatrix} \infty & \infty & \infty & \infty & \infty \\ \infty & \infty & \infty & \infty & \infty \\ 0 & \infty & \infty & \infty & \infty \\ \infty & \infty & \infty & \infty & \infty \\ \infty & \infty & 0 & \infty & \infty \end{bmatrix}$$

Figure 7.30 Path 1, 4, 2, 5; node 10

Apply row and column reduction $r = 0$.

$$\hat{c}\,(5) = \hat{c}\,(2) + A(2, 5) + r = 28 + 0 + 0 = 28$$

Since the minimum cost is 28, so select node 5. The matrix obtained for path (1, 4, 2, 5) is considered as reduced cost matrix as shown in Figure 7.31.

$$\begin{bmatrix} \infty & \infty & \infty & \infty & \infty \\ \infty & \infty & \infty & \infty & \infty \\ 0 & \infty & \infty & \infty & \infty \\ \infty & \infty & \infty & \infty & \infty \\ \infty & \infty & 0 & \infty & \infty \end{bmatrix}$$

Figure 7.31 Reduction cost matrix

Consider the path (1, 4, 2, 5, 3): The 5th row and 3rd column of reduced matrix are made infinity (∞) and element (3, 1) is also made ∞ as shown in Figure7.32.

$$\begin{bmatrix} \infty & \infty & \infty & \infty & \infty \\ \infty & \infty & \infty & \infty & \infty \\ \infty & \infty & \infty & \infty & \infty \\ \infty & \infty & \infty & \infty & \infty \\ \infty & \infty & \infty & \infty & \infty \end{bmatrix}$$

Figure 7.32 Path(1, 4, 2, 5, 3)

Apply row and column reduction $r = 0$.

$$\hat{c}\,(3) = \hat{c}\,(5) + A(5, 3) + r = 28 + 0 + 0 = 28$$

The complete state space tree generated by procedure LCBB is shown in Figure 7.33.

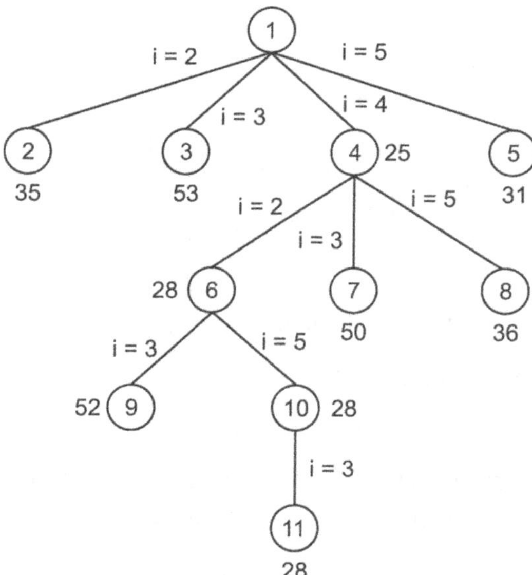

Figure 7.33 State space tree generated by procedure LCBB

Path is: $1 \rightarrow 4 \rightarrow 2 \rightarrow 5 \rightarrow 3 \rightarrow 1$

Minimum Cost $= 10 + 6 + 2 + 7 + 3 = 28$

7.9 0/1 KNAPSACK PROBLEM USING BRANCH AND BOUND

The 0/1 knapsack problem states that, there are 'n' objects given and capacity of knapsack is 'm'. Then select some objects to fill the knapsack in such a way that it should not exceed the capacity of knapsack and maximum profit can be earned. The 0/1 knapsack problem can be stated as,

$$\max z = p_1x_1 + p_2x_2 + \text{------} + p_nx_n$$

$$w_1x_1 + w_2x_2 + \text{------} + w_nx_n \leq m$$

$$x_i = 0 \text{ or } 1$$

A branch and bound technique is used to find solution to the knapsack problem. Branch and bound technique cannot be directly applied to the knapsack problem, because the branch and bound deals only with the minimization problems, whereas knapsack problem is maximization problem. The knapsack problem is modified and converted into the minimization problems. The modified problem is

$$\min Z = - p_1x_1 - p_2x_2 + \text{-------} p_nx_n$$

$$w_1x_1 + w_2x_2 + \text{------} + w_nx_n \leq m$$

$$x_i = 0 \text{ or } 1$$

7.9.1 LC Branch and Bound Solution

Let $\hat{c}(x)$ and $\hat{u}(x)$ are the two cost functions such that $\hat{c}(x) \leq c(x) \leq u(x)$, satisfying the requirements where $c(x) = -\sum p_i x_i$. The $c(x)$ is the cost function for answer node x, where lies between two functions called lower and upper bounds for the cost function $c(x)$. The search begins at the root node. We compute the lower and upper bound at root node called $\hat{c}(1)$ and $u(1)$. Consider the first variable x_1 to take a decision. The x_1 takes values 0 or 1. Compute the lower and upper bounds in each case of the variable. These are the nodes at the first level. Select the node whose cost is minimum. That is

$$C(x) = \min\{c(lchild(x)), c(rchild(x))\}$$

$$C(1) = \min\{\hat{c}(2), \hat{c}(3)\}$$

The problem can be solved by a sequence of decisions on the variables $x_1, x_2, .. x_n$ level wise. A decision on the variable x_i involve determining which of the values 0 or 1 is to be assigned to it by defining $c(x)$ recursively.

The path from root to the leaf node whose height is maximum is selected and it is the solution space for the knapsack problem. Lower and Upper Bound algorithm (Algorithm 7.2 and 7.3) for knapsack problem is given below.

Algorithm Bound(cp, cw, k)

```
       // cp is the current profit total, cw is the
       //current weight total; k is the index of the last
       //removed item; and m is the knapsack size.
 1:    {
 2:    b := cp; c := cw;
 3:    for i := k + 1 to n do
 4:    {
 5:    c := c + w[i];
 6:    if (c < m) then b :=b + p[i];
 7:    else return b + (1 - (c - m) / w[i]) * p[i];
 8:    }
 9:    Return b;
10:    }
       Algorithm 7.2 A bounding function
```

Algorithm UBound(cp, cw, k, m)

```
       // cp, cw, k and m have the same meanings as in
       //Algorithm 7.1. w[i] and p[i] are respectively
       //weight and profit of the i^th object.
 1:    {
 2:    b := cp; c := cw;
 3:    for i := k + 1 to n do
 4:    {
 5:    if ( c + w[i] ≤ m) then
 6:    {
 7:    c :=c + w[i]; b :=b - p[i];
 8:    }
 9:    }
10:    Return b;
11:    }
```

Algorithm 7.3 Function u(.) for knapsack problem

Algorithm ubound finds the upper bound where fractions are not allowed and they are stored in variable u, whereas algorithm bound finds the lower bound where fractions are allowed and stored in variable $\hat{c}$ ().

Example: Draw the portion of state space tree generated by LCBB for the following knapsack instances: n = 4 (p_1, p_2, p_3, p_4) = (10, 10, 12, 18), (w_1, w_2, w_3, w_4) = (2, 4, 6, 9) and m = 15.

Solution: Convert the profits to negative i.e., $(p_1, p_2, p_3, p_4, p_5) = (-10, -10, -12, -18)$. Calculate the lower bound and upper bound for each node. Place the first item in to the bag i.e., 2 then the remaining weight is $15 - 2 = 13$. Place second item i.e., 4, the remaining weight is 9. Place third item i.e., 6 the remaining weight is 3. Since fractions are not allowed in calculation of upper bound, so we cannot place the 4th item in the bag. The profit earned is $-10 -10 - 12 = -32$ this is also known as upper bound. Upper bound is calculated by algorithm ubound. Upper bound is also calculated as

$$= - p_1x_1 - p_2x_2 - p_3x_3 - p_4x_4$$

$$= - 10(1) - 10(1) - 12(1) - 18(0)$$

$$= - 10 - 10 - 12 = - 32$$

To calculate the lower bound, algorithm bound is used, fractions are allowed place 4th item in the bag.

After placing first three items total weights of three items is 12 and knapsack capacity is 15, the remaining weight is 3. A fraction of 4th item is allowed and it is 3/9 of item 4 its weight is $3/9 \times 9 = 3$ and by placing 3/9 of item 4 the profit earned is $3/9 \times 18$.

$$\text{Lower bound} = - 10 - 10 - 12 - 18(3/9) = - 38$$

$u(1) = - 32, \ \hat{c}(1) = - 38$

For <u>node 2</u> $x_1 = 1$ means, we should place first item in the bag.

$\hat{c}(2) = - 10 - 10 - 12 - 18(3/9) = -38$

$u(2) = -10 - 10 - 12 = - 32$

For <u>node 3</u> $(x_1 = 0)$ means, we should not place first item in the bag

$\hat{c}(3) = - 10 - 12 - 18(5/9) = - 32$

$u(3) = - 10 - 12 = - 22$

The part of LCBB tree is shown in Figure 7.34.

Select the minimum of lower bounds i.e., $\min\{\hat{c}(2), \hat{c}(3)\} = \min\{-38, -32\}$ $= -38 = \hat{c}(2)$

First object is selected i.e., $x_1 = 1$. Therefore choose the node 2, i.e., node 2 is E- node and it is expanded its

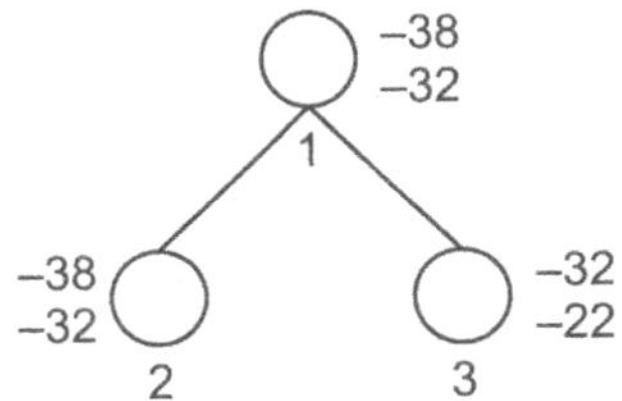

Figure 7.34 Part of a LCBB Tree

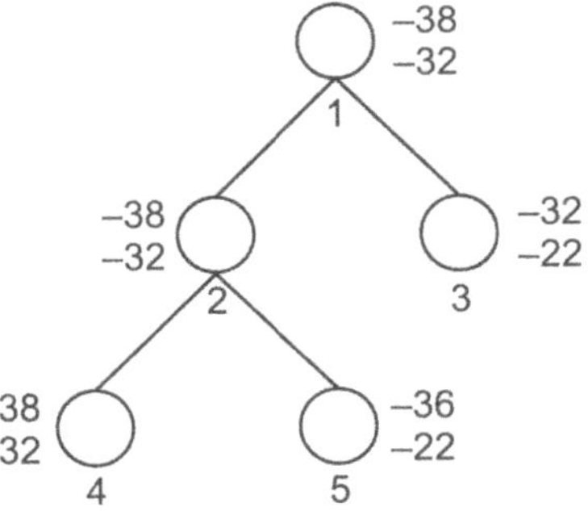

Figure 7.35 Part of a LCBB Tree

children are node 4 and node 5, the part of LCBB tree is shown in Fig 7.35. Consider the second variable to take the decision at second level.

For <u>node 4,</u> $(x_2=1)$

$\hat{c}(4) = -10 - 10 - 12 - 18(3/9)$

$= -38$

$u(4) = -10 - 10 - 12 = -32$

For <u>node 5,</u> $(x_2=0)$

$\hat{c}(5) = -10 - 12 - 18(7/9) = -38 = -10 - 12 - 14 = -36$

$u(5) = -10 - 12 = -22$

Min$\{\hat{c}(4), \hat{c}(5)\}$ = min$\{-38, -36\}$ = -38. Node 4 is selected, therefore second object is selected i.e., $x_2 = 1$. Node 4 is E-node and it is expanded its children are node 6 and node 7, the part of LCBB tree is shown in Fig 7.36. Consider the 3rd variable to take the decision at 3rd level.

For <u>node 6,</u> $(x_3 = 1)$

$\hat{c}(6) = -10 - 10 - 12 - 18(3/9) = -38$

$u(6) = -10 - 10 - 12 = -32$

For <u>node 7,</u> $(x_3 = 0)$

$\hat{c}(7) = -10 - 10 - 18 = -38$

$u(7) = -10 - 10 - 18 = -38$

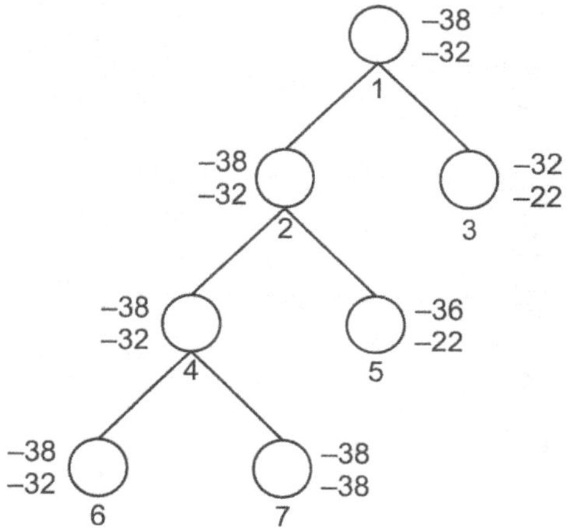

Figure 7.36 Part of a LCBB Tree

node 7 become

Min$\{\hat{c}(6), \hat{c}(7)\}$ = min$\{-29, -29\}$ = $-29 = \hat{c}(7)$

Here $\hat{c}$ of node 6 & 7 are same, so we can select any arbitrary node i.e. 6 or 7. Since u(7) is less than u(6), therefore node 7 is selected. Third object is not selected i.e. $x_3 = 0$. Node 7 is E- node and it is expanded its children are node 8 and node 9, LCBB tree is shown in Fig 7.37. Consider the 4th variable to take the decision at 4th level.

For <u>node 8,</u> $(x_4 = 1)$

$\hat{c}\,(8) = -\,10 - 10 - 18 = -\,38$

$u(8) = -\,10 - 10 - 18 = -\,38$

For <u>node 9,</u> $(x_4 = 0)$

$\hat{c}\,(9) = -\,10 - 10 = -\,20$

$u(9) = -\,10 - 10 = -\,20$

Node 9 has $\hat{c}\,(9) >$ upper and is killed immediately.

Search terminates with node 8 as answer node.

Therefore the path is $1 \to 2 \to 4 \to 7 \to 8$. The solution for 0/1 knapsack problem is $(x_1, x_2, x_3, x_4) = (1, 1, 0, 1)$

Maximum profit $= 10 + 10 + 0 + 18 = 38$.

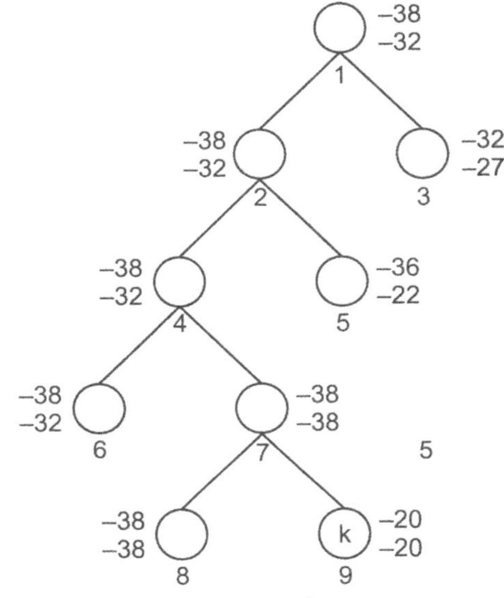

Figure 7.37 LCBB Tree

7.9.2 FIFO Branch and Bound Solution

For the above knapsack instance let us use FIFO branch and bound solution. Draw the portion of state space tree generated by FIFOBB for the following knapsack instances: $n = 4$ $(p_1, p_2, p_3, p_4) = (10, 10, 12, 18)$, $(w_1, w_2, w_3, w_4) = (2, 4, 6, 9)$ and $m = 15$.

Upper bound and lower bound for node 1, node 2 and node 3 are calculated in the similar manner as LCBB and they are

$$u(1) = -\,32, \;\hat{c}\,(1) = -\,38 \text{ and } \hat{c}\,(2) = -\,38 \;\; u(2) = -\,32$$

$$\hat{c}\,(3) = -\,32 \;\; u(3) = -\,22$$

The part of FIFOBB tree is shown in Fig 7.38.

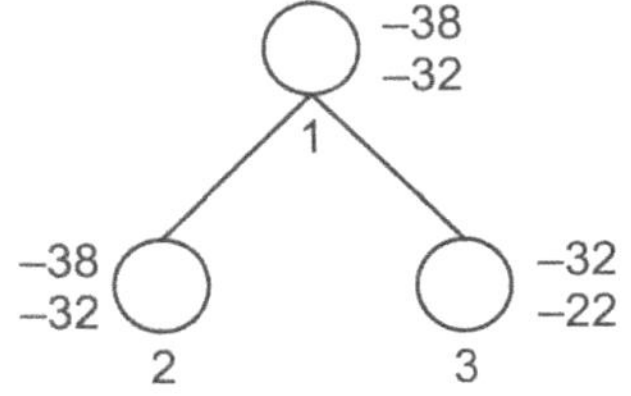

Figure 7.38 Part of a FIFOBB Tree

Node 2 and node 3 are placed in queue and let us assume that node 2 is generated first and it becomes E-node. Node 2 is expanded, its children are node 4 and node 5 they are stored in queue and the part of FIFOBB tree is shown in Fig 7.39.

$$\hat{c}\,(4) = -\,38 \quad u(4) = -\,32$$
$$\hat{c}\,(5) = -\,36 \quad u(5) = -\,22$$

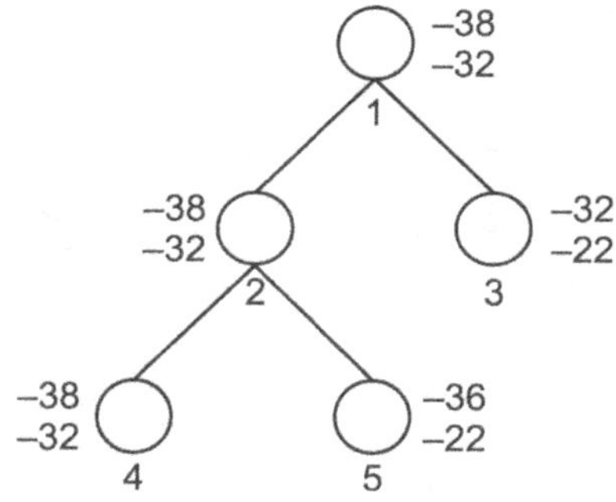

Figure 7.39 Part of a FIFOBB Tree

Now node 3 becomes E- node and it is expanded its children node 6 and node 7 are generated and the part of FIFOBB tree is shown in fig 7.40.

$$\hat{c}\,(6) = -\,32 \quad u(6) = -\,22$$
$$\hat{c}\,(7) = -\,28 \quad u(3) = -\,28$$

Node 7 is immediately killed because $\hat{c}\,(7)>$ upper and node 6 is stored in the queue as shown in the figure below

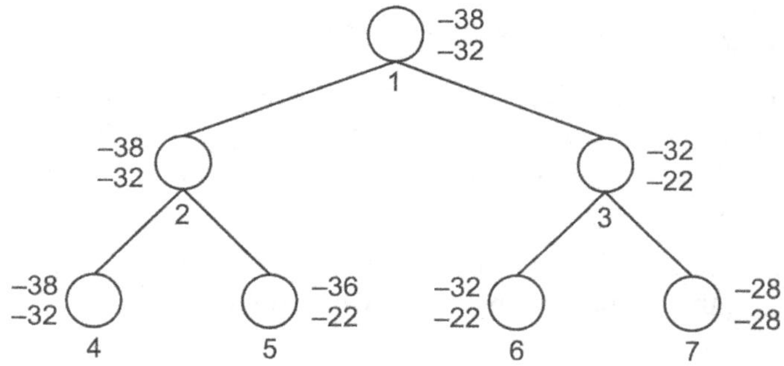

Figure 7.40 Part of a FIFOBB Tree

Now node 4 becomes E- node and it is expanded its children node 8 and node 9 are generated and added in queue and the part of FIFOBB tree is shown in Fig 7.41.

$$\hat{c}\,(8) = -\,38 \quad u(8) = -\,32$$
$$\hat{c}\,(9) = -\,38 \quad u(9) = -\,38$$

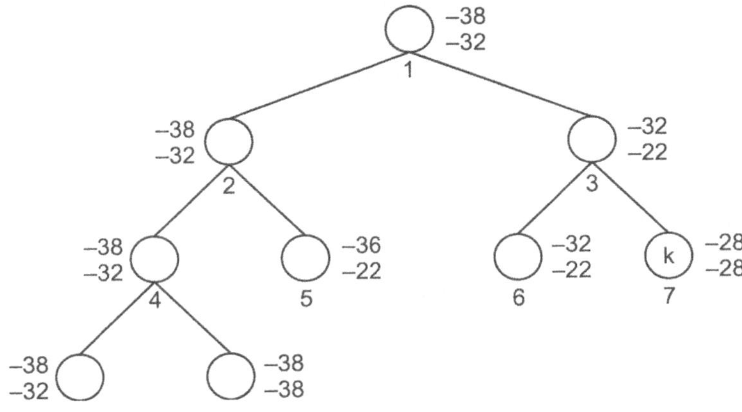

Figure 7.41 Part of a FIFOBB Tree

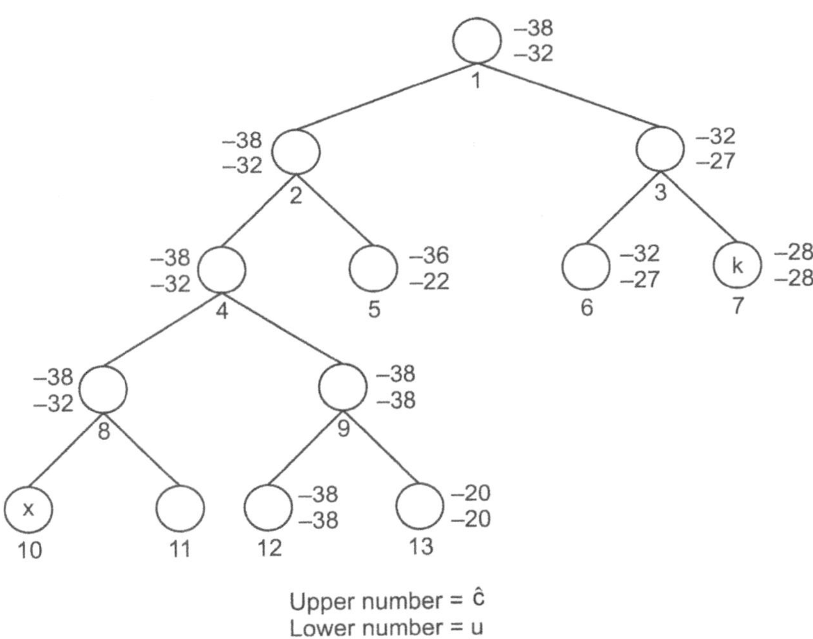

Figure 7.42 FIFOBB Tree

The next nodes in the queue are node 5 and node 6, they are the E- nodes node 5 and node 6 are not expanded because their ĉ ()> upper and therefore they are killed. Now node 8 becomes E- node and it is expanded its children node 10 and node 11 are generated and added in queue and FIFOBB tree is shown in Fig 7.42. Node 10 and node 11 are killed because node 10 is not feasible and node 11 has its ĉ (11)> upper. Now node 9 becomes E- node and it is expanded its children node 12 and node 13 are generated and node

12 is added in queue and node 13 is killed because its $\hat{c}$ (11)> upper. Node 12 is the only remaining live node and it has no children and search terminates at node 12. The value of upper is – 38.

The solution for 0/1 knapsack problem is $(x_1, x_2, x_3, x_4) = (1, 1, 0, 1)$

Maximum profit $= 10 + 10 + 0 + 18 = 38$.

Therefore the path is $1 \rightarrow 2 \rightarrow 4 \rightarrow 9 \rightarrow 12$.

Objective Question Bank

1. We start at a particular node in the graph, visiting all nodes exactly once and come back to initial node with minimum cost. This is known as [   ]
   A. traveling sales person problem
   B. minimum cost spanning tree
   C. 0/1 knapsack problem
   D. optimal storage on tapes

2. In the Least Count (LC) search, which one is the ranking function? [   ]
   A. $\hat{c}(x) = f(h(x)) + g(x)$
   B. $\hat{c}(x) = f(h(x))/g(x)$
   C. $c(x) = f(h(x)) * g(x)$
   D. $\hat{c}(x) = f(h(x)) - g(x)$

3. The FIFO search coupled with bounding functions is called as [   ]
   A. cumulative reduction function
   B. column reduction
   C. least count search
   D. FIFO BB

4. An LC search coupled with bounding functions is called as [   ]
   A. bound-and-branch search   B. state space search
   C. LC branch-and-bound search   D. least count search

5. The algorithm of FIFO branch and bound can be given with upper bound [   ]
   A. ∞ B. 1
   C. 2   D. 0

6. A search strategy that uses a cost function to select the next E-node would always choose for its next E-node a live node with least [   ]
   A. LIFO function   B. FIFO function
   C. branch function   D. cost function

7. In LC search, every time the child is checked by the condition that [   ]
    A. the child is right or left
    B. the child is answer node or not
    C. the child is dead node or not
    D. the child is problem node or not

8. In FIFO BB, square nodes indicate   [   ]
    A. answer nodes   B. dead nodes
    C. E-nodes   D. feasible nodes

9. The 15-puzzle problem was invented by   [   ]
    A. Mr. T.Ibaraki   B. Mr.C. kiarel
    C. Mr. Sam Loyd   D. Mr . S. Martello

10. We start at a particular node in the graph, visiting all nodes exactly
    once and come back to initial node with minimum cost. This is known
    as   [   ]
    A. minimum cost spanning tree   B. optimal storage on tapes
    C. traveling sales person problem D. 0/1 knapsack problem

11. In FIFO branch and bound, if cost function of the node is greater than
    upper, then   [   ]
    A. node becomes E-node
    B. the node gets killed
    C. that node is the minimum cost answer node
    D. that node is the problem node

12. For infinite state space trees with no answer nodes   [   ]
    A. LC search will terminate
    B. LC search cannot be conducted
    C. termination of LC search depends on cost function D.LC search
        will not terminate

13. Which is not true in case of LC search?   [   ]
    A. It uses the cost function
    B. LC search algorithm gives answer node, but it may not give the
        optimal answer node.
    C. LC search algorithm gives answer node
    D. among all the live nodes, we select a node which has minimum cost

14. In branch-and-bound method, for nodes representing in feasible
    solutions, $C(x) =$ [   ]
    A. 2   B. infinite
    C. 1   D. 0

15. The FIFO search coupled with bounding functions is called as   [   ]

    A. cumulative reduction function   B. least count search
    C. column reduction   D. FIFO BB

16. It is the time complexity for the traveling sales person problem, if it is solved by using dynamic programming   [   ]
    A. $O(n^2 + n)$ B. $O(n^2.2^n)$
    C. $O(2^n)$ D. $O(n^2)$

17. An LC search coupled with bounding functions is called as   [   ]
    A. LC branch-and-bound search   B. bound-and-branch search
    C. state space search   D. least count search

18. In FIFOBB, initially, the queue of live nodes is   [   ]
    A. empty   B. alternatively filled
    C. full   D. half filled

19. Functions find a live node with least cost function in LC search   [   ]
    A. Maximum( )   B. search()
    C. Least()   D. minimum()

20. For infinite state space trees with no answer nodes   [   ]
    A. LC search cannot be conducted
    B. LC search will terminate
    C. LC search will not terminate
    D. termination of LC search depends on cost function

21. In the tree of variable tuple size formulation, the nodes are numbered as in   [   ]
    A. random order   B. BFS
    C. FIFO order   D. DFS

22. The travelling sales person problem which asked for a tour that has minimum cost. Then this tour is a   [   ]
    A. principle of optimality
    B. cube connected cycle
    C. multi stage graph problem
    D. Hamiltonian cycle

Fill in the Blanks

1. The 15-puzzle consists of __________numbered tiles on a square frame with a capacity of _____tiles.

2. A ____ method searches a state space tree using any search mechanism in which all the children of the E-node are generated before another node becomes the E-node.

3. To use the branch-and-bound technique to solve any problem, it is first necessary to conceive of a ____for the problem.

4. A cost function $\hat{c}(.)$ such that $\hat{c}(x) \leq c(x)$ is used to provide lower bounds on solutions obtainable from any node x.

5. In bounding each time a new answer node is found, the value of ______________ can be updated.

6. In the 15-puzzle $\hat{g}(x)=$______________________________.

7. In branch-and-bound terminology, a BFS-like state space search will be called ____________ search as the list of live nodes is a first-in-first-out list (or queue).

8. A D-search-like state space search will be called ____________ search as the list of live nodes is a last-in-first-out list(or stack).

Review Questions

1. (a) Draw the portion of state space tree generated by LCBB for the knapsack instances:
    $n = 4$; $(P_1; P_2; P_3; P_4) = (10; 10; 12; 18)$; $(w_1w_2;w_3;w_4) = (2;4; 6; 9)$ and $M = 15$.

    (b) Explain Least cost Search.
    Set 1 December 2011

2. Write the LCBB algorithm for the 0/1 Knapsack problem. Also analyze its complexity.
    Set 2December 2011

3. Write an algorithm schema LIFOBB for a LIFO branch-and-bound search for a least cost answer node.
    Set 3 December 2011

4. Write an algorithm schema FIFOBB for a FIFO branch-and-bound search for a least-cost answer node.
    Set 4 December 2011

5. (a) Define the terms Branch and Bound. Explain about it's general method.

    (b) Explain 0/1 knapsack problem using Branch and Bound.
    November / December-2014

6. (a) Illustrate LCBB solution to solve the knapsack problem.

    (b) What do you mean by bounding? Explain how these bound are useful in branch and bound methods?
    June-2014

7. (a) Generate FIFO branch and bound on the traveling salesman problem and find the solution space tree.

    (b) What is bounding? Explain the principles of bounding.
    May-2013

8. Differentiate between Backtracking and Branch & Bound technique by considering 4- queen problem. Explain how nodes are generated and numbered in state space tree in the above two techniques.

April-May, 2012

9. (a) Draw the portion of the state space tree generated by FIFOBB using the variable tuple size for the knapsack instances: $n = 5$; $(P_1; P_2; P_5) = (10; 15; 6; 8; 4)$; $(w_1; w_2; w_5) = (4; 6; 3; 4; 2)$ and $M = 12$.

(b) Write the control abstraction of LC search.

Set 2April-May, 2012

10. Consider the Travelling salesperson instance defined by the cost matrix.

$$\begin{bmatrix} \infty & 11 & 10 & 9 & 6 \\ 8 & \infty & 7 & 3 & 4 \\ 8 & 4 & \infty & 4 & 8 \\ 11 & 10 & 5 & \infty & 5 \\ 6 & 9 & 5 & 5 & \infty \end{bmatrix}$$

(a) Obtain the reduced cost matrix

(b) Using a state space tree formulation, obtain the portion of the state space tree that will be generated by LCBB. Label each node by its $c^\wedge$ value. Write the reduced matrices corresponding to each of these nodes.

Set 3 April-May, 2012

11. (a) Describe the Traveling Salesperson Problem in Branch & Bound.

(b) Explain the principles of FIFO & LC Branch & Bound?

Set 4 April-May, 2012

12. Explain the principles of:
(a) Control Abstraction for LC-search.
(b) Bounding.
(c) FIFO Branch & Bound.
(d) LIFO Branch & Bound.

December 2011

13. Write an algorithm schema FIFOBB for a FIFO branch-and-bound search for a least-cost answer node.

December 2011

NP-Hard and NP-Complete Problems

8.1 INTRODUCTION

The problems that we intend to solve, using a computer, can broadly be divided into two types P- class and NP-class problems. The problems that can be solved in polynomial time are said to be in P-class. An example for P-class problem is a problem of searching an element from the list. It can be solved in O(log n)

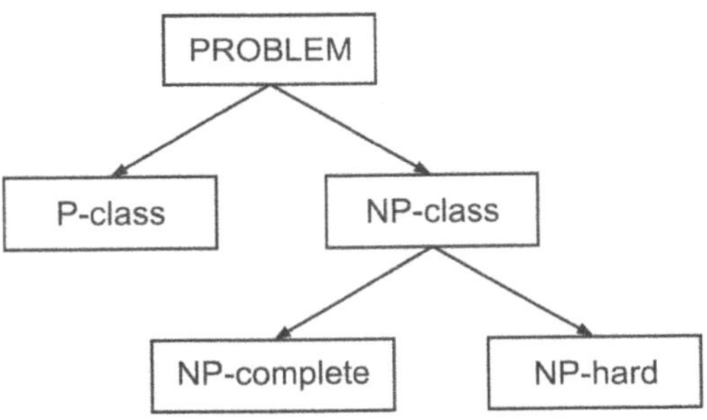

Figure 8.1 Classification of Problems

time. The problems that can be solved in polynomial time, by non-deterministic machine, are called NP-class problems. An example of NP-class problem is a Knapsack Problem whose time complexity is $(O(2^{n/2}))$, Travelling Sales Person Problem whose time complexity is $(On^2 2^n)$. In this chapter, we differentiate between problems that can be solved by a polynomial time algorithm and for which no polynomial time algorithm is known. The detailed classification of problems is shown in Figure 8.1.

8.2 TRACTABLE PROBLEMS

They are problems which can be solved in a finite duration of time. The problems that can be solved in polynomial time are called tractable problems. They are also defined as set of all problems that can be solved by polynomial time algorithms. Example: Searching of an element from the list.

8.2.1 Polynomial Time Algorithm

An algorithm for a given problem size (n) is said to be a polynomial time algorithm if it's worst case complexity belongs to $O(n^k)$ for a fixed small integer value k and an input size of n.

8.3 INTRACTABLE PROBLEMS

The problems that cannot be solved in polynomial time are called intractable problems. In real time applications, there are some problems whose solution may take large amount of time or there might not be any known solution. This might be due to nature of the input, complexity of the algorithm used for solving etc. They are called as intractable problems. The mean of intractable is difficult to manage. It is necessary to study those problems and analyze its algorithms to find a feasible solution if possible. They are problems which can't be solved in a finite duration of time. The complexity of the problems is very high.

Example: Algorithms whose worst case complexity belongs to $O(2^n)$, $O(n^n)$ etc., can't be solved in finite amount of time for larger values of 'n'.

Problems can also be classified into decision problems and optimization problems. Decision Problem is a problem for which the output is binary, i.e., true / false or 1/0. An algorithm for the above problem is called decision algorithm. Optimization problem is a problem that finds an optimal (maximum or minimum) value of a given cost function. An algorithm for the above problem is called optimization algorithm.

A deterministic algorithm is an algorithm in which the output of every operation used in it is uniquely defined. Today's computers are capable of executing deterministic algorithms. Non – deterministic algorithm contains operations whose outcomes are not uniquely defined, but are limited to specified set of possibilities. The machine executing such operation is allowed to choose any one of these outcomes. A non-deterministic algorithm is an algorithm which can be executed on a non-deterministic machine, non-deterministic algorithms cannot be executed on today's computers.

Many optimization problems can be converted into decision problems with the property that the decision problem is solved in polynomial time if and only if the corresponding optimization problem is solved in polynomial time. If there is no polynomial time solution to decision problem then its corresponding optimization problem cannot have polynomial time solution.

0/1 knapsack problem is converted into decision problem by checking whether there is 0/1 assignment of values to x_i, such that $\sum p_i x_i > = r$ and $\sum w_i x_i < = m$ where r is a given number. 0/1 knapsack optimization problem cannot be solved in polynomial time if 0/1 knapsack decision problem cannot be solved in polynomial time.

P-class is a set of all decision problems solvable by deterministic algorithm in polynomial time.

8.4 NP PROBLEMS

They are also called Non Deterministic polynomial problems. NP problems can be defined as the class of decision problems that can be solved in polynomial time by Non-Deterministic Algorithms. NP-class is a set of all decision problems solvable by non-deterministic algorithm in polynomial time. NP does not stand for "non-polynomial". It is non-deterministic polynomial, there are many complexity classes that are much harder than NP. NP consists of those problems that are verifiable in polynomial time. It means that it is possible to "guess" the solution (by some nondeterministic algorithm) and then check it. Nondeterministic is just a fancy way of talking about guessing a solution.

A problem is in NP if you can quickly (in polynomial time) test whether a solution is correct (without worrying about how hard it might be to find the solution). As of today, there are no faster algorithm (in polynomial time) to provide "exact" answers to NP-problems. The discovery of such algorithms remains a big task for researchers. Today many people think that such algorithms do not exist and so they are looking for alternative methods.

An example of an alternative method is the genetic algorithm.

Many graph problems used in CAD algorithms for computer chip design fit in class of NP.

Satisfiability Problem Closed Tour: Given n cities and an integer k, is there a tour, of length less than k, of the cities which begins and ends at the same city?

Examination Scheduling: Given a list of courses, a list of conflicts between them, and an integer k; is there an exam schedule consisting of k dates such that there are no conflicts between courses which have examinations on the same date?

Vertex Cover: Given a graph and an integer k, is there a collection of k vertices such that each edge is connected to one of the vertices in the collection?

Example: Consider the problem of searching a particular element in a binary tree. Let the depth of the binary tree be 'd'. Suppose the depth is zero, we have only one element in the tree and if the depth is 4, we have 31 elements. In general the number of elements in the tree having depth 'd' is given by $2^{(d+1)} - 1$. Note that the level 'd' starts from 0.

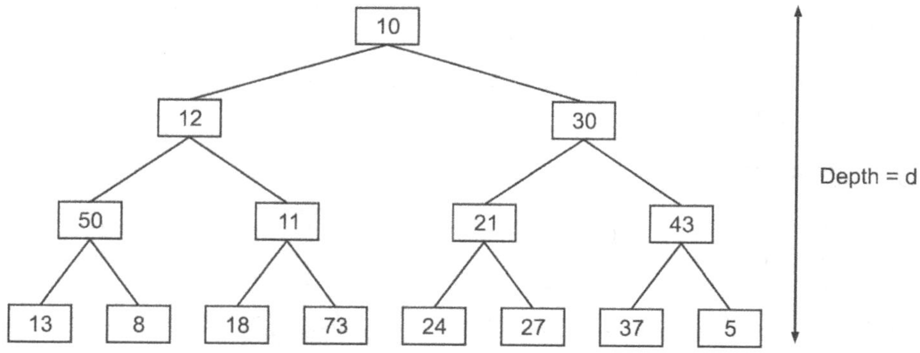

Figure 8.2 Binary search problem representation

A deterministic algorithm for this problem would be as follows:

Start from the root node (10) and keep traversing in preorder comparing each element with the search element. Because search is sequential the worst case is $O(2^{(d+1)})$ comparisons as shown in Figure 8.2. Suppose we have a non-deterministic machine to solve the above problem. Figure 8.3 represents non deterministic algorithm for Binary search problem. A Non deterministic algorithm for searching problem would be as follows:

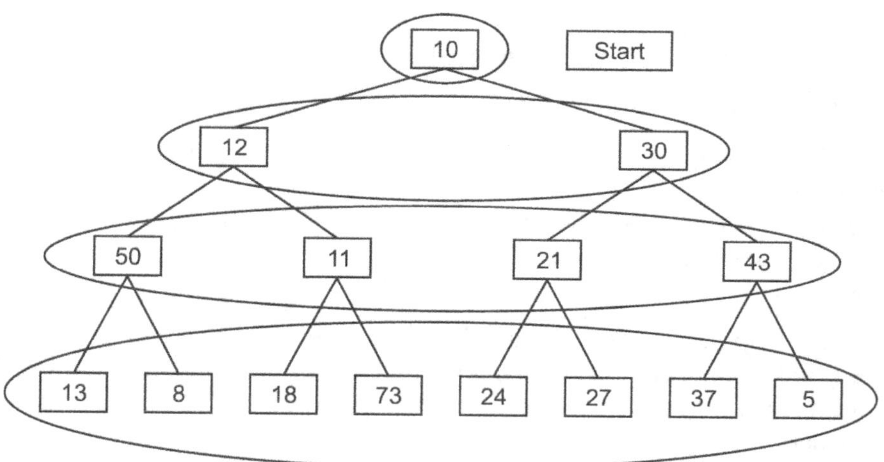

Figure 8.3 Binary Search for a non deterministic algorithm

For a non-deterministic machine which can compare the search element with all the elements at every level in one unit of time, the search algorithm will have a worst case complexity of **O(d)** $\cong$ O(n): which is in polynomial time. The key point to note here is that the search is not conducted in a serial fashion. Machines of such capability (hypothetical machines) are Non Deterministic Machines.

8.5 NON-DETERMINISTIC ALGORITHMS

A non-deterministic machine is an imaginary computer possessing computing power with limitless degree of parallelism. A non-deterministic algorithm is an algorithm which can be executed on a non-deterministic machine. That is, non-deterministic algorithms cannot be executed on today's computers.   Therefore non-deterministic algorithms are not practically useful to obtain the solution using a computer. At present, non-deterministic algorithms are intended for study purpose at theoretical level.

Non deterministic machines are hypothetical machines. The following example illustrates the working of Non deterministic machine.

Consider the following pseudo-code:

```
X=17;
If (x= =6)
{
        Call function foo
                OR
        Call function foo2      // this is possible in
                                //Non-deterministic machine
}
Else
{
        Call function foo3
                OR
        Call function foo4
                OR
        Call function foo5  // This is possible in Non-
                            //deterministic machine
}
```

In the above code snippet, it is observed that is a parallel operation subjected to 'IF ELSE' condition. If x = 6, either function foo or function foo2 can be called.

A non-deterministic machine is able to perform the computation based on the abode pseudo code in a non-sequential way while a deterministic machine, can't work in parallel.

A non-deterministic algorithm is a two stage algorithm.

A non-deterministic stage or guess stage

A deterministic stage or verification stage

A non-deterministic (guess) stage: In non-deterministic stage, choose() function is used. choose() function takes one argument of type **set** as its input and it returns ***arbitrarily*** one of the elements of the input set. We note that the return value is ***not unique*** for the given input. Therefore, it is a non-deterministic step of the algorithm.

Consider the following example of non-deterministic step of an algorithm.

$$x = \text{choose}(S) ;$$

Let us assume S = {0,1}. When the above statement is executed, two copies (which is equal to the number of the elements of the input set) of the algorithm is created. These two copies are executed in parallel. Each copy of the algorithm *arbitrarily* returns either 0 or 1. The non-deterministic machine ensures that the element leading to the successful completion of the solution is definitely returned by one of its copies. We do not worry how such operation can be performed by a computer because the operation is defined for an *imaginary* computer.

Let us now assume S = {Mon, Tue, Wed, Thu, Fri, Sat, Sun}. When the above statement is executed, *seven* copies (which is equal to the number of the elements of the input set) of the algorithm is created. These seven copies are executed in parallel. Each copy of the algorithm returns an *arbitrary day*. The non-deterministic machine ensures that the element leading to the successful completion of the solution is definitely returned by one of its copies.

A deterministic (verification) stage: In this stage it takes as input the candidate solution and the instance to the problem and returns yes if the candidate solution represents actual solution. In this stage, success() and fail() functions are used.

Example on Non-deterministic Algorithms: Write a non-deterministic algorithm for searching an element 'x' in an array 'A' containing n elements. We have to find an index i such that A[i] = x such that A[i] = x or i = 0 if x is not in A.

Non-deterministic_Search(A,x,n)

```
{
   i=choose(1..n);
   If (A[i]=x) then
   {
     Write(i);
     Success();
   }
Write(0);
Fail();
}
```

The above non-deterministic algorithm searches for an element 'x' in an array 'A' containing 'n' elements. When a non-deterministic machine executes the above algorithm, its effect is as follows.

When the control reaches the statement at line 3, it creates n copies of the algorithm and these n copies proceed in parallel. Each copy returns an arbitrary value in the range 1 to n. And we note that arbitrarily returned values *definitely include* a value leading to the correct final solution. For example, if 'x' is present at location 7, one of the copies definitely returns 7 by the statement at line 3. All the copies with unsuccessful comparison at line 4 will execute lines 9 and 10. The effect of executing fail() is to terminate the corresponding copy of the algorithm. A copy of the algorithm with successful comparison at line 4 executes the statements at lines 6 and 7. The effect of executing success() by any one copy is to terminate all the other copies of the algorithm. In the above algorithm choose will return the index value if the element is present otherwise it will return zero in one comparison only. The time complexity is O(1).

8.6   NP-HARD AND NP-COMPLETE CLASSES

8.6.1   NP – Complete Problem

There are a large number of problems in real time applications belonging to NP class. To check whether each of the NP problems have a polynomial time solution on a deterministic machine is practically impossible. Instead, it is possible to identify a small set of NP problems such that if any one problem in this set has a polynomial time solution on a deterministic machine, then the rest of all NP problems will also have a polynomial time solution on a deterministic machine. This subset of NP problems having the above mentioned special property is called **NP Complete problems**. It has been shown that if a deterministic polynomial time algorithm is found for an **NP Complete problem**, then every problem in NP complete class can be solved in deterministic polynomial time.

Figure 8.4 represents the relationship between NP and NP complete problem.

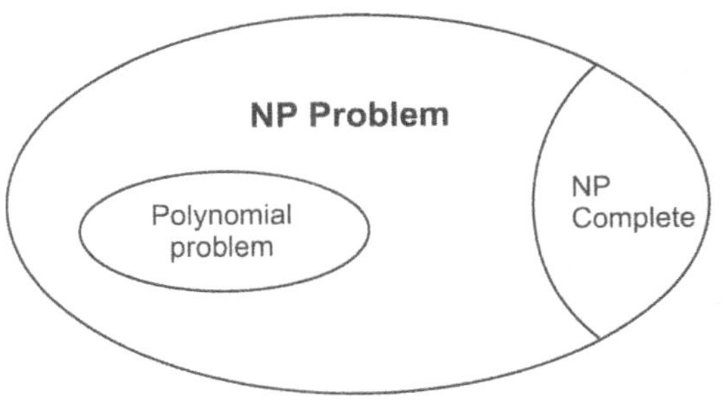

Figure 8.4 NP Complete Problem representations

8.6.2 NP Hard Problems

A problem L is NP-hard if and only if satisfiability reduces to L. If an NP-hard problem can be solved in polynomial time then all NP-complete problems are solved in polynomial time. A problem L is NP-complete if and only if L is NP-hard and L∈NP. NP and NP complete are decision problems which require Yes/No answer. These NP hard problems are ones which require optimal solution.

For example, if the coloring graph problem has used 5 colors for the nodes, NP hard problem would be to find the minimal number of colors to solve the graph coloring problem (say instead of 5, either 4 or 3 or 2).

Figure 8.5 represents Venn diagram showing the relation between NP, P, NP complete and NP hard problems.

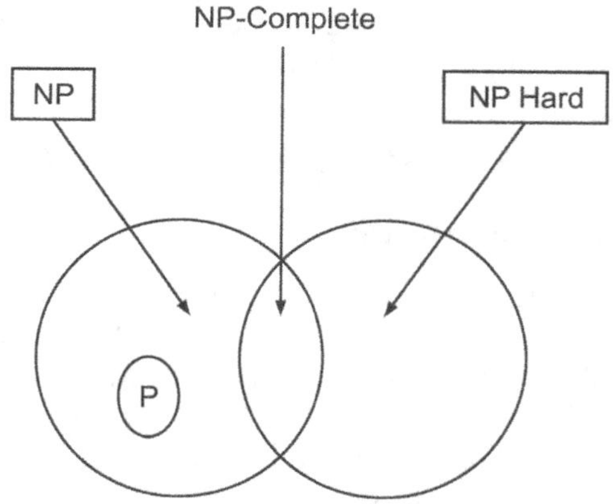

Figure 8.5 Venn diagram for NP, P, NP complete and NP Hard problems

8.7 SATISFIABILITY PROBLEM

We formulate satisfiability problem to determine whether a formula is true for same assignment of truth values to the variables.

The Boolean formula Ø is composed of,

Boolean variables $x_1, x_2, x_3, \ldots$

Boolean connectives or any Boolean functions with one or two inputs and one output such as ^ (AND),V(OR), ~(NOT), →(IMPLECATION), ↔(if and only if) and Parenthesis.

A truth assignment for a Boolean formula Ø is a set of values for variables of Ø, and a satisfying assignment is a truth assignment that causes it to evaluate to 1. A formula with a satisfying assignment is a satisfiable formula.

CNF (Conjunctive Normal Form): A formula is in CNF iff it is represented as $\wedge_{i=1}^{k} C_i$ as where C_i are clauses each represented as V I_{ij}. I_{ij} are literals.

DNF (Disjunctive Normal Form): It is in DNF iff it is represented a $V_{i=1}^{k} C_j$ and each clause Cj is represented as $\wedge$ I_{ij}. $(x_1 \wedge x_2)$ V $(x_3 \wedge \overline{x_4})$ is in DNF whereas $(x_1 V \overline{x_4})$ $\wedge$ $(x_1 V \overline{x_2})$ is in CNF.

8.8 COOK'S THEOREM

Cook's theorem states that satisfiablility is in P if P = NP. We already know that satisfiability is in NP. Hence if P = NP, then satisfiability is in P. Then it remains to be shown that if satisfiability is in P then P = NP. In order to prove this statement, we show how to obtain any polynomial time non deterministic decision algorithm A and input I, a formula Q(A, I) such that Q is satisfiable if A has successful termination with input I. if the length of I is 'n' and the time complexity of A is P(n) for some polynomial P( ) then the length of Q will be $O(p^3(n) \log n) = O(p^4(n))$. The time needed to construct Q will also be same.

A deterministic algorithm Z to determine the outcome of A on any input I may be obtained as, if (Z) computes Q and then uses a deterministic algorithm for the satistiability problem to determine whether or not Q is satisfiable. If O(q(m)) is the time needed to determine if a formula of length 'm' is satisfiable then the complexity of Z is $O(p^3(n) \log n + q(p^3(n)\log n)$. If satisfiability is in P then q(m) is   polynomial function of m and the complexity of Z becomes O(r(n)) for some polynomial r( ). Hence if satisfiability is in P then for every non deterministic algorithm A in NP we can obtain a deterministic Z in P.

Objective Question Bank

1. If there is an NP-complete language L whose complement is in NP, then complement of any language in NP is in __________   [   ]
   A. P   B. NP
   C. Both P and NP   D. none of these

2. Both P and NP are closed under the operation of__________   [   ]
   A. union   B. interaction
   C. concatenation   D. Kleene

3. Which of the following is correct?   [   ]
   A. 3-Sat <= p CNF-Sat

    B.   at the language level, 3-Satisfiable <=p CNF-Satisfiable

    C.   both 3-Sat <=p CNF-Sat and at the language level, 3-Satisfiable <=p CNF-Satisfiable

    D.   none of these

4. The language Satisfiable, or the problem Sat, is __________   [ ]

    A.   NP-complete   B.   NP-hard

    C.   both NP-complete and NP-hard   D.   none of these

5. P is the set of all decision solvable by deterministic algorithms in ______

                                                                [ ]

    A.   binomial time   B.   polynomial time

    C.   final time   D.   none of these

6. NP is the set of all decision solvable by non-deterministic algorithms in__________   [ ]

    A.   binomial time   B.   polynomial time

    C.   final time   D.   none of these

7. The computing time for Choice, Success, Failure are taken to be__________   [ ]

    A. $O(n)$ B. $O(\log n)$

    C. $O(1)$ D.   none of these

8. To define computation of the algorithm __________ signals are used   [ ]

    A.   Choice()   B.   Failure() and Success()

    C.   Choice(),Success() and Failure()   D.   none of these

9. The following: Given a sequence $a_1, a_2,$ __________, a_n of integers, and an integer M, is there a subset J of $\{1,2,....,n\}$ so that summation I belongs J $a_i = M$?

    The sum-of-subsets problem is NP-complete by constructing a reduction from

    The__________   [ ]

    A.   k-colorability problem   B.   exact cover problem

    C.   sum-of-subset problem   D.   none of these

10. Given a sequence $a_1, a_2,......, a_n$ of integers, is there a subset J of $\{1,2,...,n\}$ so that

    Summation I belongs J a_i = summation I does not belongs to J a_i?

The partition problem is NP-complete by constructing a reduction from the _________   [   ]
A.   k-colorability problem   B.   exact cover problem
C.   sum-of-subset problem   D.   none of these

11. The exact cover problem is the following: Given finite subsets $S_1,\ldots\ldots,S_k$ of a set, with $S_i = A$, is there a subset J of $\{1,2,\ldots\ldots,k\}$ so that for any two distinct elements I and j of J, S_i intersection S_j = theta and union I belongs J $S_i = A$ _________   [   ]
A.   NP-complete by constructing a reduction from the k-colorability problem
B.   exact cover problem
C.   sum-of-subset problem
D.   none of these

12. In measuring complexity of an algorithm, _________ length is used as the parameter   [   ]
A.   output   B.   input
C.   input and output   D.   none of these

13. _________ classes of problems are used in computational complexity
[   ]

A.   three   B.   four
C.   one   D.   two

14. A machine capable of executing a non-deterministic algorithm is called-
[   ]
____
A.   deterministic machine
B.   non-deterministic machine
C.   non-deterministic machine and deterministic machine
D.   none of these

15. The subset-sum problem is defined as follows : Given a set S of n positive integers and a positive integer W, determine whether there is a subset of S whose elements sum to W.

An algorithm Q solves this problem in 0(nW) time. Which of the following statements is false?   [   ]
A.   Q solves the subset-sum problem in polynomial time when the input is encoded in unary
B.   Q solves the subset-sum problem in polynomial time when the input is encoded in binary
C.   The subset sum problem belongs to the class NP
D.   The subset sum problem is NP-hard

16. Let f be a function in PF, the set of functions from summation* to summation* computable in polynomial time. Let A(a language in

summation*) be in P. Then f inverse(A) is in P, where by definition, f inverse(A) = {z belongs to summation*| f(z) belongs to A}.   [   ]
    A.   true   B.   false
    C.   uncertain   D.   none of these

17. Which of the following decision problems are in P?   [   ]
    A.   DNF-Satisfiability: Given a Boolean expression in disjunctive normal form, is it satisfiable?
    B.   CNF-tautology: Given a Boolean expression in CNF, is it a tautology?
    C.   The colorability problem
    D.   All of these

18. _________ problem is used in the non-deterministic polynomial time algorithm   [   ]
    A.   Knapsack decision   B.   sum of subsets
    C.   k-colorability   D.   none of these

19. The distinction between problems that can be solved by a _________ algorithm   [   ]
    A.   non-deterministic knapsack   B.   deterministic
    C.   polynomial time   D.   none of these

20. CNF formula g(x) is the conjunction of_________ clauses   [   ]
    A.   six   B.   five
    C.   seven   D.   eight

Fill in the Blanks

1. A problem that is _________________________ has the property that it can be solved in polynomial time if and only if all other _____________________ problems can also be solved in polynomial time.

2. If an _____________________________ problem can be solved in polynomial time, then all NP-complete problems can be solved in polynomial time.

3. The Choice(S), Failure( ), Success( ) are the 3 new functions of _______________ algorithms.

4. A _____________________________________algorithm terminates unsuccessfully if and only if there exists no set of of choices leading to a success signal.

5. A machine capable of executing a non deterministic algorithm is called a _____________________________ machine.

6. Any problem for which the answer is either zero or one is called a ________________________problem.

7. Any problem that involves the identification of an optimal (either minimum or maximum) value of a given cost function is known as an ________________________________problem.

8. An optimization algorithm is used to solve an ______________________________ problem.

9. Satisfiability is in P if and only if ______________________________.

10. A problem L is NP-complete if and only if L is __________________ and ______________.

Review Questions

1. Explain the P, NP, NP-Hard and NP- complete classes with suitable examples.

   December 2014

2. (a) What makes a problem to fall into class NP?

   (b) Explain the differences between decision and optimization problems.

   December 2011

3. (a) You are in front of a wall that stretches indefinitely in both directions. You know that there is a door in the wall, but it is dark and you only have a dim light that allows you to see no more than one step in either direction. Find the door. Is this Problem P or NP. If it is P, give an outline of the algorithm.

   (b) Write short notes on NP, NP-Hard and NP-complete problem.

   December 2011

4. (a) Compare and contrasts between NP-HARD and NP-COMPLETE.

   (b) Briefly explain Cooks-theorem.

   November / December-2013

5. (a) Explain the classes of NP-Hard and NP-Complete.

   (b) Discuss about deterministic and non-deterministic algorithms.

   June-2014

6. State and explain cook's theorem and also discuss about NP complete classes.

   May-2013

7. (a) Write short notes on Cook's theorem.

   (b) Explain about different types of NP problem.

   April-May, 2012

8. What are differences between NP-Hard and NP-Complete classes? Explain with examples.

April-May, 2012

9. (a) Describe some classic NP problems and why they are important.

   (b) Write about tractable and intractable problems.

December-January, 2011-2012

10. Write about Graph Coloring Problem and Subset Sum Problem. Are they NP problems. If yes, Justify your answer to include them in to NP Problems.

December-January, 2011-2012

ANSWERS

Chapter 1: Introduction

Answers

1.	A	2.	A	3.	D	4.	A	5.	A
6.	B	7.	C	8.	B	9.	A	10.	D
11.	B	12.	B	13.	A	14.	B	15.	A
16.	A	17.	A	18.	B	19.	D	20.	C
21.	A	22.	B	23.	C	24.	A	25.	B
26.	B								

Fill in the Blanks

1. An Algorithm
2. Program
3. Computational Procedures
4. Program Verification
5. Time complexity, Space Complexity
6. Debugging
7. Records
8. Read, write
9. Space complexity
10. Time Complexity
11. Compile Time, Run (or execution) Time
12. $f(n) = O(g(n))$
13. $f(n) = \Omega(g(n))$
14. Omega
15. O-notation
16. Asymptotic
17. $O(n^2)$

Chapter 2: Searching and Transversal Techniques

Answers

1. A	2. B	3. A	4. C	5. D	6. A
7. C	8. B	9. B	10. A	11. C	12. C
13. B

Fill in the Blanks

1. Articulation points
2. Root node
3. Breadth First Search
4. r, r
5. Disjoint sets
6. Union Find
7. BFS
8. BFT
9. $\theta(n + e)$
10. Breadth first spanning trees
11. An articulation
12. Biconnected
13. Biconnected
14. Articulation
15. Two
16. Back edges
17. Depth first spanning
18. min { dfn[u],min { L[w] | w is child of u },min {dfn[w] | (u,w) is a back edge } }
19. DFS
20. $\theta(n + e)$
21. Collapsing rule
22. Breadth First
23. No Articulation Point
24. Disjoint
25. Articulation
26. Implementation

Chapter 3: Divide and Conquer

Answers

1. D	2. B	3. D	4. C	5. D	6. A
7. B	8. A	9. C	10. A	11. B	12. B
13. B	14. B	15. A	16. B	17. B	18. B
19. D	20. C	21. D	22. A	23. A	24. D
25. C	26. D

Fill in the Blanks

1. log n
2. Divide and conquer
3. Divide and conquer
4. Program Verification
5. Divide and Conquer
6. $O(n^{\log_2 7}) = = O(n^{2.81})$
7. $O(n^3)$
8. $O(100)$
9. $O(\log n)$
10. $O(\log n)$
11. Linked List
12. Sorted
13. Quick Sort
14. $O(\log n)$
15. $O(100)$

Chapter 4: The Greedy Method

Answer

1. C   2. A   3. D   4. A   5. B   6. C

7. C   8. C   9. A   10. D   11. A   12. C

13. A

Fill in the Blanks

1. Compatible
2. Acyclic
3. Safe
4. Repeatedly merges two components
5. Kruskal's algorithm
6. Disjoint-set data structure
7. One
8. Light edge
9. Priority queue
10. O(E lg V)
11. O(E + V lg V)
12. Minimum spanning tree(MST)
13. By the SET and UNION method
14. SET
15. UNION
16. $O(|E| \log|E|)$
17. $O(n^2)$
18. Activity On Edge
19. Critical path method(CPM)
20. 2-way
21. extended binary tree which is used in the 2-way merging problem

$$\frac{1}{n} \sum_{j=1}^{n} t_j$$

22. O(nlog n)
23. $O(n^2)$
24. Single-Source Shortest Path problem

Chapter 5: Dynamic Programming

Answers

1. A	2. C	3. C	4. C	5. C	6. A
7. A	8. B	9. A	10. A	11. A	12. D
13. A	14. A	15. A	16. A	17. C	18. C
19. C	20. A	21. A			

Fill in the Blanks

1. Principle of optimality

2. 5

3. $1-(1-R)^2$

Chapter 6: Back Tracking

Answers

1. A	2. A	3. A	4. A	5. C	6. D
7. D	8. C	9. C	10. B	11. D	12. D
13. C	14. A	15. B	16. C	17. C	18. D
19. A	20. B	21. D	22. C		

Fill in the Blanks

1. Backtracking

2. Depth first

3. Backtracking

4. D.H.Lehmer

5. Explicit

6. Criterion

7. State space

Chapter 7: Branch and Bound

Answers

1. A	2. A	3. D	4. C	5. A	6. D
7. B	8. A	9. C	10. C	11. B	12. A
13. B	14. B	15. D	16. B	17. A	18. A
19. C	20. B	21. B	22. D		

Fill in the Blanks

1. 15 16
2. Branch and bound
3. State space tree
4. $\hat{c}(x) \leq c(x)$
5. Upper
6. Number of non blank tiles not in their goal position.
7. FIFO(First In First Out)
8. LIFO(Last In First Out)

Chapter 8: NP-Hard and NP-Complete Problems

Answers

1. A	2. D	3. C	4. A	5. B	6. B
7. C	8. B	9. B	10. C	11. A	12. B
13. D	14. B	15. B	16. A	17. D	18. A
19. C	20. C				

Fill in the Blanks

1. NP-complete, NP-complete
2. NP-hard
3. non deterministic
4. non deterministic
5. non deterministic
6. decision
7. optimization
8. optimization
9. $P = NP$
10. NP-hard $L\epsilon$ NP

INDEX